CHASING
THE
DRAGON'S
TAIL

THE
STRUGGLE
TO SAVE
THAILAND'S
WILD CATS

Anchor Books
DOUBLEDAY
New York   London   Toronto   Sydney   Auckland

CHASING THE DRAGON'S TAIL

ALAN RABINOWITZ

AN ANCHOR BOOK

PUBLISHED BY DOUBLEDAY

a division of Bantam Doubleday Dell Publishing Group, Inc.
666 Fifth Avenue, New York, New York 10103

ANCHOR BOOKS, DOUBLEDAY, and the portrayal of an anchor are trademarks of
Doubleday, a division of Bantam Doubleday Dell Publishing Group, Inc.

Chasing the Dragon's Tail was originally published in hardcover by Doubleday in
1991. The Anchor Books edition is published by arrangement with Doubleday.

ANCHOR WORLDVIEWS is an imprint of Anchor Books.

Book design by Marysarah Quinn

Library of Congress Cataloging-in-Publication Data

Rabinowitz, Alan, 1953–
    Chasing the dragon's tail : the struggle to save Thailand's wild
cats / Alan Rabinowitz. — 1st Anchor Books ed.
        p.   cm.
    "Anchor worldviews books"—T.p. verso.
    Includes bibliographical references and index.
    1. Leopard—Thailand—Huai Kha Khaeng Wildlife Sanctuary.
2. Tigers—Thailand—Huai Kha Khaeng Wildlife Sanctuary.   3. Forest
fauna—Thailand—Huai Kha Khaeng Wildlife Sanctuary.   4. Huai Kha
Khaeng Wildlife Sanctuary (Thailand).   5. Wildlife conservation—
Thailand.   6. Wild animal trade—Thailand.   7. Ethnology—Thailand.
I. Title.
[QL737.C23R32   1992]
333.95'9—dc20   92-1739
                                                                    CIP

ISBN 0-385-41518-4
Copyright © 1991 by Alan Rabinowitz

ALL RIGHTS RESERVED
PRINTED IN THE UNITED STATES OF AMERICA
FIRST ANCHOR BOOKS EDITION: November 1992
10 9 8 7 6 5 4 3 2 1

TO THE MEMORY OF SEUB NAKHASATHIEN,
WHOSE WORK WAS DEDICATED TO THE CONVICTION THAT
OTHER CREATURES HAVE AS MUCH RIGHT TO LIFE AS HUMAN BEINGS.
REST IN PEACE, MY FRIEND.

Hard is the Journey,
Hard is the Journey,
So many turnings,
And now where am I?

Li Po (A.D. 701–62)

CONTENTS

CHASING
THE
DRAGON'S
TAIL

Wildlife Sanctuaries

Thung Yai

Huai Kha Khaeng

HQ

DWM

HYY

UPPER KWAE YAI R.

HUAI KHA KHAENG

Tu Fu Found Dead

First Male Leopard Snared

Tu Fu + Li Po Captured

Supanyo + Jangair Captured

TIBET

CHINA

BURMA

LAOS

THAILAND

CAMBODIA

VIETNAM

SOUTH CHINA SEA

MALAYSIA

SUMATRA

BORNEO

Huai Kha Khaeng Wildlife Sanctuary

waterways ====

trails ———

PROLOGUE
TAIPEI, MARCH 1987

"Your element is fire but you were born in the month of water," the voice said quietly, eyes and fingers moving between different sets of charts.

"There are clashes, conflicting elements in your life. The fire gives you an intense personality with great life force. But as water, you're not centered. You flow, you adapt well, but you do not come to terms easily with your surroundings. It will be many years before your life stabilizes, before the fire is subdued. Travel, instability, and conflict are the dominant forces in your life." He paused, glanced at me momentarily, then went back to his charts. I searched his face for any hint of deceit but detected only intense concentration.

In the silence that followed, I looked around me. I was sitting in a comfortable office facing a well-dressed Chinese businessman whose secretary had interrupted our session twice with papers for him to sign. Although this man's reputation as a fortune-teller was well known throughout Taiwan, he was also an executive employed by an international foundation. He knew nothing about me and had agreed to this appointment only through the intercession of a mutal friend.

"What about death?" I asked abruptly. "Will I die young or violently?"

He looked up at me, as if he had forgotten I was there.

"Your life is complex," he answered diffidently, "sometimes hard to interpret. But do not worry about death. Your life force is strong, too strong for you to die easily. It may help save others close to you."

I wanted to believe him, but there had been so many near misses over the last few years. I thought of the plane crash that had almost killed me, the jaguar that had slashed my chest, the near-fatal virus that had attacked my bone marrow. In the end I decided that I had to believe him. Otherwise, I wouldn't have the courage to continue my work.

"You are an interesting man," he continued. "Your life will be filled with difficulties, and the battles will not always be external. But you will persevere." He smiled, while his eyes narrowed and hardened. He had said all he was going to say.

1

HUAI KHA KHAENG WILDLIFE SANCTUARY, THAILAND, MARCH 1986

I was tired. Not just physically tired but that deep, bone-weary tired that comes from having pushed beyond your limits not just once but every day for months. I was finishing up more than twelve weeks of difficult tracking through some of the largest forested areas in Southeast Asia, where I was searching for the clouded leopard, one of the most elusive cats in the world. The hardships of the jungle were beginning to take their toll. Now, fighting fatigue, I was just trying to make it through the last leg of the survey before going home.

This was my first time in Thailand, and my fourth day in the Huai Kha Khaeng Wildlife Sanctuary, one of the few remaining "forest gems" of this country. But after having spent the last few months tracking leopards in the dense, lush vegetation of Borneo's rain forest, this dry semi-barren area seemed anything but gemlike. Efforts to find clouded leopard tracks in the area of a recent sighting had, so far, proven futile, though there were abundant signs of tigers and Asiatic leopards. Normally, this would have excited me, but right now, this hike seemed like just another delay in my quest for a cold drink and a soft bed. As my Thai guides jabbered away in a language that sounded completely nonsensical to me, I calculated the days, hours, and minutes before I might reach Bangkok.

Six hours out from camp, and a little after midday, when the heat was at its most merciless, we reached the Huai Kha Khaeng, the main river which runs through the heart of the sanctuary. (Huai means river in Thai.) This watershed is one of the most pristine forest areas remaining in Thailand, and it contains some of the richest wildlife populations in the country.

Racing ahead of my companions, I veered off from the old elephant trail we'd been following to get a drink of cold water from a small feeder stream nearby. As I knelt to scoop the water in my hands, I heard a high-pitched squeal, followed by the sound of something crashing into the water. Looking up, I froze. Twenty-five feet in front of me was a large prehistoric-looking beast. After being scared by my approach, it had leaped into the main river. All my weariness vanished at the sight.

It was a Malayan tapir, a hulking, secretive creature whose starkly contrasting black-and-white coloration helps render it inconspicuous during its travels through the forest. Its six-hundred-pound bulk had been moving quietly through the dense undergrowth parallel to our trail, reaching the riverbank at the same time as I did. I watched its wet hippolike body glisten in the midday sun as it stopped abruptly in midstream and turned its head in my direction. Raising its fleshy snout like an elephant's trunk, it bared large white teeth that could easily have inflicted a severe bite, then emitted a harsh, grating sound. I knew this action was meant to threaten me but I couldn't help but smile. He was brave, this one. He would have presented a tempting target for a hunter.

It was my first sighting of this species in the wild, which is considered rare even by men who have lived in this part of the world. The tapir's preferred habitat of lush lowland rain forest made its presence here, at the drier northern extremity of its range, unusual. Yet even where tapirs are more common they are not often encountered. This strange-looking relative of horses and rhinos, considered one of the most primitive mammals in the world, is now on the list of the most threatened.

Realizing that I posed no immediate threat, the tapir continued to thrash his way across the river, then disappeared into the forest undergrowth with a speed that seemed impossible for such an ungainly animal. The other men, only one of whom had ever seen a tapir before, had caught up and were standing behind me, watching quietly. We were all smiling. Many years earlier, a traveler in Burma had described the tapir as "an enigma," a survivor of a "more gentle and legendary time . . . wandering in unique isolation in a world not yet mature enough for its wisdom." I suddenly remembered what had brought me to this part of the world. I was seeking a little of what was left of the "wisdom" of the forest. For the remainder of the day, I looked upon the terrain with new eyes, no longer in a rush to be anywhere else.

Shortly afterward, I returned to Bangkok to meet with officials of the Royal Thai Forestry Department and to share with them my impressions of the areas I had surveyed. I explained that signs of the clouded leopard were scarce, but that I was impressed with some of the forests and wildlife that I had seen. However, I was worried about the future. Even the country's largest cats were now restricted to only a few forest pockets, and not enough was known about these animals to estimate their current populations or carry out proper forest management.

Later that day, I presented a slide show to Thai government officials outlining the ecological research I had completed with jaguars in Central America. I explained how I had captured the jaguars, attached radio collars, and over a two-year period determined the cats' movement and activity patterns, the size of their home areas and the kinds of habitats they used. Jaguars had never been studied in a tropical rain forest this way before and this data helped the government set up a new reserve and establish management criteria for the jaguar to help ensure the future of the species. I also said that the situation for wildlife populations worldwide was steadily worsening. Biological diversity is currently at its lowest level in 65 million years. Even in protected forests, species that require large amounts of land are losing the battle for survival. In forest patches up to eight square miles in size, 20 percent or more of the species that we know exist will disappear in fifty years.

When the slide show was finished, I explained that by protecting large areas of forest for the use of the wide-ranging predators, smaller species that are not as easily studied can be preserved as well.

"People listen when you talk about saving big cats," I said. Humans show an empathy for these creatures that they often don't extend to many of the less noticeable species.

On my last day in Thailand, I was called to the office of the man who had hosted my survey there, Phairote Suvannakorn, deputy director of the Royal Thai Forestry Department, a powerful and controversial figure. There were many stories circulating about this man, who had been schooled in the United States and made no secret of his desire to rise to the top of the Thai Forestry Department. He had risen through the ranks of the Wildlife Conservation Division (set up in 1975), instead of through the more politically powerful forestry divisions whose ninety-five-year history has simply been a mandate to oversee logging operations. Phairote and I had met only twice during my stay, and both times I felt uneasy in his presence. His face reminded me of a stone lion at the entrance to a Chinese temple. We had said our goodbyes at the last meeting; this summons was unexpected.

The atmosphere in his office was stiff and formal, and the first five minutes of our conversation were filled with the obligatory Thai small talk that precedes any serious discussion. Then as Phairote started talking about the slides I had shown and my work with the jaguars, he became increasingly animated. Leaping up from behind his desk, he rushed around the office handing me pictures of Thai wildlife and pointing out areas on a map of Thailand where good forests still existed. His finger, moving up and down the country, always came back to one place, the Huai Kha Khaeng Wildlife Sanctuary.

"I got it protected myself," he said proudly. "It was not easy. I made enemies, but it doesn't matter. Conservation is not easy in Thailand . . ."

Shaking his head, he went back behind his desk.

"We need your help," he said to me. "There are so many problems—hunters, tribal people, rich powerful Chinese . . . You know Huai Kha Khaeng is special. You saw. Everybody wants it. But we know nothing about it. We need a study like the one you did with the jaguar."

"A study on what?" I asked. "Research has already been done in India and Africa on tigers and leopards, and Thailand isn't the best place to study clouded leopards."

"India and Africa do not mean anything here. Thailand is different. We have to save what is left of our forest."

"Just a study will not save the forest here," I said.

"It will help. I want you to work in Thailand, in Huai Kha Khaeng. It is the best place, but for how long, I don't know. You will have my help."

I was silent for a moment, taken aback by Phairote's uncharacteristic candor. Should I voice my doubts to him? I wondered. The national parks I had visited in Thailand seemed like little more than playgrounds for the wealthy. Logging camps and rice fields hovered on the perimeter of wildlife sanctuaries, like vultures on carrion. Young forest rangers in tattered clothes pointed out birds and trees with the barrels of their automatic rifles, which were always close at hand. I hadn't been able to sort the situation out yet, but I had seen enough to make me wary.

"I appreciate your invitation," I said, still trying to pull my thoughts together. "This is unexpected. I'm returning to New York tomorrow. I'll have to think it over."

While I was figuring out a way to make a polite exit, there was a knock at the door and another official entered the room. Seeing my chance, I stood and quietly made my way to the door, smiling a goodbye that Phairote acknowledged with a nod of his head. As I left the building, I wondered if there had been more to the conversation than I had understood. This man's thoughts were unreadable to me.

I rehashed our discussion that night in my hotel room. My trip to Thailand had been almost an afterthought to my original plans. Because Thailand is one of the fastest-developing nations in the world and has one of the highest rates of deforestation, I hadn't thought there was much potential in this country for good research and conservation. I had come here hoping only to find out more about the status of the clouded leopard. But now I was faced with this startling request.

As a staff zoologist for Wildlife Conservation International (the field research division of the New York Zoological Society), my job was to carry out scientific research on endangered animal species that would help in their protection and management. Now I was looking for my next long-term research site. I had finished my work on jaguars in Central America nearly a year ago, and since that time my plans had centered on Borneo. There, the largest cat on the island, the clouded leopard, still remained unstudied in the wild. If I could obtain good ecological data and draw attention to this rare species, as I'd done with the jaguar, my work might help protect one of the largest existing tracts of tropical rain forest in the world. Now, out of nowhere, I was being asked to get involved in a situation in Thailand that I knew virtually nothing about.

Phairote's earnestness had impressed me. It was unusual for a high government official to realize the importance of field research and ask for assistance in such a forthright manner. But there was something more. Thailand had reached the point that most underdeveloped tropical countries in the world were moving toward: the remaining forests were contained in mostly small, isolated pockets and already many of the larger animals that once roamed the area had disappeared. Only a few remote areas of extensive protected forest remained, places like Huai Kha Khaeng. If these places could not be saved, then what were the prospects elsewhere? In Borneo, there still seemed to be time. But here in Thailand, the situation was more urgent.

Comprehensive scientific data on the wildlife community in Thailand was virtually nonexistent, as was good ecological information on most Southeast Asian mammal species. Places such as Huai Kha

Khaeng were legally protected on paper, but without any basic knowledge of how the animals lived and what role they played in maintaining the forest, it was difficult for officials such as Phairote to justify continued protection of such large areas. More and more schemes were being cooked up in government circles to "utilize" these forests, and illegal encroachment was rapidly increasing. Phairote believed that Huai Kha Khaeng represented Thailand's last hope to save anything substantial.

The idea of working in the Huai Kha Khaeng Wildlife Sanctuary was, in many ways, intriguing. This thousand-square-mile sanctuary forms the core of a forest area more than four times that size, one of the largest protected forests in Southeast Asia. Still relatively pristine and remote, this preserve supports wild populations of tigers, leopards, tapirs, wild cattle, and elephants; it is the last refuge in the country for the wild water buffalo and green peafowl. Much of the sanctuary is comprised of dry deciduous forest, containing trees that shed their leaves seasonally. These forests contain good soil for agricultural development and thus have been quickly destroyed in most areas where they once existed.

Phairote had convinced me that the Huai Kha Khaeng Wildlife Sanctuary was in danger, despite the size and remoteness of the area. A long history of tribal occupation, illegal hunting and timbering was threatening to kill the very heart of this forest. The allegedly corrupt government was doing little to stem the tide of these forces. A 1969 survey called the valley of the Huai Kha Khaeng "Thailand's greatest wilderness," yet even at this early date there was evidence of "tree platforms, campsites with animal bones, gun cartridges, and racks for drying and smoking meats." The report concluded that the wildlife of Huai Kha Khaeng had survived, not because of law enforcement, but because of the area's vastness and relative inaccessibility. Twenty years later, little had changed.

It was now midnight, and the street noises of Bangkok outside my hotel room were just reaching a crescendo. As my mind drifted back to the nights I had spent at Huai Kha Khaeng, I thought how different these sights and sounds were from those of the forest. There

I had been lulled to sleep by the monotonous rhythm of geckos, called *too-kay* in Thai because of the strange throaty sound they make to each other, and I had awakened to the howling of male gibbons. Fresh tiger and leopard tracks lined the riverbanks and trails, the various shapes and sizes telling a different story about each animal. I remembered the huge clumps of fresh elephant droppings and the afternoons when I'd been shaken from my reverie by the high-pitched, almost mournful trumpeting of an elephant herd nearby.

My most vivid memories didn't stem from anything I had seen or heard in the forest, but from what I had felt. This forest possessed what I can only describe as an "oldness." Inside this sanctuary the modern world had yet to fully intrude. The pure essence of this place was still somehow undisturbed.

Two scenes in particular played back in my mind. I remembered sitting on the steps of a thatched hut in the forest watching a golden-backed woodpecker search for its morning meal. Peering around a corner of the hut to follow the bird's flight, I found myself instead facing the calm countenance of a thin, medium-sized man. I'd had no idea he'd been standing there. His head was completely bald and he was wearing nothing but an orange cloth around his body. I had just met my first forest monk.

We stared at each other for several seconds, then he pointed to the bird, which had landed nearby, and said something in Thai. Seeing I couldn't understand him, he smiled and beckoned me to follow him down the path from which he'd come. I wanted to go with him but to my surprise I turned away instead, and walked quickly back toward camp.

Two days later, I was following leopard tracks along an old elephant trail when I smelled a strange, sweet odor. Glancing around until my eyes adjusted to the shadows, I suddenly noticed there were people standing quietly among the trees watching me. They were Hmong tribesmen whose villages were near the Burma border, at least a two-day hike from where we were standing. There were five of them—three boys and two old men—and a water buffalo, making their way to purchase or trade supplies in the nearest village outside the sanctuary. As I moved among them, the boys looked at me curiously, while the glassy-eyed old men looked toward the ground. The strong, sweet smell that had first caught my attention permeated their clothes. It was the smell of opium.

As I finally drifted off to sleep, fragments of other events flashed through my mind. I had been told about the recent killings of forest rangers who had been shot to death by poachers. I remembered the desolate, parched look of the forest after recent fires; I had been surprised when I learned that the fires had been set by the forest guards themselves.

During my last night in the sanctuary, while looking into the darkness of this forest that extended virtually unbroken into Burma, chills had raced down my spine. I had never felt so small, standing on the verge of something far beyond my control.

In the morning the street noises filtering through my window were the same as in any big city. My hotel room looked like dozens of others. But for some reason I felt unsettled. I threw on some clothes and stepped out into the stifling heat and humidity, looking for a place to grab a quick breakfast.

Without thinking, I steered clear of the restaurants that catered to tourists and settled for a street vendor down a small alleyway. The food that hung from hooks above his stand was mostly unrecognizable to me, and I didn't speak enough Thai to ask him about it, so I pointed at the freshest-looking piece of meat and sat at the single table he kept beside his stall. The vendor, amused by my confusion, his face catching some of the hot oil as he flipped the meat into the wok, squeezed his eyes shut and laughed, shaking his head vigorously from side to side. I laughed too, thinking of the tapir in the middle of the stream shaking his long snout at me.

It dawned on me then what was different about this morning. As I looked at my bowl of rice porridge with pieces of unidentifiable organs floating around in it, I knew now I had made my decision. Borneo could wait.

2

DANCING
WOMAN
MOUNTAIN

I returned to New York to talk over my plans with George Schaller, the scientific director of the field program at the New York Zoological Society. After having spent thirty years studying large mammals in Africa, Asia, and South America, Schaller is a legend in wildlife research. He also has strong opinions about the practical side of conservation biology which often prove correct. Although Schaller appears aloof to many of the people who meet him, beneath this seemingly unsympathetic exterior is a warm, caring human being who has spent his life helping to save what remains of the world's wildlife. George is a man who simply prefers a snow-covered hilltop in the Himalayas to a crowded office in New York City. For many years, he has been my mentor and my friend.

We first met in 1982 at the University of Tennessee, where I had just received my Ph.D. in ecology and I was burning with ideas about saving the world. After Schaller read my dissertation on the ecology of raccoons, we spent a day hiking together in the Great Smoky Mountains National Park. Luckily for me, I knew too little about George to be in awe of him. My thoughts were far removed from him anyway as I contemplated the potential academic career I didn't want and wondered what my next move would be. While I listened to George compare the forests of the Smoky Mountains with areas of Giant Panda habitat in China, a familiar restlessness stirred inside of me.

It was a long time since I'd left the streets of New York City, an angry, lonely young man trying to cope with a severe stuttering problem. Four years at Western Maryland College, then graduate school in the hills of Tennessee had helped lessen many of my insecurities. It had taken me a lot to get this far yet I felt I was ready for a new challenge. I had no idea what that challenge might be.

At the end of George's visit we said our goodbyes and wished each other luck. I never expected to see him again. A week later Schaller called from New York and spoke with one of my professors. That night, at a party, my professor relayed their conversation to me. George had wanted to know if I was interested in spending a month in the country of Belize assessing the status of the jaguars there.

"Tell him yes," I said. I had no idea where Belize was.

My professor smiled broadly. "He wants you to think about it and call him within a week."

I left the party early and stayed up late staring at a tiny little speck called Belize, barely a quarter inch long on my world map. But to me, this small Central American country on the Caribbean Sea filled my vision. I phoned George the next day and accepted the job. It was the beginning of an adventure that would span more than two years and would change the course of my life forever.

Now, four years later, I felt a bit nervous telling George about my decision to work in Thailand. I was still unsure what exactly I was getting myself into. The situation in Huai Kha Khaeng was more complex than anything I had handled before. I would not be dealing with a single endangered species like the jaguar, but with an entire wildlife community in a complex forest mosaic that was severely threatened and, given current trends, would not survive intact much longer. The best approach seemed to be to combine research on the large, wide-ranging cats with studies of some of the smaller carnivore species. Carnivores often suffer the most from encroachment and development of forest areas. The data collected could be used to put together management and conservation strategies for the sanctuary and other areas like it. My plans were much more ambitious than what Phairote had asked for, but it was what he would need to help conserve this forest.

Laying down a map of Thailand with its protected areas clearly delineated, I pointed out to George how little of the forest system was still intact—and how many of the larger species of wildlife had already disappeared from these areas. The neighboring countries of Burma, Laos, and Cambodia still showed good pockets of forest on paper, but this land remained largely unprotected. By the time research and conservation opportunities opened up in these areas, much of the forests and wildlife would probably already be gone.

"I'll concentrate on the two big cats, tigers and leopards, as showpieces for the government, because they need so much space. They'll help justify the preservation of large areas of forest. But I'll study some of the smaller cats as well. We don't know anything about most of these animals in the wild. This area is so complex ecologically, I think we need to know more than just what the big animals are doing."

I paused, waiting to see George's reaction. He remained silent, eyes still on the map.

"Of course, it's not as straightforward as this," I went on, tempering my enthusiasm. "There are socioeconomic and political factors strongly impinging on the protected areas in the country, and on Huai Kha Khaeng in particular. And there are very few officials or academics nearby who are trained in any sort of wildlife research or conservation techniques. But if I start building a foundation of good research data, train some young Thais, and draw attention to the sanctuary, it'll be a beginning."

Schaller looked up at me.

"What about Borneo and the clouded leopard?"

"It can wait," I said, returning George's stare.

"Maybe not," George replied. "Do you really think this one place in Thailand is more worthwhile than trying to get things going in Borneo?"

"Yes," I said. "This place is special. It feels right to me." I thought again of the strange little monk and the smell of opium hanging on the old Hmong men's clothes. Please let me be right, I prayed silently.

"It's your decision," he said. "Put together a budget and a proposal for spending at least two years there. Don't try to do too much at first. This is a tough project, tougher than you think."

The months that followed were taken up with the dozens of details that need to be worked out before embarking on any intensive research project. Despite Phairote's help, there was still the tedious process of getting permits and letters of support from the necessary Thai bureaucracies, working out the specific field techniques I'd use once I was over there, and ordering field equipment. In my spare time, I read everything I could get my hands on about the country, the culture, and the wildlife of the area.

The most important equipment to be ordered was the drugging gear and radiotelemetry hardware—collars, antennas, and receivers. Without this equipment in the forest, anything more than the most cursory of observations on large cats and other carnivores would be virtually impossible. Most of these Southeast Asian species were secretive and nocturnal, and only the most wary animals survived the poachers' guns. Indirect evidence such as feces and tracks could tell me many things, but it was only by closely monitoring individual animals that I could get good ecological and behavioral data.

Radiotelemetry tracking is done by capturing animals and affixing small radios around their necks. Each radio has a different frequency and a simple activity switch that changes the pulse of the radio signal according to the animal's head movements. When an animal is resting, the beeps from the radio are slow; when it is moving, the beeps become faster. The tracker listens to these signals by using special receiving equipment hooked up to an antenna. Once a signal from a particular animal is located from several places, a map and compass are used to determine the location, movements, and activity patterns of individual animals. Many locations over a long period of time show the home range or territory of the animal.

I had already used these techniques with black bears, raccoons, jaguars, and ocelots, and had learned that each species reacted differently to the collars. Capturing and collaring wild animals is always unpredictable. In order to anticipate difficult situations and minimize the danger to the animal, I had to consider the requirements of each species carefully. Not only were factors such as body size, shape, and weight important, but I also had to think about the behavior patterns of each species, seasonal fluctuations in temperature and rainfall, and variations in topography, elevation, and forest types.

By the time I returned to Thailand, I had done everything I could think of to ease my transition into the forest. My equipment, which had been sent ahead, was waiting for me at the airport customs depot, and I was being loaned a four-wheel-drive Toyota Landcruiser from a nongovernment group called Wildlife Fund Thailand. As I moved up in line at the customs counter and handed over my documents, I figured that in twenty-four hours I'd be in the forest.

"Twenty-five thousand baht [$1,000 U.S.]," the official said after looking at my papers and going through another file he had pulled from a cabinet behind him.

"Shipping was already paid," I said.

"Customs duty," he said, unable to speak enough English to explain further.

"I am exempt from customs duty." I handed over signed endorsements from the Royal Thai Forestry Department, the National Research Council of Thailand, and the Department of Biology at Mahidol University, all written in Thai. He glanced at the papers and handed them back to me.

"Customs duty, twenty-five thousand baht," he repeated, looking past me to the next person in line.

As I walked away in frustration, I was immediately accosted by a man claiming to be a customs broker. His English was passable, so I hired him to help me. Wasting no time, he cut back into the line and talked to the same official who had just waved me on.

When he returned, he explained to me that I wouldn't have to pay the customs tax as long as I filled out the forms and got the proper signatures that guaranteed that the equipment would be taken back out of the country once the project was finished. That seemed easy enough. Except that nobody knew which forms were needed for the kind of equipment I had.

"Can the radio receivers pick up military frequencies along the Thai-Burmese border?" I was asked.

"No," I replied.

"Can the blowpipe or dart pistol be used as a weapon?"

"Only to put someone to sleep," I said.

"Can the antennas be used to pick up television broadcasting?"

"No," I lied.

Question after question followed for the next couple of days, and soon I was on a first-name basis with Suchet, my customs broker. As we moved from one office to another, we were told either that we didn't have all the proper forms, that the forms were filled out incorrectly, or that additional signatures were needed from officials who weren't in just now. I checked into a hotel in Bangkok and started dreaming about the customs office.

An entire week passed before all of the problems were resolved —except for the radio collars, which I had explained were to be attached to animals in the forest and therefore would be staying in the country after the project was finished.

"What about the forms that say the radios will be given to the government?" I asked.

"I tried that," Suchet said. "He says you will not be giving the radios to the government. You will be giving the radios to animals."

"So I'll get the animals to sign the forms," I said. Suchet smiled.

Finally, by chance, we met an official who was interested in wildlife. After I promised him a chance to visit me in the forest, he got on the phone and spoke with a friend of his in a different office.

"He is saying that you are a special case," Suchet whispered to me. "They have a form for that."

After six trips to the customs office, and countless hours of waiting, all the forms were in, some money exchanged hands, and the officials who had been "unavailable" before magically affixed their stamps of approval. I could pick up my belongings in a few days once all the new papers were in order. When I parted company with Suchet for the last time, he looked like he was losing one of his oldest friends.

Now that the daily ritual of going to the customs office had come to an end, I didn't know what to do with myself. I wandered the streets of Bangkok, recalling descriptions of this crazy city from dozens of books and articles: "the capital of dynamic languor, the city of angels, Sin City, hedonistic heaven, a happy-go-lucky Buddhist capital, a city of snap-crackle-pop eclecticism." All of it fit.

During the day I weaved my way through bumper-to-bumper traffic, a large portion of which was made up of Mercedes-Benzes and BMWs. I walked through hotels and shopping malls that matched anything in New York City. At the Grand Palace, former residence of the royal family, I was awestruck by the towering golden pillars and giant mythical figures. At tourist attractions such as the floating market, the alligator farm, and the Temple of the Reclining Buddha, foreigners mingled easily with smiling Thai faces.

Eventually I wandered away from the crowds toward the edges of the city and found myself in the slums. Here along the open sewage canals children sifted through garbage heaps with their mothers. There were no tourists.

In many parts of Bangkok my inability to communicate even the simplest desire made me feel completely isolated. I tried learning simple Thai words and phrases from a book and a cassette I'd bought in New York, but it seemed hopeless. Thai was originally a Chinese-influenced monosyllabic language which borrowed and adapted both Mon and Khmer words. Later, it absorbed polysyllabic Sanskrit and Pali words as Brahmanism and Theravada Buddhism asserted their influences over the culture. Grammatically, the language is not complicated, but a Thai word spelled phonetically in English can have up to five or more different Thai meanings according to your tone and/or enunciation. For example, one of the most commonly used words, the word meaning "rice" or "cow," is said with a rising tone and a long pronunciation. But with different tonal variations it can also mean "white," "news," or "smells fresh." With a short, more forceful pronunciation using the same tones, it can mean "knee," "go in," "you," or "mountain." Many Thai sounds can't even be spelled phonetically, such as the nasal "ng" sound or the explosive, but soft "bp" sound.

I must have eaten shrimp fried rice at least two dozen times during that first week because it was the only food I could properly request in Thai. Finally I learned to say "noodles," *gwi-tee-oh*, hoping to vary my diet a little, but I was horrified to learn that there were five different kinds of noodles: *sen mee* (very thin white noodles), *sen lek* (thin white noodles), *woon sen* (transparent very thin noodles), *sen yi* (large, rectangular white noodles), and *ba mee* (thin yellow noodles). I stuck with the rice.

At night, I tried letting taxi drivers be my tour guides, but because I was a young male on my own, they inevitably took me to Patpong, Bangkok's infamous commercial sex district, which thrives in a city where prostitution is illegal. In reality, Patpong is no more than a few small side streets which transform after dark into a Las Vegas-type strip where attractive women bombard you with enticing smiles. But all rules of normalcy are left behind once you enter its confines.

I wandered from one bright light to the next, at first mesmerized by it, then a bit intimidated, afraid to let myself be drawn in completely. Buddha statues with food and flower offerings sat beside bars where naked young girls danced and sold themselves for the hour or for the night. Up darkened stairways, past young Thai boys shoving menus of sexual delights in your face, there were sex shows. Here you could sit back and enjoy your beer while attractive little girls pulled razor blades or live snakes out of their vaginas, then rubbed fire down their undulating bodies after dripping hot wax on their tongues and nipples. The grand finale, depending on the bar, was either a homosexual or a heterosexual sex act in numerous gymnastic positions. Back outside, nestled among the bars, were rooms to rent by the hour, deaf-mute children selling Thai crafts, and pharmacies with any manner of drugs you might need: medications to keep you awake, to put you to sleep, to enable you to have more frequent erections, or to remove the newly acquired sores on your genitals.

When the bizarreness of this scene finally became too much, I started wandering on my own again into the quieter parts of the city where the lights were dimmer and smiles didn't rise so easily to the surface. Here, youth and beauty were replaced by limbless beggars sleeping in doorways and deformed children selling flowers along the road. Wherever I went, a tremendous energy, passion, and pathos permeated everything about this city, at levels I couldn't begin to grasp. It became obvious to me that, beneath the glitter, Western values didn't account for much here. The problem was that I didn't know what to replace them with.

One night as I stood by the window in my hotel room, I noticed a young girl, a child actually, no more than fifteen, squatting in the darkness between two parked cars. I turned off the lights in my room and watched her as she held her head between the palms of her hands, eyes toward the ground. Her body gently trembled and I saw the tiredness and pain emanating from her. Then I realized she was crying. Not flowing tears, but dry, heaving crying, the kind when the tears are inside.

From her clothes, I knew she worked in a bar nearby. When a man stepped out from the darkness and motioned for her to come with him, she got up without hesitation. Just before she turned away and disappeared, the lights from the parking gargage caught her face. I'd never seen a look like that on a child before. It was a look of futility, and incredible weariness.

Finally I received the letter I'd been waiting for, telling me to remove my belongings from the customs depot or start paying a storage fee. I was there within the hour. I was told how my "special case" had involved thirty sheets of paper signed by twelve different officials over forty times. I humbly apologized for the trouble I had caused them.

I hired a truck to take the three trunks and two crates back to my hotel in the city. I wanted to pack up and get into the forest as soon as possible. That young trembling girl had made me wonder how conservation could fit into a society where the lives of humans are held so cheaply.

The next morning I packed the Landcruiser and took off in the early-morning free-for-all loosely termed Bangkok traffic. I'd only driven the vehicle once before, so I concentrated on staying on the left side of the road, hoping that the traffic signs in Thai weren't too important. Everything went well for the first ten minutes.

Then, as I merged into a massive entanglement of cars at a place called the Victory Monument traffic circle, I misjudged the width of the Landcruiser and sideswiped a three-wheeled open taxi—called a *tuk-tuk*—cleanly removing its side mirror. The driver, looking a bit shaken, jumped out and started rambling on in Thai, gesticulating at his vehicle. As cars backed up behind us, images of a day in the police station, a fine, and possibly even a lawsuit raced through my mind.

I must have looked pitiful, my face a mixture of utter panic and confusion. I didn't understand a word that was being said, horns were blaring, people on the street had stopped to watch, and I had no idea what to do. The *tuk-tuk* driver suddenly stopped talking, stared hard at me, then shook his head and smiled. He went over and picked up his mirror. Waving it in the air, he kept repeating, "*Mai pen rai, mai pen rai*," one of the few phrases I'd learned, which meant "It's okay, it doesn't matter," before climbing back into his *tuk-tuk* and racing off in a blaze of exhaust fumes. I stood there dumbly, not quite sure what to do next, until the sounds of the car horns told me to just get moving. I jumped into my truck and continued out of Bangkok. Maybe the day wouldn't turn out so badly after all.

By early afternoon, I was in Uthai Thani, the nearest town to the sanctuary. From here, the highway turned into smaller village roads until it reached a little outpost called Lan Sak. After this the pavement turned to dirt. Several miles down the dirt road, I spotted a large brown sign, which I recognized from my first visit as the entrance to the forest reserve. This government forest area borders the Huai Kha Khaeng Wildlife Sanctuary.

Once inside the reserve it was slow going. The road was narrow and rough. Log bridges sagged under the weight of the Landcruiser, and deep crevasses from the previous rainy season had to be circumvented carefully. I passed several clusters of simple wood-and-thatch houses, some with corrals for cattle, others beside large, newly cut clearings. Technically these people were illegally encroaching on government land, but historically they were homesteaders establishing ownership by presence and use. Once forest reserve land became badly enough degraded, the land was often turned over to the people who settled there. There was no clearly enforced government policy regarding these reserve areas.

When I finally crossed the river bordering the sanctuary, it was late afternoon and I was tired, dirty, and hungry. I skirted the buildings that comprised the headquarters and stopped the truck at the beginning of a smaller dirt track. This would take me to my final destination, nine miles ahead.

I looked out the truck's window into a little clearing which contained two black wooden markers put up several years earlier—monuments to the two forest guards shot and killed by poachers in the sanctuary. The black paint was faded and chipped. No one had wanted to talk about these markers when I had been here last.

I knew I was close to my destination when I had to engage the four-wheel drive and shift into low gear in order to take a long steep hill. A couple of miles beyond that was Khao Nang Rum, or Dancing Woman Mountain, site of Thailand's only wildlife research station. The station had a colorful history. Placed at the junction of a major smuggling route for opium, arms, and ivory that ran between tribal villages and the town of Uthai Thani, this station had been the first "guard post" when the sanctuary was established in 1972. A few months after it was built, it was burned to the ground, supposedly by Communist insurgents. When it was rebuilt, it was given the less provocative title of "research station." This was to be my base camp for the next two years. I would be the only full-time researcher there.

I killed the engine at the top of the hill to cool it off and get myself oriented before the final stretch. For the umpteenth time, I thought about whether I had forgotten anything. All the equipment I should need for at least the next year was in the back of the truck. Money had been mailed several months earlier to the chief of the station for building a small research base. I had my permits, a year's visa, a bank account in Bangkok, and I had put out word at various universities that I was interested in finding a graduate student to work with me.

I looked off toward the north. A few miles through the woods were five simple little monk huts. For the first time, I freely admitted to myself that those huts were a major factor in my decision to return to this place. Something about that particular spot was as important to me as the forest itself.

I started up the truck and was about to move on, when I noticed a miniature wooden house atop a low hill to my left. It was the spirit house, a shrine to the mother spirit of the mountain, the dancing woman, who watched over this area. I had been told about it during my first visit, when the men stopped to pay obeisance on our way in. This dilapidated little structure, with its tiny plastic figurines of Thai classical dancers inside, had been built by previous forest workers here. The strange pyramidal rock pile it rested upon was part of a two-hundred-year-old spirit structure built along the old opium trail that still continued back into the hill tribe areas near Burma.

I honked my horn twice as I had seen the Thais do to get the attention of the mother, then nodded my head toward the spirit house to thank her for a safe trip into the valley. My hands on the steering wheel tensed with excitement. Spirits, monks, tigers, and leopards? I had no idea what to expect next.

3

INTO
THE
CAULDRON

The station at Dancing Woman Mountain sits in a secluded forest pocket fifteen hundred feet high at the confluence of two streams which eventually join to flow into the Huai Kha Khaeng. Mountains ring the perimeter. The highest, called Khao Khieo, rises to over four thousand feet southeast of the station. The climatic fluctuations in this area, more extreme than in other parts of the sanctuary, contribute to a forest structure that is unlike many of the other "monsoon forests" of Southeast Asia. Drought and fire during the dry months and heavy rains followed by flooding during the wetter months help maintain a mosaic of tropical habitats ranging from open, savannalike forest to dense, moist areas of evergreen forest. My previous trip had shown me that this area had a rich wildlife community, including at least several large cats.

My arrival at the station was heralded by the barking charge of three tawny-colored Thai dogs, though my truck had been heard long before I reached the first house. The station chief, Noparat, was waiting alone in front of the kitchen area to welcome me. As a huge grin broke across his face, I realized how glad I was to see him again.

Noparat had been an enthusiastic supporter of my research at this station. At thirty-seven, he was only three years older than I and had a college degree in forestry and wildlife. He rushed over to the door of the truck before I could get out.

"Good to see you again," he said in university-taught English. He seemed nervous, unsure whether to clasp his hands together and bow in a traditional Thai greeting or to shake my hand.

"Your house is not finished yet. Too many other things for the men to do. But *mai pen rai*, one room is ready. You can stay there. So glad you have come back. Everybody has been waiting for you." He waved his arm to encompass the station.

I turned and scanned the hill and open areas behind me. There was no one else around.

Over the next few days I settled in, and tried to learn more about my new home and its inhabitants. There were fifteen men currently at the station, many with wives and children. Five of the men, including Noparat, were employees of the Wildlife Conservation Division of the Royal Thai Forestry Department. The others were young hired workers from local villages around the sanctuary and were paid from the station's budget.

The station sat on several acres of cleared forest in a little valley pocket. There was a large grassy soccer field in the lower part of the camp. Nearby sat the station chief's house and the open-sided camp kitchen alongside one of the two main streams in the area, the Huai Chang Tai. Past the kitchen and up a hill were two long wooden buildings off to the right. These were subdivided into one-room dwellings for the workers and their families. To the left was the office building, which contained a recently acquired wireless radio. The radio allowed daily contact with the sanctuary's headquarters and other, smaller substations in the area. Beyond the office was a small concrete guesthouse that was usually empty. Farther up the hill and beyond the edge of the forest was my new house.

I had chosen the site of my house carefully, but I had left its design up to Noparat, telling him to keep it simple. He had done so for the most part, but had also decided that a Westerner needed some special comforts. These extra luxuries took the form of glass windows, concrete floors, and a sit-down toilet (versus the stand-over squatting type toilet typical throughout most of Asia). I could have done without the windows and floors but I was ecstatic about the toilet. Having used the Asian kind all too often, I was very pleased to realize that I wouldn't have to squat for the next two years.

However, all these amenities seemed trivial when I stood in front of the half-finished wooden structure and looked around me, remembering why I had chosen this site. The house sat on a knoll higher than the rest of the camp and was set back into the forest so that I couldn't see or hear the activities of the station. The bedroom faced south, as I'd requested, so that when I woke in the mornings I could look out my window into the forest.

At mealtimes, I ate at the communal kitchen with Noparat and some of the staff. Although Noparat spoke to me in English when I asked questions or if he needed to explain something, all other conversation was in Thai. At first, everyone was nervous around me and unsure how to behave. Few other foreigners had passed through the station, and I was the first to settle in there full-time.

I quickly threw away my Thai-language learning cassette once I realized that no one in Thailand spoke anything like the voices on those tapes. Instead a Thai-English dictionary became my constant companion, and every day I made flash cards of new words to memorize. In the meantime, I was forced to communicate mostly with sign language.

My first efforts at speaking Thai were met with friendly laughter and seemed to help break the ice between the men and me. They never tired of my constant mistakes. I was a good source of entertainment when I pointed to the dogs and called them horses or tried explaining how I had seen shirts in the forest when I meant tiger tracks.

After a few weeks life fell into a routine, and my spirits, which had lowered considerably in Bangkok, started to revive. My house was almost finished. With Noparat's help, I hired Beng, the wife of one of the workers, to do my laundry and carry water up from the stream to fill my washtub and toilet, which drained into the forest behind my house. Bathing was done as elsewhere in rural Thailand, by pouring buckets of water over your head.

While I helped the men work on my house, I made my first friend, Supakit, the camp's general engineer and handyman. Supakit was a dark, rugged-looking Thai with a quick wit and an easygoing personality. We were the same age. He was Noparat's foreman, and he completed his tasks with such quiet skill that I often enjoyed just sitting and watching him work. Despite the language barrier, we were drawn to each other immediately. In the evenings after dinner, we'd sit together over a bottle of Mekong (a Thai whiskey made from rice) teaching each other Thai and English.

Supakit's wife, Amporn, a striking twenty-six-year-old from the Chiang Mai area of northern Thailand, was the camp's cook and my most diligent Thai teacher. If I went to the kitchen while she was preparing dinner, she would drill me on what I had learned the previous day, correcting my pronunciation and making me repeat new words that she wanted to teach me.

At mealtimes, Amporn would whip up our usual fare of white rice with side dishes of assorted spicy vegetables and eggs. If fresh meat was still available from the last trip to town, it was chopped into small pieces and added to the dishes. Sometimes a plate of flat, dried fish was served, the ony food I never learned to like. It looked and smelled like it had been run over by a truck and left to rot for several days before being sold at the market.

White boiled rice was the major staple of our diet and it was usually served at every meal. For a change of pace, we'd have rice porridge for breakfast or fried rice for lunch and dinner. When we were flush with supplies, Amporn would prepare a delicious dessert called *cow neeoh biak*, sweetened sticky rice with coconut milk.

The food took some getting used to and I was often hungry after a meal, but eventually I realized what an incredible job Amporn did with the little money she was given. Still, since I was bigger than all of the Thais at camp (and I had no desire to get as thin as they were), I decided to start supplementing my diet with a private stock of canned food.

By the end of the month, I was regularly patrolling the roads and elephant trails looking for signs of animals. Sometimes I'd follow compass bearings through the forest or walk along a stream bed to see where it would lead. I wanted to get a feel for the forest and the wildlife community before I went about methodically collecting data and trapping animals. I needed to know more than just what species were in the area and what signs they left behind; I needed to grow comfortable here as well. I had to feel that I was moving through the forest, not against it.

However, the forest was always quick to remind me that becoming too comfortable was dangerous. One day, while crossing a stream, I was busily concentrating on the pronunciation of some Thai words when I stepped up onto the opposite bank; a break in the normal pattern of the grass made me freeze instinctively. Just inches below my boot was the mottled, diamondlike pattern of a coiled Russell's viper, one of the most poisonous snakes in the region.

As I pulled my foot back slowly, the snake became rigid, head up, ready to go into action. I froze, holding my breath with my foot still in the air, not wanting even the backward movement to appear threatening. Finally the snake uncoiled and moved off into the underbrush.

I sat down on a rock by the stream, letting my heartbeat return to normal, and pictured the consequences of this snake's bite. Descriptions of vomiting blood, bleeding out of the eyes and nose, organ failure, and cerebral hemorrhaging came easily to mind. That was enough. The snake had reminded me to tread much more carefully.

Once I knew what species were in the area, I never tired of finding their fresh spoor, smelling the glandular scent that they had rubbed against a tree or into the dirt, or seeing where they had bedded down the previous night. I was thrilled when I discovered where a little leopard cat had crossed the trail or when I followed the tracks of an Asian wild dog, called a dhole, along a stretch of road. Although the animals were usually long gone, I could still feel their presence and picture their actions in my mind.

Along stream banks, I'd see where civets, mongooses, or hog badgers had come to drink. At salt licks, areas where some animals come to lick up mineral deposits that break through the ground's surface, I could discern regular visits by deer, elephants, and wild cattle species. But it was the big cats I was always on the lookout for, and so I was especially excited to find their tracks and feces along almost every path I traveled. When more than one big cat was in the area, the trail would often be littered with scrapes, the distinctive scratch marks large cats make with their paws in order to mark their territories.

Most of the big cat tracks I found were medium in size, approximately three inches long by nearly three and a half inches wide. Feces near the tracks averaged an inch in diameter. Experience told me that these were most likely left by leopards. In some places, however, I regularly found tiger tracks that were almost six inches square with feces up to three inches in diameter. Although leopards had been spotted in the area much more frequently than tigers, I still had to confirm that these sightings were indicative of the leopard's greater abundance and not just due to chance.

I started to determine how many big cats were around by drawing and measuring many of their tracks and scrapes. But although I could usually tell leopard's tracks from tiger's, it was not easy to differentiate between individual members of the same species. One animal can show a lot of variation in its track size depending on whether the track is made with the front or rear paw, how quickly the animal is moving, and whether the track is found in mud, hard dirt, or sand. However, if I looked closely enough, I could sometimes find slight, consistent anomalies in a track that singled out an individual leopard.

Sometimes the toes or footpads would be shaped differently from those of other cats, or an old wound would cause an irregularity in the track's pattern.

In the evenings, I transcribed my field notes, practiced Thai with my flash cards, and watched the camp activities. The men, in spite of long days of hard physical work, usually played soccer or takraw in the early evening. Takraw is similar to volleyball, but you can use only your feet and head and the small ball is made of light rattan. They played until dark, and then the station's generator clicked on, providing two to three hours of electricity during dinnertime. Most of the camp was in bed by ten o'clock.

By now I'd gone out into the forest with most of the men, but I only knew a few of the workers by their first names. There was Ot, a tall, thin thirty-three-year-old who had worked at the station for nine years and was one of the best forest men in camp; Muuk, who had bad teeth and a quick smile, and always dressed in torn, ragged clothing; Intah, a short Burmese powerhouse with the body of a weight lifter; Sombat, a handsome, slow-moving bachelor who was Beng's older brother; Samut, the camp's mechanic, who had been born with a congenital deformity that left parts of his fingers missing; Anant, who at seventeen years of age was the youngest worker in camp and whose smile spread over half his face; and Riap, a fifty-five-year-old who looked twenty years younger and whose overly shy mannerisms seemed almost furtive.

I didn't know any of the women except Beng and Amporn. Most of the village girls were not used to dealing with foreigners and in the beginning they'd usually scatter or go inside their house whenever I approached. In the evenings, they would gather at the front of their apartments to gossip and breast-feed the newest additions to their families. The older children played nearby with toys made from sticks, buckets, and shiny cans. Little girls hunched over imaginary fires pretending to cook rice, while the boys turned sticks into guns to go out and hunt the local game.

Thai children are allowed to roam and play freely, and are only gradually made to help with their family's work. But childhood is still short. By the age of eight, girls are expected to help with the house-work and boys start to assist with the farm chores. Fifteen-year-old girls and sixteen-year-old boys are considered fully mature laborers. Boys usually marry at about twenty after spending some time as a monk. For girls, marriage can come as early as fourteen or fifteen.

Once I became more settled at camp, the days flowed by. The gibbons would rouse me in the morning with their early wake-up calls, and I would watch sambar and barking deer feed in the grassy open forest around my house. Sometimes I'd spot the majestic great hornbills flying overhead in the early evening. My Thai was improving and I was no longer treated like a stranger in camp. But I still felt like an outsider. Rather than call me by my name, I was always referred to as the *farang*, a Thai word meaning Westerner, which can also have negative undertones.

I knew that Thais expressed emotion differently than Westerners, but I didn't expect the adjustment to this alien culture to be so difficult for me. Despite my growing friendship with Supakit and Amporn, there was still a strong cultural wall between me and everyone else, and the initial euphoria I had felt upon arriving here was slowly being replaced by loneliness. I worked harder than ever to learn Thai, hoping that this was the key to breaking through some of the barriers.

Since my arrival, Noparat had been my only real channel of communication with the rest of the camp. He had helped smooth my transition and often had patiently helped clarify the events taking place around me. But recently he'd started to shift all our conversations around to his personal failures and frustrations. It became clear that this seemingly self-effacing man was fighting internal battles which were eating him up.

When I'd met Noparat during my first visit, he had just left the monkhood. The practice of becoming a monk at some point during a man's life is still highly regarded in Thai culture. In the past, a Thai man who had never been a monk was regarded as *khon dip*, an unripe person, and was not readily accepted as a suitable marriage partner.

But for Noparat, the transition back to his old world was proving difficult. He was now a middle-aged bachelor with no belongings and no home other than the forest station. Torn between returning to the monkhood or living out his life as a layperson, he wavered between the two, trying to maintain vows of celibacy and selflessness, but having a difficult time dealing with the realities of his life and his job, which unfortunately now included me.

I respected Noparat. He loved the forest and he treated his workers like family. When government funds were late or never materialized, he'd keep the station running with money from his own pocket. When children were sick, he'd make a special trip to bring them to the nearest clinic which was several hours away. The workers, in turn, were unwavering in their loyalty to him, treating him like a benign monarch. But the familylike atmosphere at this isolated station also provided Noparat with a safe haven from the pressures of the outside world that occasionally troubled him.

In the beginning, I listened patiently and let Noparat vent whatever was building up inside him. But my enjoyment of our conversations lessened. Eventually I began to avoid him and we talked less openly, which caused our friendship to cool.

After more than a month of hiking through the forest around Dancing Woman Mountain on foot, one morning I decided to take my truck along one of the dirt tracks that had been cut by the poaching patrols to allow access for their vehicles. I hoped to use these routes to haul traps and other equipment into the forest's interior. Since the roads were minimally maintained and rarely driven, they were the preferred travel paths of many animals.

The day before, Belinda Stewart-Cox, a British researcher investigating the status of the green peafowl in Thailand, had come to visit the station. We got on well together and I invited her to accompany me on my trip, which would take us to the river. I avoided telling Noparat because he had recently requested that I take a fully armed worker with me whenever I went into the forest. I understood his concern because of the illegal hunters in the area, but I had found that having a guard constantly at my side hindered me from moving through the forest quickly and quietly, so I kept my plans to myself.

Belinda and I drove the truck two and a half miles to the larger of the two main streams, the Huai Ai Yo, and then separated. I spent my time looking for cat tracks along the bank while Belinda went off by herself. There were signs of animal activity everywhere. It was the beginning of April, the middle of the dry season, and ground fires were sweeping through much of the area. Many of the smaller streams had dried up, forcing much of the wildlife to come here to the main river for water.

For a while, I sat on a rock along the bank near a large tiger track, feeling that uneasy tingle I often get when I'm alone in a wild place. I closed my eyes and listened to the water moving through chutes in the rocks. In the distance, I could hear the crackle of a fire burning. Every now and then sounds like gunshots went off, telling me that the fire had just reached a bamboo thicket. The bamboo blew apart as the heated air inside its sealed compartments expanded. The word "bamboo," Malay in origin, is believed to imitate the explosive sound bamboo makes when it burns. I listened to more bamboo blowing up; this time the noise was closer. Having seen how quickly fires could sweep through an area, I decided it was time to leave.

I met up with Belinda, and we started back. On my left side fires were already within sight of the road, but the truck could still easily get by them. Then, just as I topped a small hill, the truck's left wheel broke through the edge of a deep rut, snatching the steering wheel out of my hands and sending us veering off the side of the road. I slammed on the brakes, but I couldn't stop the truck's forward momentum. We smashed into a tree and then were thrown backward into the same rut that had caused me to lose control in the first place.

When I tried to get the truck going again, the engine started immediately—but none of the gears engaged. I got out and crawled under the truck to investigate. One look confirmed my worst fears. The transfer case of the front differential had cracked open and all the fluid had drained out. Some of the gears inside the housing were probably broken as well. Clearly the truck was not going anywhere.

I laid my head back in the dirt trying to figure out what to do next when a loud explosion went off nearby. I swerved around, peering out at ground level between the two front tires.

"I think we've got another slight problem," I heard Belinda say above me.

The line of fire we had seen while driving was now no more than twenty yards away. My first instinct was to put as much distance between myself and the truck as possible. The gas tank was nearly full, and if the fire reached the truck, it would go off like a bomb. For a moment, I considered just letting it happen and using the accident as an excuse to abandon both the truck and the project, and return to New York.

I crawled out from under the truck and turned to where Belinda had been standing, but she was no longer there. Then I saw her breaking branches in the forest close to the advancing fire.

"Let's get on with it, Alan," she called out to me. "We don't have all day." I followed her toward the flames.

Using burning branches, we started our own fire between the flames and the truck before clearing all the flammable debris from around the truck. If this went as planned, then our fire would meet the advancing flames and they'd stop each other. But if the advancing fire got larger, it would simply jump ours. We did all we could before starting back to camp on foot. We were both quiet, keeping an ear out for a major explosion. Luckily it never came.

I told Noparat the news over dinner. He sympathized with me at first but then blamed me for going out without one of his men and not being careful. Belinda, sensing the rising tension, diverted the conversation. I ate the rest of the meal in silence while Noparat talked with the men about the higher price of rice in town. Finally he told Supakit to tow my truck back to camp the next day. After dinner I returned to my house and started in alone on a bottle of Mekong. Nothing was going as planned. Half a bottle later, I finally got to sleep.

In the early-morning light, some of the gloom of the previous night left me, replaced by a slight headache. I went outside in my underwear to listen to the chatter of the birds and squirrels. I never made it two steps beyond my front door.

There, at the entrance to my house, was a long, distinctive double paw scrape, the smell of fresh urine emanating from a wet patch at its base. Several feet away, in a shaded area of softer dirt, was the outline of a track four inches long and three and a half inches wide. The lower lobes of the footpad had a slight, almost unnoticeable angular shape. I knew this animal, having frequently seen and drawn its tracks while walking along the Huai Chang Tai, the stream closest to my house. It was a big male leopard.

I sat in the doorway of my house staring at the scrape. Sometime during the night while I lay in a stupor, this leopard had walked up to my front door and left his calling card. Had he seen my tracks following his once too often? I wondered. Had he growled a foot below my bedroom window as I slept?

I got up and went to the edge of the clearing that defined my "front yard." An area of matted grass indicated this was where he had come from. Kneeling down, I made a long, deep scrape in the dirt with my hands. Then I stood up and urinated behind it.

"Okay, you've told me," I said. "But I'm here to stay."

4

FOREST
CATTLE

It took ten workers most of the day to pull my truck the two miles back to camp. After disengaging its transfer case and attaching a tow bar cut from a tree, we hitched the station's Toyota pickup to the dead weight of my heavier Landcruiser, and the two trucks inched their way along. When we came to an incline, the men jumped out and pushed the Landcruiser. At the last hill before camp, no amount of muscle power could move my truck up the short, steep grade. So everyone grabbed their shovels and picks and, within a few hours, we had flattened the hill.

Feeling guilty about the extra work I'd caused the men, I compromised with Noparat and agreed to let one of his workers accompany me on a regular basis until I found someone to assist me permanently. He chose one of the strangest, most colorful characters in camp: a gnomelike, toothless, sixty-year-old former elephant hunter called Lung Galong, who had lived over forty years in these forests. (Lung is a term of respect in Thai which means Uncle.) Galong had first come to this area in his mid-teens, while working with a forest survey team. Later he became an opium courier for a high-

ranking policeman. When opium trading was banned, he fled deep
into the forest. There he lived for more than ten years among the
Hmong and Karen tribespeople, carrying their opium out to other
villages and hunting elephants for ivory. Sometimes he'd kill bears
and tigers and take their paws to sell to Chinese restaurants.

The end of Lung Galong's freewheeling jungle career came when
he lost three fingers from his right hand after his muzzle-loading rifle
blew up while he was shooting an elephant. Convinced that this
accident was in retribution for killing too many animals for profit,
he swore to the spirit mother that he'd never hunt again. Sometime
after that Noparat adopted him, letting him earn his keep by doing
odd jobs around the station.

Any misgivings I had about Galong's abilities were dispelled on
our first day in the forest together. As he cut our way along old
elephant trails with unflagging energy, he jabbered away in Thai,
pointing out birds, trees, and animal sign, not caring whether I understood anything he was saying or not. Sometimes he'd burst forth
with a few garbled, mispronounced words in English, German, or
French that he'd picked up from various foreigners over the years.
Then he'd break out in a high-pitched cackling laugh, obviously
pleased with his own worldliness. His smile, energy, and good nature
won me over quickly, despite the many times I wanted to gag him
just to remember what silence sounded like.

By now I had delineated the boundaries of the study area. For
the large cats, I confined myself to forty square miles, encompassing
all the lower riverine habitat around the station and extending a short
distance beyond the range of Dancing Woman Mountain. The focal
area encompassed about twelve square miles surrounding the station.
This area was where I planned to study some of the other carnivores.
The first task was to use compass and tape measure to accurately map
the more than eight miles of roads and the five to ten miles of dirt
tracts and trails within these areas. This would enable me to plot the
location of tracks and animal sign and eventually to plot the locations
of the animals I hoped to radio-collar. It was slow, monotonous work.

Initial efforts to identify spoor of different cat species was proving more difficult than I'd expected. Cat tracks ranged in size from those of the little leopard cat (about a square inch) up to the six-inch tracks of tigers. The vast majority fell somewhere in between and could belong to any of five different cat species known to be in the sanctuary: the fishing cat, jungle cat, Temmick's or golden cat, clouded leopard, and Asiatic leopard. Because many of the cat-track sizes and shapes overlapped, it was often impossible to tell species apart.

While Lung Galong proved to be invaluable in helping me map the area and get acquainted with the forest, I had to sift through his statements carefully. He knew it was my interest in clouded leopards that had first brought me here, so now he insisted that every medium-sized cat track we saw was from that species. I knew, though, that Galong had never seen a clouded leopard or several of the other cat species in the area. Though his knowledge of the forest was extensive, so was his imagination. He would find a few spots of dried blood in matted-down grass close to big cat tracks, then act out an entire stalk-and-chase scenario between a tiger and a barking deer, almost convincing me he had seen it happen. His clouded leopard tracks later turned out to be those of a female Asiatic leopard.

After a week of Galong's constant chatter, I was anxious to be by myself again. One morning I sneaked away at 5 A.M, an hour before dawn, to look over an area in the evergreen forest where I wanted to put my first big cat trap. The male leopard had not marked in front of my house again, but his tracks along the Huai Chang Tai told me that he was still in the area.

The trail was dark under the closed canopy of the evergreen forest, so I walked slowly and carefully, thinking about the king cobras, Russell's vipers, and reticulated pythons that might be lurking nearby. As I rounded a bend in the trail, there was an abrupt movement ahead of me and I looked up to see a huge black mass emerging from the darkness. My first thought was elephant, but as my eyes adjusted and focused on the golden forehead beneath two long, outward-curving horns, I realized that I had just stumbled upon a gaur, one of the two wild cattle species in the sanctuary. A breeze came up behind me and, as the gaur angled his head in my direction, he suddenly caught my scent.

I stepped into the shadows at the edge of the trail and froze, watching him disappear as quickly as he had come without making a sound. I couldn't believe how big he was. I waited nearly half a minute before moving again. Then as I was about to step forward, a second gaur emerged onto the trail, following the first one but, as yet, unaware of my presence.

While I was sneaking closer for a better look, there was a loud snort behind my left shoulder. I crouched down, wondering if I had walked into the middle of a large group as they were bedding down for the day. The second gaur, suddenly alert, was looking right at me. I was at eye level with his yellow-white stockings, which reached from his hooves to above his hocks. Then he was off with a crash, joining the first somewhere in the darkness.

I had read stories about gaur circling around people quietly, then charging suddenly and spearing them with their horns. Many hunters considered this animal one of the most difficult and dangerous beasts on earth. George Schaller, who had studied them in India, said they were one of the few wild animals formidable enough to stand their ground successfully against a tiger.

There was no further movement, and as we waited each other out, I peered through the undergrowth trying to spot their huge black bodies among the greenery. The largest of all the Asian wild cattle species, the gaur has a body length of up to eleven feet and stands seven feet at the shoulder; they can weigh up to two thousand pounds. I was amazed that these two had disappeared so completely. I wondered if there were others out there, since they often travel in groups of twenty or more.

My legs were cramping and I knew I couldn't remain crouched much longer, so I stood up and started talking loudly, telling the gaur to "go away" while making rustling noises in the brush around me. Immediately there was a crashing, like a tractor moving through the forest, and I saw the two gaur running away, up the west slope of Khao Khieo Mountain. There were just the two of them, probably both bulls. As I had hoped, they wanted nothing more than to get away from me. Two jungle fowl scurried off into the undergrowth at the same time. These birds sometimes trailed gaur, supposedly taking advantage of the insects that the cattle stirred up. I went over to where the gaur had first emerged from the forest and sat on a log nearby, smelling their odor and letting the excitement sink in.

Wild cattle, with names like gaur and banteng, are a distinctly Asian phenomenon. In Thailand, these two species are becoming increasingly rare with some of the last large herds found in the forests of the Huai Kha Khaeng Wildlife Sanctuary. Gaur, also known as seladang in Malaysia, are found primarily in hilly, evergreen habitats containing dependable sources of food and water. Capable of roaming over thirty to fifty square miles, they need large, relatively undisturbed forest areas to survive. Poaching, loss of habitat, and diseases spread by domestic cattle have already decimated the gaur population in Thailand. In 1977 there were estimated to be fewer than five hundred individuals, and the gaur's numbers are still decreasing.

I still hadn't seen a banteng (or wild ox), which is believed to be the possible ancestor of domestic cattle. This bright reddish-brown ox is smaller and less aggressive, but more wary than the gaur. Often found in large herds alongside deer and wild pigs, bantengs were less common in the hilly forests around the station because they preferred the open, grassy lowland plains for grazing. Both wild cattle species are greatly prized by hunters.

It was now the middle of May and the increased rainfall at the end of the dry season was bringing color and life back to the forest. It amazed me how, virtually overnight, burned and dry forest was transformed from a bare, blackened moonscape to a green, grassy, almost pastoral scene. During my first visit here, I had been surprised to learn that many of the annual fires were started by forest guards. Although this was against the government's official policy, local sanctuary workers often saw fires as beneficial. Fires produce new grass and edible young shoots for the deer and wild cattle, keep paths clear, and help control pests and diseases. Poachers within the sanctuary often started fires for the same reasons. Outside the sanctuary, fires that were started to clear land, fertilize soil, and remove stubble from old rice harvests often spread into the forest. But I wondered what these fires were doing to the forest over the long term. Lung Galong had said that in the past the forest had been so thick that the canopy nearly blotted out the light from the sky. Now there were many open, dry areas. And where did the rodents, the ground-nesting birds, and the small cats go during fires? I noticed a paucity of snakes, frogs, and other animals that I had expected to see here in greater abundance.

One of the main habitats around the station, the open, savan-nalike, dry dipterocarp forest, is thought to be a product of fires. Althouth dry dipterocarp forest can occur naturally in certain restricted areas, fire helps spread this kind of habitat into the fire-intolerant and richer evergreen forests. Around Dancing Woman Mountain, the soil was rich enough to support more evergreen forest than was present. If the fires were damaging this vulnerable evergreen forest, then the situation here was not as stable as I'd first thought.

Fire advocates argue that regular burning eliminates much of the land's underbrush and dry litter, which is the major fuel for fires. This supposedly protects the sanctuary from potentially hotter, more destructive fires. There is some truth to this argument but fires that occur too frequently further damage the more fire-adapted open areas as well.

The socioeconomic conditions in Thailand also favor the creation of man-made fires. Most forest and wildlife communities are already little more than isolated pockets, surrounded by an ocean of humanity. The destruction of parts of these forest pockets by fire provides a good excuse for immediate expansion by surrounding communities. The impact of this local exploitation on newly "degraded" land is irreversible. When I left the sanctuary and saw the new huts, cleared fields, and felled trees eating into the forest like a leprotic sore, it upset me to see how easily this newly burned land had been taken away from the wildlife.

·   ·   ·

With the start of the rainy season came the monks. I'd been passing the monk huts almost daily while looking for cat sign, but they had remained empty since my arrival. Now Noparat informed me that three monks had come in on the truck that brought our weekly supplies. When he asked if I wanted to go with him the next day to visit them, I immediately agreed.

We met one of the monks sweeping the dirt path to his hut and were immediately invited to join him for late-afternoon coffee. While the monks usually eat only one meal a day provided by the local people, they are allowed other foods categorized as "medicines" whenever they want. Coffee and tea, usually laden with numerous heaping teaspoons of sugar, are "medicines." We removed our shoes and sat opposite the monk on a bamboo platform that was raised several feet off the ground and protected from the rain and sun by a slanted thatched roof.

Two other monks shortly emerged, coming up from the Huai Chang Tai, where they had been bathing. One was an elderly man, accompanied by a young boy who looked to be no more than sixteen. The boy was a novice, Noparat explained, forbidden to enter the monkhood until he was at least twenty. As a novice, he had to adhere to only the 10 basic rules or precepts of Buddhism, as compared with the 227 for a monk. The older monk, walking behind the boy, had a cigarette dangling from his mouth. I wondered if tobacco was also classified as a "medicine."

They were all curious as to why I was living in the forest and how I was able to eat Thai food. In turn I asked them, using Noparat as my translator, why they had come into the forest and what they hoped to achieve here. The younger monk replied with answers that were nebulous, almost apathetic. The older monk gave a simpler answer.

"To mediate," he said, "and to help a novice along the path." He flicked his cigarette off into the forest. I kept silent while Noparat chatted with them for another fifteen minutes. As we drove back to camp, I expressed some misgivings.

"The problem is with you," Noparat said to me, not unkindly. "The monks are men, but you expect more."

"I thought they're supposed to be special," I said, flashing on scenes of incense-filled temples and golden Buddhas.

"They are not special, they are different. They are men who have given up normal life to live simply and reflect on Buddha's teachings."

I was confused. If Buddhism meant devotion to a simple way of life, then why all the ceremony surrounding special holidays, the obeisance involved in the giving of food by the laity, the large ornate temples?

"Oh, I almost forgot. I found someone to help you," Noparat said, interrupting my thoughts. "Lung Soowan, a hunter like Galong, but not so old. He'll be here in two days."

"Thanks," I mumbled, my mind still distracted with thoughts of the monks. Was Thai Buddhism more style than substance? I wondered.

In addition to the monks, the beginning of the rainy season brought other visitors as well: ants, a group of animals that must have evolved solely to torture man. At first there were just the tiny, innocuous varieties. I'd find them stuck between the bristles of my toothbrush, running across the pages of my book as I read, emerging from the switches on my tape player, or floating in their final resting place in my morning coffee or rice. After a while I stopped picking them out of my food and just ate them along with the vegetables. When I finally adjusted to their constant presence, another, more insidious species entered my life.

Lying half awake in the darkness slapping at myself, I wondered how mosquitoes had gotten inside the net. Then I felt painful little stings and I switched on the flashlight that I kept under my pillow. Large red ants, which until now I'd only seen in little groups around camp, were all over the lower part of my body. They were moving en masse through the window beside my bed. I slapped at them frantically and jumped out from under the net, only to have them retaliate by biting me more ferociously. When I felt them marching across my feet, I swung the flashlight around to see that they were all over the floor and spreading quickly into the other two rooms of the house.

I ran into the bathroom, dumped water over my body, and then ran outside feeling like I had just emerged from a late-night horror movie. Around me the forest was dark, quiet, and peaceful. It was peaceful, I thought—except for the ants, scorpions, snakes, gaur, elephants, tigers, and leopards. I crawled into the front of my truck and tried to sleep, but my heart was still racing. Every now and then I'd feel the movement of an ant that had been stranded somewhere on my body. It was two days before I could move back into my house. It was much longer before I could sleep easily again.

When Lung Soowan appeared at my door the day after the ant invasion, I found myself staring into the face of a scarred, tough-looking forty-two-year-old man. He was dressed only in a short, saronglike wraparound called a *pacomah* and his chest and back were covered with tattoos, a practice common among men from the north-eastern part of Thailand. He'd never worked with a *farang* before and spoke mostly Isarn, a northeastern dialect, different from both the northern dialect Amporn was teaching me and the more common central or Bangkok Thai which I had been learning on my own. I was just beginning to make myself understood, I thought. Now this.

Soowan arrived alone. His family had remained in his village about an hour from the sanctuary. After agreeing on a salary of fifty baht (two dollars) a day, he moved into part of Beng's house and started coming over every morning at sunrise to go into the forest with me. Though he understood my Thai, at first he rarely acknowl-edged anything I tried to say. I made the situtation worse when, several days after we had started working together, I gave Soowan a hunting knife as a present. When he refused it, I thought he was being polite, so I stuck the knife in his belt. He turned and left

abruptly. When I told the story to Noparat, I learned that in Thailand
a knife is only given to someone whom you wish to hurt. It can be
given as a friendly gesture only if you accept something in return.
Noparat talked with Soowan, and the next day I accepted one baht
(four cents) for the knife.

Despite the initial lack of rapport between us, I could tell from
our first day together that Lung Soowan was at home in the forest.
He would glide through the underbrush, clearing vegetation with no
more than a flick of his razor-sharp knife, all the while pointing out
sights and sounds that I had difficulty discerning even after being
shown them. Sometimes he'd pull up and freeze suddenly, eyes flashing,
as he watched a sambar deer grazing by the water or a group of
macaques moving through the trees overhead. But when it came to
communication, he was Lung Galong's exact opposite. Words were
spoken only when necessary.

The initial breakthrough came during the third week we worked
together. As we chopped our way through a rough, scrubby area, I
grabbed a thorny, poisonous plant that caused me extreme pain and
made my hand start to swell immediately. This sent Lung Soowan
into fits of laughter, producing the first smile I'd seen from him.

"What was that?" I demanded in Thai, not at all pleased.

"Elephant scream plant," he answered, a big grin still on his face.
"Even elephants cry when they touch it. It'll hurt for many days."

"Why didn't you tell me about it?" I asked unreasonably.

"I forgot you're a *farang*," he said, laughing.

I suddenly realized that not only did Soowan have a nice smile
but we had just held our first conversation. I laughed too in spite of
the pain. Later, I learned how Thais often laugh at the misfortunes
of those closest to them. If Lung Soowan had disliked me, he would
have shown no emotion.

From that point on, our relationship improved. I learned to communicate with him in his Isarn dialect mixed with some common
Thai, and layers started peeling away. Soowan could make my day
just by giving me a smile or a nod of approval. These small gestures
meant a lot to me. Once Soowan understood what I was trying to

do, we could divide up the work. Now I had him start building the first of our big cat traps which Supakit helped to design.

The first chance I got, I went to Bangkok for a week to look for a new front differential for the truck. While I was there, I purchased a punching bag and two forty-pound dumbbells. Although the field-work was exhausting, exercising helped me vent some of my frustra-tions and had an important therapeutic effect on me. I already jogged almost every day along the road to the monk huts but that was never enough.

At first my exercise routines went unnoticed, but as the punching of the bag resounded throughout the quiet evening air, some of the children came wandering up to watch this strange display. Soon the men who came up to retrieve their children stayed to watch. Even-tually some of the men started coming on their own, especially when I'd entice them with whiskey.

In the beginning only Supakit actually exercised with me. He enjoyed the weight lifting because it "made his arms fatter" and his wife, Amporn, liked the effect. He even helped expand my little outdoor gym by building a wooden bench press and hooking up a pipe between two trees to make a chin-up bar. Then Anant, the youngest of the workers, started coming by. He was a bachelor on the lookout for a wife, and he asked me to help him get muscles so that he could look more like a man. The only other regular was a worker named Prateep, who had been a *muay Thai* (Thai kick boxing) competitor in his village. He came every evening to kick the bag.

Some of the other men tried playing around with the equipment but soon gave it up, seeing no reason to do physical work on their time off. Most simply came by to drink whiskey, talk, and listen to the music I played while exercising. That was fine with me. I felt less lonely and was learning Thai more quickly.

. . .

One morning just after sunrise, Soowan burst into my house and beckoned me excitedly to follow him. He talked rapidly while I put on my boots and the only word I could make out was *seu-uh*, the generic Thai word for a large cat. We took off through the forest, climbing over two small hills behind my house. When we reached the Huai Chang Tai, we went upstream for less than a hundred yards before Soowan stopped and pointed.

There lying on the ground was the upper half of a dead sambar deer, fresh blood still dripping from where its hindquarters had recently been. In the soft mud of the stream bank were large leopard tracks. We were less than a quarter of a mile from my house. Before I even examined the tracks, I knew this was the cat that had marked at my door. Soowan told me that he had heard a big cat vocalize a few hours before sunrise, followed by the dying screech of a sambar deer. Curious, he had gone out at first light and followed the blood drippings through the grass and along the stream. The leopard ran away when he saw him.

I looked at the carcass and saw that the blood was just starting to congeal. The leopard had followed his regular pattern of eating a large kill: the hindquarters and the marrow-rich ends of the upper hind-limb bones were already gone. If he had had time, he would have eaten the ribs, internal organs, and vertebrae next; then the nose, facial flesh, and throat; and finally the upper forelimb bones.

"What do you want to do?" Soowan asked me, crouching down and poking at the kill.

"The big trap isn't finished yet," I said. "We have to wait."

"The cat will come back for his food," Soowan stated. "It is hard to find a kill so fresh in the forest. You have something else." Soowan was referring to a set of cable snares I had brought with me to Thailand. They were made for capturing large mammals but had the potential to injure. I didn't want to use them.

The forest suddenly went silent around us. Lung Soowan stood up from the kill and became rigid.

"He's coming back now," Soowan said quietly.

5

LEOPARD CAPTURE

I had to make a decision. The big trap we'd been building was nearly finished, but the door was still not ready. The box trap was the only capture technique I was really comfortable using. Some animals are too wary to go into these traps, but those that do are usually calm in the protected confines of the enclosure.

Cable leg snares are an altogether different story. Made from a steel cable loop that is laid over a triggering mechanism, these traps are carefully hidden at ground level in places where the animal will step. Once the animal's weight triggers the release lever, a spring mechanism throws the loop up onto the animal's leg, and the cable automatically tightens and locks as the animal tries to pull away. The other end of the cable is secured to either a spike in the ground, a large log, or a tree. A spring and a swivel linkage hook on to the secured end, allowing free rotation of the cable if the animal continues to fight and pull. Cable traps have been used effectively on bears, canids, and cats in the past, but individual animals react differently. Left out in the open with one leg suddenly immobilized some animals sit and wait while others fight ferociously.

After much debate with myself, I decided I couldn't let this opportunity pass. Finding a fresh kill in the forest was unusual in itself, but with the cat nearby waiting to retrieve his food, it was a perfect setup for a capture. I was afraid there might not be a second chance. I decided I would use a cable snare and monitor it closely.

Soowan didn't have his gun with him and he refused to stay and watch over the kill alone, so we used vines to tie what remained of the deer up in a tree, then hurried back to camp for both the capture equipment and Soowan's gun. The house was close by and we could be back in less than half an hour. I was sure that the leopard would be too wary to do anything within that time. I was wrong.

When we returned the kill was gone. The leopard had scaled the tree and cut the vines with his claws. The dragging of the carcass had left a clear trail, but I was *not* enthusiastic about stealing this cat's kill a second time. Before I could voice my apprehensions, Soowan disappeared along the cat's trail.

Less than a quarter of a mile later, Soowan pulled up short in front of a large thorny scrub and bamboo thicket and looked around uncertainly. Circling the area, we saw no further sign of the cat. Soowan looked at me and pointed into the thicket.

"He's in there," he said calmly, clicking the safety off his gun.

"We can't go in there," I said. "It's too dangerous."

Soowan got down on his hands and knees and entered the thicket.

"You're crazy," I mumbled. "I'm not following you in there."

As he disappeared, I imagined what it would be like to stand there alone as the cat suddenly rushed out in my direction. I got on my hands and knees and followed him.

Old Jim Corbett tales say that large cats, even man-eaters, avoid confrontation whenever possible. But a kill is one thing that a cat will often fight over. I learned later that Soowan had reasoned that, because the cat had already eaten half the sambar deer, he was satiated and wouldn't risk fighting for the rest of it. I was glad he hadn't explained that to me at the time; it wouldn't have been enough to keep me crawling through a thicket at eye level with a large male leopard. Whether Soowan's assumption was right or not I'll never know, but as we made our way into the heart of the thicket, the leopard, after a series of growls, left his kill again.

We grabbed the deer, which was already a bit ripe, and got out of there. I planned to set the snare up closer to camp in an area that was relatively open and flat. I had seen a good place where Soowan first found the kill. There was a small ravine there where we could watch the snare from the top of a hill, out of the leopard's view.

As I hastily cleared brush from around the trap site, I saw Soowan's hands tighten around his gun as he looked back in the direction we had come. The hair on my arms stood on end. The leopard was already coming back.

I quickly gathered branches and logs to build a small V-shaped wall out from the base of a tall tree to which I anchored the end of the cable. The remains of the deer were placed in the angle of the V between the tree and the hidden snare. Unless the cat had had previous experience with a trap like this one, he should approach the kill from only this one direction, stepping right onto the triggering mechanism of the snare.

It took three-quarters of an hour to set up the trap and make the area look as natural as possible. Once I was satisfied, Soowan and I returned to my house to wait. A few hours later we returned to the site to see the results of our efforts.

When we got back my hopes immediately sank. The leopard had not come back after his kill and there was only an hour of daylight left. Obviously the cat was more wary now. Realizing there was no choice but to wait him out, I looked up at the cloud-filled sky and groaned. It would be a dark night.

Once the sun went down, a wall of blackness enveloped us beneath the forest canopy. It was unsettling, not being able to see more than a few feet ahead and knowing that the leopard was close by. As the hours ticked by, we heard nothing but the normal night sounds of the forest. Leopards have keen sight and hearing despite a poor sense of smell. It was likely that this leopard knew exactly where we were and was probably playing his own waiting game.

Soowan and I kept drifting off to sleep, and around midnight I realized the futility of our staying there any longer. If the cat already knew we were there, he was not going to reappear while we were still around. He was more careful now, and if we deterred him from his kill again we might lose him for good. I decided to return to camp and come back at first light, less than six hours away.

Despite my exhaustion, I couldn't sleep. Finally tired of tossing and turning, I got up and sat outside in the darkness. As soon as there was enough light to safely see the trail we'd cut to the trap site, I went back. There was no point in waking Soowan yet.

When I reached the spot where we had been sitting several hours earlier, I didn't hear anything in the darkness below. My heart sank. Then I looked more closely and I noticed that the wall of branches had been scattered all over the ground. Almost simultaneously I heard a low, deep growl from the shadows. We had him! I ran back to camp to get my equipment and wake Lung Soowan.

Supakit returned with us, and by the time we got back, there was enough light to see clearly into the ravine. My first sight of the leopard took my breath away. He was even bigger and more beautiful than I had pictured him when I found his mark at my door. I moved forward, cracking a branch under my feet. Suddenly sensing our presence, the leopard became wild, roaring and pulling at the snare.

I motioned Soowan and Supakit to stay quiet. The cat was sideways to us and, using my blowpipe with a compressed-air pistol attachment, I could shoot him with a tranquilizing dart from where we stood about twenty yards away. I estimated the leopard's weight at about 150 pounds and loaded a dart with 750 milligrams of a drug called Telazol, then aimed and shot. There was a quick "pop" as the dart left the blowpipe and hit the cat above his left hind leg. We backed further into the trees and waited. After five minutes, when there was no further movement from the leopard, I approached cautiously.

As I had thought, it was an adult male and, judging from the area around the snare, he had put up quite a fight after being trapped. When I turned to speak to Supakit, I saw that he and Soowan were waiting about ten yards behind me with their guns ready. Both these

men, who were so competent and fearless in the forest, looked completely unsure of this situation. Soowan had faced down an angry
leopard with his kill in the underbrush just hours earlier, but he was
not about to approach this same cat now that he was sleeping peace-
fully at my feet. I motioned them over, assuring them the cat was
out cold for at least fifteen minutes.

I checked the cat's pulse and respiratory rate while Soowan and
Supakit went to release him from the snare. Almost immediately I
heard an ominous grunt from Lung Soowan and looked up. He was
holding the cat's left front paw, which was the leg that had been
caught by the snare. It was covered with blood.

I wiped the blood away and saw that the cable had caught the
paw around the middle digits instead of higher up above the wrist,
as was intended. He must have pulled back quickly after having sprung
the trigger and nearly escaped. His subsequent fight had ripped the
top of two digits open to the bone. Luckily nothing was broken, but
it was still a deep, open wound. Wounds like this are always dangerous
in a tropical, parasite-filled environment.

As the cat quietly stirred, I injected him with more of the drug
to keep him sedated longer. I was rethinking the previous night's
actions, going over all the things I should have done differently. But
I knew that this was not the time for that. I had to consider the
options still open to me.

Unfortunately there was no holding area to keep the leopard in
while he healed, and even if there had been, I doubted whether a
large wild cat would tolerate such confinement. The wound was in
a place where, despite the fact that walking might be painful, the
leopard could keep the cut clean and free of parasites. Wild animals
had survived much worse injuries than this. From what I could see,
his chances of healing were good.

While Supakit gently cleaned the paw with antiseptic, Soowan
helped me take the leopard's body measurements and fit a radio collar
around his neck. He was eight feet long from head to tail and weighed
almost 150 pounds. I injected him with a long-acting antibiotic and
rubbed antiparasite powder deep into the wound. I decided not to

suture the wound because the stitches might create a greater risk of infection by preventing the cat from keeping his injury clean himself.

After testing the radio collar, we moved the leopard over to a shaded area near the stream where he could awaken from the drug. Then we packed up the equipment and left. Everyone was quiet during the walk back, our earlier enthusiasm over the capture dampened by the cat's injury.

I began monitoring the leopard's collar almost immediately. This was the closest I could get to being at his side, although there was little I could do other than listen to the impersonal beeps of the radio. The pulse rate of the beeps told me if he was awake or asleep, and the changes in the signal's intensity, caused by interference from the forest vegetation, indicated if he was moving. Over the next few hours, I could tell that the leopard had woken up and moved a short ways off.

That night I hooked up an antenna to the roof of my house to better monitor his signal and ran a long wire through the window beside my bed. At nearly midnight, the radio indicated he was resting. There were occasional short bursts of activity which I thought might be just head movements. I pictured him licking the wound with that sandpaperlike tongue that cats have for scraping meat off the bones of their prey. Was he trying to figure out what had happened? I wondered. I fell asleep to the beeps.

I stayed with him closely for the next two days, listening to an erratic pattern of activity and resting. Although he had still not moved far from the place of capture, I wasn't concerned, because I assumed his lack of movement was due to the injury. Several times I started walking in on his signal, but I always stopped before I got too close. I didn't want to interfere any more than I already had, and I wasn't at all certain how tolerant a wounded leopard would be of my presence. But by the third day I was worried. He had moved less than a quarter of a mile from the capture site, and the pulse rate of the radio signal indicated too many long periods of inactivity. Although he was already close to water, he should have been traveling more to find food.

By noon of the fourth day, the continued slow beeps of the radio signal seemed ominous and I felt a sinking in the pit of my stomach. I couldn't wait any longer. Soowan was away from camp, so I asked Supakit to come with me. Starting from the point of capture, we followed the direction of the strongest signal and isolated it inside a low-lying boggy area near a tributary of the Huai Chang Tai. After walking in concentric circles, I zeroed in on a patch no more than a hundred and fifty feet in diameter and started making loud noises to arouse the cat. If the radio went active, we would leave. When the signal remained unchanged, I fired off an air pistol. There was still no sign of any movement.

I then walked directly toward the signal into a tangle of fallen trees and branches. Supakit cocked his rifle. This was a potentially dangerous situation. The leopard, hungry and hurt, could be lying totally still, waiting for us to get close enough before leaping. Or he might have ripped the collar off and been stalking us from behind as I followed the signal. I looked over at Supakit, his face set in hard lines and dripping with sweat. Because I had the headphones on, only I could hear any changes in the radio signal. Supakit was walking blind.

Soon the signal was blasting in my ears, even with the volume turned low. I disconnected both the antenna and the headphones and listened to the beeps through the external speaker. The beeps were still slow and steady, but were emitting with equal intensity from all directions. Evidently we were right on top of the cat. The radio receiver was of no use to me now so I turned it off and began to search visually. While I looked up into the trees, Supakit scanned the dense, tangled undergrowth around us. Neither of us saw anything.

I stepped up onto the trunk of a large fallen tree, and just before coming down on the other side, I jumped back, letting out a short scream of fear which quickly turned to anguish. There at my feet was the leopard, eyes open, staring past me into the sky. His head lay just at the entrance to an underground den created by the root system of the tree I was standing on. I threw my equipment to the ground and called Supakit.

We pulled the leopard from the den. The body was still warm, but rigor mortis was setting in. I closed his eyes and told Supakit to cut down a small tree so we could carry him back to camp. Supakit gave me a hard, questioning look, but I would not meet his gaze. We returned to camp, the leopard hanging between us like hunters returning from a kill.

Many months would pass before I could objectively reflect back on this incident and think about what I should or shouldn't have done once I found the leopard dead. At the time, I was acting on my emotions, without giving any thought to how my behavior might be seen by the Thais. Later I would realize my actions were irrational. But what happened that day was to affect both me and the project for the remainder of my time in Thailand; I was never forgiven for this incident.

We lay the leopard in front of my house and I sat beside it, stroking its fur. Word quickly spread through camp and a crowd gathered at the house. The women and children would not come very close; even a dead leopard seemed to terrify them. The women's usually gay chatter was replaced by quiet whispers.

When Noparat asked me why I had brought the carcass back to camp and what I would do with it, I didn't answer him. When he saw the look of anguish on my face, his tone softened. He told me it wasn't my fault. He quietly explained that Buddhism differentiates between good and evil intentions, regardless of the outcome. The thought that the leopard's unintentional death would not add to my burden of karma didn't make me feel any better. What Noparat didn't know was that my instincts had warned me not to use the cable snare, but I'd been greedy for the capture. I had acted selfishly and thus, for all practical purposes, the leopard's death might as well have been intentional.

Soon people started to leave. There was too much emotional intensity in the air, something that many Thais generally prefer not to confront. Only Noparat, Supakit, and Soowan stayed. I looked up at Noparat and said there was no reason for the animal to be wasted. We could save the skin and skull and keep them at the station or send them to a museum in Bangkok. Organ parts should be preserved for parasite analysis.

No one said anything and I sensed disapproval. Then Noparat spoke quietly.

"That does not show the leopard the respect you say you have for it."

"He's dead already, Noparat," I said angrily. "I'm not going to just dump him back in the forest and act as if this never happened." Noparat turned and left.

The job took several hours with Soowan and Supakit helping. We worked in silence, the only sounds coming from the camp dogs fighting over the pieces of meat we were cutting away. I still wasn't sure why the leopard had died four days after capture. Severe trauma seemed the only feasible explanation. But severe trauma from what? From fighting the snare for several hours? Had he given up before I even reached him, or did that happen later as he lay in his hole for three days? The thought that I should have left him where I had found him flashed through my mind. Maybe Noparat had been right.

When the men left, I bathed and sat alone at the house. The camp generator had been turned on, but I preferred the comfort of the darkness. I didn't go down for the evening meal, and when Beng and Amporn came up later to bring me some food, I pretended not to hear them.

In the morning, I returned to the den where we had found the leopard. When I looked at it more closely, I was surprised to see a rear entrance, which I hadn't noticed before. The cat's tracks showed that he had gone in through the rear entrance and not come out again.

I got down on my hands and knees and followed the tracks into the den. It was a comfortable place, snug but not tight, kept clean and smooth from repeated use. A slight musky smell permeated the air. Had he come to a safe haven to die? I looked out the hole where I had found him, putting my head in the position where his had been.

When I returned to camp, I put gas in my truck, packed some clothes, and told Noparat that I was going into Bangkok for a few days. I needed to send the cat's tissue samples off immediately, I said. He nodded, recognizing the lie but not challenging me. I just couldn't stay in the camp a second longer.

I reached Bangkok with mixed emotions of rage and grief building inside. Over and over again I thought of what I should have done differently. I should never have left the kill, I told myself. I should never have used a cable snare when I knew it had the potential to cause injuries. I should have gone back to get the leopard the first day after I saw he wasn't moving as I knew he should. I should have waited until the box trap was finished. This last thought lingered in my mind the most. I could have waited a little while longer. I had acted in my own best interests, but not in the best interests of the animal.

I wandered the streets of Bangkok at random, drinking too much and looking for trouble. Finally, at some point in the early-morning hours, I had drunk enough alcohol to melt my anger. As I headed back to my hotel room with some faceless person I had picked up along the way, a deep weariness came over me.

She lay naked on the bed, her pretty powdered face framed by long, black, silky hair. I ran my hands through her hair and stroked her breasts, talking in English, knowing she couldn't understand, and not wanting her to understand. Then as I touched her face and she smiled, I noticed the red streaks lining the insides of my fingers. I realized with a shock that the leopard's blood was still on my hands. The formaldehyde used in preserving the tissue samples had burned the blood into my skin. When she asked me what was wrong, I couldn't tell her. I couldn't tell her that I was stroking her as I had stroked the leopard and there was blood on my hands.

6

BUDDHIST MONKS

I cried out and sat up quickly, feeling afraid and suffocated by the heat and darkness, alone and disoriented. It was 4 A.M.—the "hour of the tiger" according to the Chinese. I lay on the sweat-soaked sheets unable to get back to sleep while memories that hadn't surfaced in years found their way through. The next thing I knew I heard Beng rustling around outside the house, picking up the day's wash and checking the water levels in my bathroom. Another night had passed.

I went down early to try out some of the new Thai words I'd memorized with Amporn as she prepared breakfast. As I passed the workers' houses, the women, with pots of rice already boiling on their little charcoal stoves, smiled shyly. Some of the men, returning from their morning ablutions at the stream, smiled and called out to me: "Sawadee krap, by ny?" (Good morning, where are you going?) I answered back and asked them how they were feeling today. The night before, they had had one of their long drinking sessions, which had lasted well into the early-morning hours. The men smiled, telling me they felt better this morning after a little kohn mah, or "hair of the dog," an expression I had taught them. They seemed genuinely pleased now that they could finally speak with me a little.

The person I was growing closest to was Beng, my housekeeper. Beng, an attractive twenty-three-year-old, had taken on the roles of both mother and sister, and for some reason she was completely loyal to me. Though Beng was from a poor, rural northeastern village, she was more industrious than any of the other women from similar backgrounds in camp. She was constantly active—planting a vegetable garden, making clothes, or tending to her beautiful little six-year-old, Yui. Sometimes I'd return home from the field in the early evening and find Beng sweeping the dirt in front of my house just because all her other chores were done.

It was months before Beng was confident enough to talk to me at any length, but I learned from Amporn that she was staunchly protective of me, telling others when to stay away and leave me alone. After the leopard died, I found pretty little yellow flowers planted around my house. When Beng learned that I liked early-morning coffee, she would leave hot water outside my door at 5:30 A.M. If I couldn't bring myself to face another meal with the staff, I would find a little plate of food (usually hot, spicy northeastern food) at my desk.

I asked the men why Beng was different from the other women, and they explained it to me in terms of her "bride-price" or dowry, which, at 10,000 baht ($400 U.S.), had been somewhat high for a poor, up-country girl. Though there was never any mention of Beng's keen mind, strong spirit, or good heart, I was sure that these qualities must have figured into her "value." Although a bride-price is usually set according to the wealth and status of the girl's family, it can be higher than usual if a girl has special qualities that increase her potential productivity and worth.

Over dinner I was told that an English-speaking German monk and a novice Thai monk had arrived that day in camp. At least a dozen monks had come and gone since I first encountered them that day with Noparat, but I had done no more than jog or walk by their huts and observe them from a distance. By now I had finished reading two books on Thai Buddhism and I thought I had found answers to some of the technical questions that had puzzled me. I understood now how the forest monks who came through the sanctuary differed from the monks I had seen in the towns and cities. The town or village monks, characterized by a practice known as *bariyat*, or "thorough learning," usually have their temples in more urban areas. Their daily routines include chanting, lessons in Pali, ceremonies, festivals, and counselling members of the local community. Forest monks, characterized by *batibat*, or "practice," stay in temples on the outskirts of towns or in the forest. These monks lead more highly disciplined lives, with fewer interruptions. They place a larger emphasis on individual meditation. In the evenings, these monks often force themselves to meditate until sleep overtakes them.

Although my readings clarified some things, they didn't explain the contradictions I sensed. Attempts to discuss Buddhism with No-parat usually left me unsatisfied. His English wasn't proficient enough to allow him to explain some of the finer points, and he often felt, like many Thais, that my questions stemmed from my Western mind's inability to comprehend Buddhism within the Asian framework from which it was born. I, in turn, was surprised by the unquestioning acceptance by many Thais of the basic rules and assumptions of Buddhism. Buddha himself had felt that his teachings should be questioned, that they were not dogma, but basic truths, to be tested and discovered for oneself. There were many things I wanted to ask this new *farang* forest monk who had somehow merged his Western upbringing with traditional Buddhist philosophy.

I was surprised when I encountered a Thai novice dressed in white, not the usual orange robes. I later learned that he was not a novice at all, but a *khon teu sin*, or a man who follows the eight precepts. He was trying out monkhood, so to speak, rigidly adhering to the more basic rules but not yet on the path to becoming ordained. Without questioning why I was there, he directed me to the hut of the German monk, which sat furthest back in the forest. No one was around, so I sat in the open doorway and waited.

The belongings of the German monk were laid out neatly in a

space that was no more than seven feet square. A little thatch sleeping mat was rolled up against one wall below a small opening that looked out into the forest. His *baht*, or bowl in which he accepts and carries food, was sitting in a dark corner, its orange lid blending in with the shadows. A toothbrush and tube of toothpaste lay next to a little portable alarm clock to the right of the doorway, placed in a groove between two bamboo slats making up part of the floor. That was it. His only other belongings, as I soon learned, were his robes, a small sewing kit to repair the robes, a razor, a strainer to exclude small creatures from his drinking water, and a bar of soap that was currently with him at the river.

I was daydreaming when I first heard his gentle chanting coming along the path that led to the hut. Then a tall, thin, pale-looking character came into view. When he saw me, his chanting stopped and his already large smile spread out into a huge tooth-filled grin.

"Ahhh, so good to see you," he said in clear Germanic English as if we had long been friends.

I couldn't help but smile back, feeling the kind of immediate bond that I so rarely experience with people. His English was music to my ears.

After that first visit, it became part of my daily routine to join him for coffee in the late afternoon. If I happened to come by earlier, he was usually away from the hut, meditating or exploring new areas in the forest. He encouraged me to visit whenever I could, and if he wasn't there, to beat on the *graw* that was hanging by his hut. The *graw*, one of the oldest Thai instruments, is made from a piece of hollow bamboo with a small vertical slit cut between the joints at each end. When a wooden beater is tapped against the bamboo, its deep, hollow sound carries easily through the forest.

This monk had been given the Thai name Supanyo, meaning "good thinking." At first, we spent most of our time together discussing Buddhism, and he seemed to get great pleasure when I challenged him, voicing doubts or criticisms. I told him of my early encounters with the monks and how I had felt that some of them were just going through the motions, making them seem like little more than beggars.

They were supposed to be humble, righteous men, I said. They were supposed to follow Buddha's teachings, but many of their actions seemed hypocritical to me. And what about the rules that Thai monks allegedly lived by? I asked him. A set of ten basic precepts was understandable, but why the additional 217 rules that told the monks how to hang their robes after washing, specified when a crack was big enough to justify replacing a food bowl, or said you couldn't open your mouth until the rice reached your lips?

Even when I did little else but berate Thai Buddhism, Supanyo just listened and gently explained.

"Monks are not beggars. You must understand this first," he said. He told me that when monks go on morning food rounds, they walk silently, often concentrating on meditation. Anything that is given is accepted. A monk doesn't thank those who give him food or show either pleasure or disappointment at what is given, because the food itself is of no concern other than for nourishment. It is the act of giving and allowing to give that is important.

"But if monks are just regular people, then why do Thais kneel and bow their heads to them?" I asked. "What is this 'merit' that is gained by giving to the monks? Does merit wipe out bad deeds?" To me it sounded suspiciously like the sins and absolution of Christianity.

"A monk is thought to be elevated, set apart from the normal world. The title 'Pra' that a monk is given means holy and exalted. When people bow before a monk, it is simply a show of respect. It doesn't have to be done. You thank the monk for allowing you to gain merit, which, though often misunderstood, means teaching you to be giving and compassionate. You are thanking the monk for helping to carry on the teachings of the Buddha. Such teachings can make the world better, even if some people choose not to be involved in them. And bad deeds are not wiped out so easily. They are a burden for you alone to carry."

"What about all those rules?" I pressed on. "Why should it matter if a monk's cheeks bulge while he eats or where he goes to the bathroom?" Supanyo grinned broadly. "It doesn't matter. The rules can be cast aside once you rise above them. But remember again, my friend, monks are simply men trying to do better with their lives. Most men need rules; they need something which defines their world and helps set patterns of behavior and good habits. Though you may think monks are above worrying about such mundane behavior, this kind of understanding can come only after much striving and meditation.

"Buddhism is faith combined with wisdom. At first you accept certain practices on faith alone, and then when you come to understand the truth inside yourself, you attain wisdom. Many people get stuck on the rules and practices alone and do not attain wisdom. Not many monks are truly 'noble' and you cannot take 'refuge' from all monks. You should seek the real refuge within yourself."

He made himself another cup of coffee with the mandatory four heaping teaspoons of "medicinal" sugar.

"Be careful of trying to think through everything or gaining understanding just from books," Supanyo said, offering me the pot of hot water so that I could make my own coffee. (A monk doesn't serve a layperson.) "Of course, it is good to question as you do. Buddha wanted people to question. But don't expect understanding to come so easily."

"Will it come to me in this lifetime?" I laughed.

"Ahhh, you wish much," he said, smiling. "I am only a little older than you. I have worn the robes for eight years now, and have been seeking much longer than that. I am far from wisdom yet."

"I'm not greedy," I said. "I only want a little wisdom."

"Me too, my friend, me too. Maybe you have more than you think."

We smiled often during our times together but we didn't always talk. Sometimes, we'd just sit in silence looking off into the forest. Usually the *pra-cow*, or white monk as I now called him, would join us and sit quietly to one side staring at me.

"He is very impressed by you," Supanyo said to me one day. "He thinks you are—how do you say it?—'a real man'. He told me that he dreamt about you one night. He believes that your strength and spirit come from a former life in which you were a warrior prince or a religious crusader. But he believes you are incomplete."

I looked over at the white monk and he dropped his eyes to the bamboo mat.

"Why?"

"He believes that in this life you should wear the robes. That you will not be complete otherwise."

"What do you think?" I asked.

"I dreamt of you with your head shaved once," he said, smiling. "But it doesn't matter. Maybe it would be fun, though."

One day I returned from Uthai Thani after seeing an old, hunch-backed woman vacate her seat so that she wouldn't accidentally touch the robes of a young monk who had sat down beside her.

"What is this attitude about women?" I asked Supanyo. "Why can women provide food and serve monks but not touch a monk or even look a monk in the face?"

"Women are asked to stay away from any physical contact with monks in order to help monks avoid temptation," Supanyo replied. "A monk must not get distracted by women."

"Supanyo, you might as well bag women up like Muslims or isolate monks in cells if you believe that the monks aren't strong enough to avoid temptation. And why aren't women allowed to become monks?"

"Woman can be nuns . . ." he began.

"Don't tell me about nuns," I interrupted. "This is a bone you throw to women. Nuns are held in such low esteem by Thai Buddhists that they often have to beg on the streets for their food. Monks pay half fares on trains while nuns pay full fares. Their assigned roles in Buddhism are menial. Often they are no more than temple helpers, preparing food for the monks and washing dishes after meals. They are never invited to preside over any religious ceremonies. Yet Buddha had women disciples."

Supanyo touched my knee and smiled, but his expression had no pleasure in it. "You have read well. Yes, Buddha had women disciples and discrimination was never part of his teachings. After Buddha's death, things changed in different places. In Thailand, there were once fully ordained Buddhist nuns, but the practice died out over a thousand years ago."

"So why can't this practice be revived, especially since Buddha himself set the precedent?"

"Oh, you will not like this answer, my friend," Supanyo said. "Buddhist regulations require that a woman be ordained as a *bhikkhuni* [female monk] only by another group of *bhikkhunis*. Since there are no *bhikkhunis* in Thai Buddhism today, nobody is qualified to ordain a woman.

"In India in Buddha's time, women were considered the incarnation of sin. They were seen as an obstacle to men's practice of religious discipline and it was thought that they could never be saved from suffering. Then Buddha said that everyone is equal and that everyone can attain Buddhahood. Unfortunately people often listen but do not hear."

One evening, after finishing my daily workout with Supakit and Anant, I paid an unexpected visit to Beng's house to bring over some sweets for her daughter and some whiskey for Lung Soowan. I rarely went over there because Beng would go out of her way to make me feel comfortable. I was surprised to see that several of the men— Muuk, Riap, Lung Galong, and Lung Soowan—were already at her house sharing a bottle of *lao-cow*, a cheap (two dollars a bottle) potent Thai whiskey that looked and tasted like car radiator fluid. Although it was well after dinner, Beng immediately started a fire going and soon had several plates of food in front of me. I ate a bit of each one, as etiquette dictated, then passed them around.

The men were already working up a good drunk by the time I got there, but the bottle of Mekong I had brought was more than welcome. Eventually the conversation, which I could only partly understand, came around to the death of the leopard. Soowan and

Galong starting talking about *san jow mae*, the mother of Dancing Woman Mountain, and suddenly all the faces turned toward me.

"Everyone thinks that the mother is angry with you," Lung Soowan said loudly, his speech a bit slurred. It took me a few seconds to realize what mother he was talking about.

"You didn't ask her permission to do what you are doing. Maybe the leopard died because of this. Then you cut the leopard up. She is angry now and it is bad for everyone."

I could see that the workers had discussed this subject before. Until now I'd known nothing of their feelings, and I might never have known if the whiskey hadn't loosened their tongues.

"Why didn't you tell me this before?" I asked Soowan.

"I know *farangs* don't believe in these things. But these are important things," he said.

"Maybe some *farangs* don't believe," I said, "but I know there is much I don't know. Maybe what you say is true. You should have told me before. What can I do now?"

My response met with approving nods, followed by an intense, fast-moving exchange in Thai among the men. Lung Galong was the focus of attention. As the oldest and the longest resident in the area, he was the appointed spirit medium of the mother.

"We can apologize to the mother and ask for her help," Soowan said, conveying the general consensus. "Galong and I will tell her that you are a foreigner and did not know better. We must do it soon."

I was given a list of supplies to buy as offerings to the mother. It included a chicken (dead and cleaned), a pig's head, incense, candles, flowers, cigarettes, and at least one bottle of whiskey. The incense, candles, and flowers were traditional Buddhist offerings. The candles represented the transitory nature of life; the flowers, the impermanence of beauty; the incense, the fragrance of a pure life. The food offerings were part of animistic traditions symbolizing sacrificial slaughter for the spirits. The cigarettes and the whiskey were a more recent Thai innovation. The Thai men figured that the mother would like a smoke and a belt every now and then. The station's truck was going into town the next day, so we planned for an emergency evening ceremony two days hence.

"Spirit houses and Hindu shrines are beside Buddhist temples everywhere around here—yet everyone claims to be a true Buddhist. How can that be?" I asked Supanyo the next evening.

"Alan, you look close and are disappointed when you don't see what you want to see. You expect too much from people. A good Buddhist may be many things. He fashions his own future. You were the one who talked of throwing out the rules. Don't be so quick to judge." He was quiet for a moment.

"You know, I have some of my best meditations after talking with you," he said suddenly. "Let me know how the spirit ceremony goes."

My truck was jammed with seven lively men chatting away as I parked at the base of the hill to the spirit house. Then their voices became hushed as we approached the little wooden structure and lay the food at the base of the rock pyramid. The tastiest morsels—the head and feet of the chicken and the ears and nose of the pig's head—were placed on the rocks themselves. A glass of whiskey and a lit cigarette were jammed into little niches among the stones. Finally, two candles were lit on either side of the little dancing figurines at the entrance to the house.

Lung Galong handed me nine incense sticks and instructed me on how to ask forgiveness for my earlier transgressions. Then I was told to make the promises we'd worked out the day before. As I kneeled at the base of the rocks, I read off the items that I would give if I captured certain species, covering all possibilities:

A tiger: 5 pig heads, 3 chickens, 8 bottles of whiskey, and 2 packs of cigarettes.

A leopard: 2 pig heads, 2 chickens, 3 bottles of whiskey, and 2 packs of cigarettes.

A medium-sized cat: 1 pig head, 2 chickens, 2 bottles of whiskey, and 1 pack of cigarettes.

A small cat (leopard cat): 2 chickens, 1 bottle of whiskey, and 1 pack of cigarettes.

Other small carnivores: 1 chicken, 1 bottle of whiskey, and 1 cigarette.

When I was finished, Galong approached the spirit house and gave a long discourse about who I was and how I was trying to help the animals. After assuring the mother that I was good at heart, despite my stupidity concerning the spirit world, he translated my promised offerings into Thai. Then each of the men approached the spirit house individually to light incense, offer their support, and make their own requests. When everyone was finished, we sat off to one side and chatted quietly while the spirit mother smoked her cigarette and sipped her whiskey.

Then Lung Galong repeated the history of this old rock pyramid. He told us that the opium trail we were on had also been a main route for Thai soldiers on their way to fight the Burmese. Soldiers would dance around the house three times, Galong said, to ask for luck, health, and safety. Tribal people paid their respects by leaving little caches of food and gifts. A previous chief of the station had come here with offerings of chicken and liquor when one of his men was lost in the forest for several days. He promised to dance naked around the spirit house if his man came back safely. When the missing man wandered out of the forest the next day, the chief returned that night to fulfill his promise.

Galong cackled, enjoying his own story. Then he turned to me with a stern look on his face. "Remember, you must fulfill any promises that are made here." After half an hour, we got up to leave. While Galong had been talking, Soowan had been carving on a two-foot-long hardwood pole that he'd picked up in the forest. Now, as I watched him, he went over and placed what looked like a large wooden penis at the base of the spirit house.

The men packed up all the food and whiskey, except for the few choice morsels that had been laid upon the stones. Galong handed the food to me, explaining that after it was offered to the mother I could eat it. I looked down at the pig's head, its tongue sticking out the side of its mouth.

"I just had pig's head the other day in town," I said, handing the food back to Galong. "You and the men share it among yourselves. I'll just take the whiskey."

I let the men go down the hill first so that I could be alone for a minute. I looked over at the spirit house. The candles were still burning, causing the little shadows of the plastic figurines to reflect against the inner wall of the house. As the flame of the candles flickered, the shadows danced on the wall. The smell of incense permeated the air and my eyes fell upon the large wooden penis that Soowan had carved. What am I to believe? I wondered.

7

SPIRITS
AND
GHOSTS

Now that the mother of Dancing Woman Mountain was placated, I could get back to work. The first large trap was finished. It was two and half feet wide, three feet high, and five feet long, with a platform at the back where a pig would be tied as bait. The trap door's triggering mechanism was a net of thin green string set between the pig and the door. Because these forest cats usually make a quick, charging kill, the trap was long enough so that the cat's entire body would be inside before the door came down. We also had six wire-gauge box traps for smaller carnivores that were ready to be put out.

One evening a truck brought in a group of university students for a two-week wildlife field course. The next day a shy, young Thai named Saksit showed up at my door. He had heard about the offer I'd made months earlier to train a graduate student in wildlife research. He wanted to know if the offer was still open.

Barely able to suppress my pleasure, I said that I was still looking for an assistant. I explained that the work was not at all glamorous, and was often painstaking and monotonous. There would be very little handling and observing of the animals. He smiled and shrugged. He'd already spoken with his professor, who had said that he could work with me for several days to try it out.

Saksit and I got along well despite some initial struggles with communication. Because he was a university student, he could speak some English, but he preferred to use Thai. In the days that followed, we set out traps, collected and analyzed feces, and explored new parts of the study area. He also helped me refine my Thai, teaching me how different forms of address for someone indicated where you stood in relation to that person. There were at least seven different ways to say both "you" and "I" to indicate status, age, sex, circumstances, friendship, anger, and wealth. By the time Saksit rejoined his class, we'd made plans for him to work with me on an extended basis.

Although I knew Saksit was due to leave soon, I was taken aback when I returned from the field one day to learn that his class was gone. I looked but there was no message left for me. When I questioned Noparat that evening, he said that Saksit was being *greng jy*, meaning that Saksit didn't want to impose on me in any way by telling me when to expect him next. This seemed to be a strange way to deal with a graduate research project.

The traps remained empty for the first week. Soowan and I checked them and fed the bait animals every day. Meanwhile Soowan started building two more large traps in different parts of the study area. One afternoon, I went to check on his progress.

He was cutting and shaping hardwood logs, fitting them together with as much care as if he were building a house. He had removed his shirt, and I could see the tattoos that covered his torso. The various animals and symbols permanently inked onto his skin glistened and contorted with his body movements. After a while, he squatted and rolled a cigarette from a plastic bag containing a strong, foul-smelling tobacco that I had long since gotten used to. His dark features blended into the forest.

I asked Soowan about the tattoos but he was reluctant to talk about them. Supakit later explained their importance—how they signify manhood, courage, and supernatural powers. Tattoos of certain animals imbue men with different traits such as amiability and strength, while particular symbols and patterns protect the body from evil forces. This once common practice of tattooing dates back to the 1600s, but now it is most often seen on men from northeastern Thailand. In earlier eras, a woman wouldn't easily accept a man as her husband without some of these tattoos.

I continued my visits to the monk huts, although with my increased work load they became less regular. One afternoon when Supanyo told me that he had seen fresh feces along one of the trails, I jokingly said that he could help me by collecting them. After that day, I'd often come down to breakfast and find a neatly wrapped bundle of leaves tied with vines waiting in the kitchen for me. Inside were little hard balls of feces. Amporn, who served Supanyo his daily meal every morning, would tell me where they'd been collected. If I hadn't visited Supanyo for a few days, there would be a little note inside.

How do we listen to the sound of falling in drops? By leaving no sound between ourselves and each drop, and by not clinging to any special drop. At this very moment can you be alive to this sound? Can you be aware of the process of your own life falling in drops, without freezing a drop of it?

Some of my most bizarre memories of this time involved the *pra-cow*. Often I'd return from the field and find the *pra-cow* at my house, wanting to tell me about his latest spirit dream or sighting, both of which occurred regularly. Other times he would bring me multicolored iridescent bird feathers that had been left for him by forest spirits. Supanyo passed these visions off lightly as the *pra-cow*'s way of dealing with his inner emotions and energies.

Sometimes I'd find the *pra-cow* stripped down to a white diaperlike piece of cloth, performing some strange form of self-abuse with my dumbbells. He'd be standing on one leg trying to balance a dumbbell on his head, or holding it with his fingers at arm's length like a Hindu ascetic. I noticed that most of the workers avoided my house during these times.

One afternoon the *pra-cow* presented me with a bamboo water container that had taken him a week to make. I turned it over in my hands, admiring the beauty and ingenuity of this simple piece of work. It was incredible how many uses I'd seen bamboo put to here: houses, fences, ladders, furniture, household utensils, musical instruments, weapons, water pipes, rafts, hats, baskets, jewelry, food containers. Bamboo shoots are even eaten as food. The British naturalist Alfred Russel Wallace wrote in 1856 that bamboo is "at once the most wonderful and the most beautiful [plant] of the tropics and the best gift of Nature to uncivilized man."

Recently it has been thought that bamboo might provide an important clue for anthropologists, who have always wondered why so few stone tools, except crude chopping tools, have been found in Southeast Asia. In the past a popularly accepted theory among anthropologists implied that the Far East never played a dynamic role in human evolution. But this is probably not the case at all. Scientists now realize that Asia was a bamboo culture whose roots date back more than a million years. Only stone axes or choppers have been found in the region because other types of tools were probably made from bamboo, and have long since disappeared. The importance of bamboo to Thailand is still obvious. Amid the concrete and steel of modern Bangkok the Thai people have a saying that is meant to give hope in even the most despairing situations: *"Pai mai koi dy."* (Bamboo never dies.)

Because the traps still remained empty, I spent much of my time looking at cat feces. Though I was anxious to actually collar some animals, I was compiling an enormous amount of information in the meantime on tiger and leopard eating habits; I was also getting some idea of the diversity of small mammal species in the area. The track and scrape data had already given me a feel for the territorial boundaries and areas of overlap between individual large cats. My study area was like a large jigsaw puzzle, with each new feces or scrape adding one more piece to the picture.

The large cats' broad range of prey items made me realize the importance of the smaller carnivores' feces to my research. If I was to understand predator-prey interactions and get a picture of the carnivore community as a whole, I needed to look at the prey base that was sustaining these animals. Many of the carnivore species were eating similar prey. But feces from animals such as civets, leopard cats, jackals, and martens often contained tiny rodent bone pieces and hair which I found difficult to identify. Also, because of similarities in the size, shape, and consistency of the different feces, I often couldn't be sure which species of predator they had come from. I knew I needed more help out in the field in order to systematically collect and analyze these feces.

I enlisted the help of the workers, who were always telling me about feces and scrapes they'd seen on their poaching patrols. I offered them ten baht (about forty cents) for every feces sample they brought to me if they could tell me where it had been collected and whether it was near a scrape or a track. Soon the men were going feces hunting during their work breaks and days off. Feces piled up so quickly that I had to put a limit on how many I'd accept in a day.

After Saksit left, I received word that a Malaysian graduate student who was studying for his doctorate in Thailand wanted to work with me. Though I preferred a Thai assistant, Soowan and I were tiring from the increased work load. I sent word for the student to come as soon as possible.

Ramesh's arrival caused a noticeable stir at Dancing Woman Mountain. He was a Malaysian by birth, but his father was Thai, his mother was Indian, and he was a Buddhist who looked Indian and spoke Thai, English, and Hindi. The Thais didn't know what to make of him, but his fluency with the Thai language and his easygoing manner quickly won the workers over. Only Noparat took a strong dislike to him, and his presence helped to further chill our relationship.

Ramesh was a quick learner and was soon doing much of the fecal analysis himself. As camp life fell back into an easier routine for me, I had more opportunities to step away from the day-to-day chores and look more closely at the data. Some days at the house, the weirdness of my current situation hit me head-on. One afternoon I recorded the following scene in my field notes:

> Lung Galong is at the house finishing off half a bottle of my whiskey while he rambles on to the Thai boxer, who is practicing his kicks and elbow throws on my punching bag. Under a tree the *pra-cow*, with a look of intense concentration, is doing contortions with a dumbbell. An Elvis Presley tape is blasting from the house, while Ramesh, in bathing trunks and a surgical mask, is picking apart feces. Every few minutes Ramesh steps outside, surveys the scene, and throws the unusable parts of the feces into the forest. It's just another normal day.

By the second week, the large cat trap was still empty. It had been placed along the road to the monk huts because there were regular signs of both leopards and tigers in this area. But once the trap was opened, there was no further activity along that section of road. One morning Ramesh returned to camp and told me calmly that he had seen "a spirit jester sitting on top of the trap laughing." He described a dwarflike man making comical movements with his head. The next day the *pra-cow* had a "vision" of a spirit in white robes walking the road where the trap was. I couldn't believe it. Along with Buddhism, magic tattoos, and the mother of the mountain, now a spirit in white and a ghost that sounded like it came out of Hindu mythology were disturbing my traps. I went to consult Supanyo.

"Do you believe in spirits?" I asked him. "Does Thai Buddhism teach that spirits exist?"

"Buddha taught that your mind exists, that you are in control of your mind. That is all," he answered.

"So what does that mean? There really are no spirits out there? But why will monks often help select the proper site for placing a spirit house? I've heard that some even conduct rituals involving magic. Do Thai Buddhists support this imaginary world?"

"True Buddhism is inside, Alan. The Buddha's teachings help in ordering your life forces. But there are other things that help people deal with what they don't understand about the world around them. Eventually, the inner truths will be recognized. Sadly, many monks don't understand this themselves." He shrugged and smiled. "But let's ask the spirit expert," Supanyo said, turning to the *pra-cow* and speaking with him quietly. He turned back to me.

"If you want to placate the spirit, our expert says, bring incense and flowers to the trap."

"But you don't believe in this, Supanyo," I said. "Why don't you help the *pra-cow* clarify and separate Buddhism from these spirit practices? Why don't you teach him what's real and what's not?"

"What is real and what is not," he repeated slowly, as if he were tasting the words on his tongue. "I cannot say, Alan. Just follow your heart. Maybe you should do as the *pra-cow* says."

I left feeling annoyed with Supanyo. But the next morning when I went to check the big trap, along with the usual food and water for the pig I carried incense and flowers. Five days later, the trap remained empty and the road trackless. To Ramesh's relief, I moved the trap into a new area.

"Did you expect differently?" Supanyo asked me when I told him all that had transpired.

As I became more friendly with some of the workers, I spent more time questioning them about their beliefs. Intah, Muuk, and Anant would come up for a drink in the evening and try to teach me about the complexity of Thai animism. The most common Thai word for ghost, *pee*, usually meant evil ghosts or devils. Heavenly or good spirits were referred to as *thewada*. Some spirits, called *jow pee*, were half *pee*, half *thewada*. The mother of Dancing Woman Mountain was *jow pee*. Since the forest was full of unseen ghosts who usually wanted to do you harm, the *jow pee*, or guardian spirits, looked after the forest.

This was their domain. These spirits were reverently referred to as the lord father, *jow paw*, or lord mother, *jow mae*. The mother spirit, *jow mae*, was the more powerful. The little wooden houses in the forest were built as dwellings for these guardian spirits. The spirits' houses were the places to go and make offerings and ask for the spirits' goodwill and protection. Anyone wanting to cut trees, hunt, or radio-collar wildlife must ask the *jow pee* for permission.

When I first watched the men at the spirit house, I wondered why I kept hearing the word for elephant. Now I learned that, when addressing the mother or guardian spirit, the local people often referred to themselves as *look chang*, or elephant calves. This is a symbolic reference to the social structure of elephant groups. The large, powerful adult elephants, fearing nothing in the forest, tenderly care for their young and fiercely protect them with their lives.

Beneath the guardian spirits, there is a whole hierarchical range of lesser spirits that reside in particular species of trees and animals. Spirits that live in trees in the forest rank higher than those that live in trees around houses; male tree spirits rank higher than female tree spirits. Such spirits can be good or evil depending on one's behavior. If respect is paid, spirits will act properly. If you do something foolish, like urinating under a tree that contains a spirit, you can get sick, and will recover only after proper offerings are made. Animal spirits, particularly the spirits of species such as tigers, leopards, and wild cattle, are not as well defined in Thai animism because the animals themselves are generally feared more than their spirits.

The strictly malevolent spirits are the most feared, and they have to be constantly guarded against with tattoos, amulets, and prayers. These were often the spirits of the *pra-cow*'s "visions." The men, after a few drinks, loved to describe these ghosts to me in all their gruesome detail.

Those spirits restricted to the forest are called *pee bah*. They include the *pee gong goi*, a ghost that jumps around at night on its one leg, and the *pee boang khang*, a ghost in the shape of an animal that lives in trees near salt licks. Then there are more gruesome ghosts which live close to villages. There's *pee graseu*, the old, ugly woman spirit who goes around feeding on raw meat and human excrement with her entrails hanging out; *pee grahang*, a male demon with a long tail; *pee pong*, a spirit that prowls during rains; *pee kamote*, who appears as a luminous light at night in marshy areas; *pee prai*, who appears in the form of a beautiful woman and entices men to fall in love with her; *pee pret*, who lives in cemeteries and assumes a tall, ugly human form to feed on pus and blood. . . . The list goes on and on. I suddenly realized why I was having difficulty getting workers to go out into the forest with me at night.

Supanyo and the *pra-cow* requested permission from Noparat to remain at Dancing Woman Mountain for "Cow Pansa," Buddhist Lent, or the rainy-season retreat. This is a period of three months, beginning on the first full moon in July, when monks cannot travel and must remain relatively sedentary at a temple or fixed abode. Supanyo had planned to return to his temple in the north, but he was having good meditations here, he said, and he and I had more to talk about. I was pleased when Noparat agreed.

The tradition of the rains retreat was said to have begun in India when Buddha and his disciples led itinerant lives. The people criticized the monks for traveling on foot during the rainy season because their footsteps caused suffering to small creatures, such as insects and crabs, which had been flooded out of their underground homes by the rains. The Buddha, hearing these complaints, made a rule that all his monks must remain within their own abodes during the rains and stop their usual traveling.

Now the custom is maintained primarily for health and comfort considerations—monsoon winds and heavy rains make travel difficult at this time of year. This is also a good time for the monks to meditate, study, and teach disciples. Many reside in the temples where they were first ordained; few choose to remain in the forest, where comfort in the simple thatched dwellings is minimal. This is also the time when many young men temporarily enter the monkhood for a period of study.

. . .

By now it was the end of June and I was feeling restless. Lately my talks with Supanyo had left me unsatisfied. There were more than 300,000 monks and 27,000 Buddhist temples in Thailand. Yet there seemed to be little connection between the Buddhist reverence for all living things and the Thais' continued destruction of their country's remaining forests and wildlife.

When Noparat asked me why I spent so much time "playing with feces" and not out in the forest, I realized how little even the best-trained Thais understood about modern research methodology. Saksit had explained to me that the field research training in Thailand's universities was based primarily on principles of forest management. Training in wildlife research involved little more than teaching basic survey techniques and the recording of cursory observations. The amount of time spent walking in the forest determined the level of your expertise; an "expert" on a particular species was someone who had seen that animal more often than others. Despite a growing awareness of conservation issues in Thailand, the lack of good ecological training was severely hampering the proper protection and management of remaining forest areas.

In bed at night, I would hear gunshots ring through the forest close to camp. The men said that the shots were fired by poachers—tribal people coming in from the other side of Khao Khieo Mountain who were hunting wild cattle or deer at the salt licks or in the new grassy areas that had burned during the fire season and were now turning green.

I had never been to the other side of Khao Khieo Mountain, and I knew little about the forest outside my study area. In order for me to fully understand what was going on with certain species, it was necessary for me to concentrate my research in one place. But unless I also understood what was outside of my area, I wouldn't be sure how applicable my research was to the sanctuary as a whole.

One morning while I was checking the traps, I looked up the trail to see strangers walking toward me. Their ragged, emaciated appearance, discernible even through their loose-fitting black clothes, immediately identified them as Hmong. These tribal people of Chinese origin are the ethnic group most disliked by the Thais, who consider Hmong to be lazy, dirty, and aggressive. The Forestry Department claimed that this tribal group was behind much of the destruction of Thailand's remaining forests and wildlife.

I thought of my first encounter with these people during my initial trip here. The Hmong didn't seem as strange to me now as they had then, but my curiosity about their way of life had not lessened. The various Hmong that lived between Dancing Woman Mountain and the Burmese border were some of Thailand's last remaining indigenous forest dwellers. Some had never even traveled as far as the nearest Thai village.

This morning the sun was at their backs, giving them an almost otherwordly appearance. Suddenly I knew I wanted to visit these people. This trip might be my last chance to see life in these hills as it existed in centuries past. The present was catching up quickly.

8

CHASING
THE
DRAGON'S
TAIL

Ever since I had first come to Thailand, I'd been hearing about the hill tribe people. Phairote had called them "illegal squatters" and had gone on to elaborate at great length about the deforestation, encroachment, and wildlife poaching they caused. They had to be relocated out of the sanctuaries, he insisted, in order to protect the remaining wildlife. At the time I had wondered how much truth there was to his accusations. Politicians often use "environmental policies" as a catch-all phrase to disguise more deeply rooted development and resource distribution problems.

There are seven hill tribes in Thailand, with a combined population of about 750,000. Most of these tribal people are settled in the relatively inaccessible, higher-elevation areas of the north, and only an estimated 25 percent are official, card-carrying Thai citizens. The favored cash crop of many of these tribes is opium. Its growth and distribution have always been controversial, causing the Thai government problems internationally.

Much of the forest in areas where the hill tribes live has disappeared. Huai Kha Khaeng and the adjoining Thung Yai Wildlife

Sanctuary contained some of the most remote and "natural" tribal settlements left in Thailand. But these settlements of Karen and Hmong are fairly recent, dating back no more than thirty years.

The forests around Huai Kha Khaeng were, at this point, a major testing ground for government policy regarding hill tribe relocation. In 1986, at the time of my initial survey, the Forestry Department was forcing the relocation of Huai YuYee, a Hmong village of 176 people. This was the last remaining Hmong settlement within the Huai Kha Khaeng Wildlife Sanctuary. But an estimated three to five thousand Hmong, and several thousand Karen still remained in the adjoining sanctuary of Thung Yai.

The Hmong back in these forests were not easily bullied by government agencies. This is the same tribal group that fought with the American Army and suffered heavy casualties in the Vietnam War. In the 1970s, when student activists hid and lived among the Hmong, the Hmong who helped them were branded "Communist party sympathizers." Now the Thai government wanted greater control over these people, who often felt they owed allegiance to no one but themselves.

The government's relocation policy was opposed by anthropologists and human rights organizations, who argued that these tribes had been in residence prior to the establishment of the sanctuary. These groups challenged the government's assertion that the hill tribes were destroying the forest. They claimed that, in fact, these people were living in a "sustainable" manner, and that their activities were maintaining and in some instances even protecting the forest.

Phairote had asked me for my opinion on the hill tribe situation when I first came to work in Thailand. After he learned that the jaguar preserve I helped set up in Central America had caused the forced resettlement of several Mayan Indian families, he assumed that I would support him in this quest for relocation. But I had avoided siding with him at the time, not wanting to take a definite stand on an unfamiliar situation. Now he was pressing me again for my endorsement of the relocation program.

. . .

Another event stirring up great controversy in 1987 was a project called the Nam Choan Dam. This project, proposed by the Electricity Generating Authority of Thailand, would dam the main river in the heart of the Thung Yai Wildlife Sanctuary.

Ecologically, the dam project would be a disaster for one of the best-protected forest areas left in Southeast Asia. Politically, the situation was so volatile that people on both sides of the issue were concerned that the government might fall if the "proper action" wasn't taken. The dam would create a forty-six-mile-long reservoir flooding all the lowland forest in the river valley—up to almost 1,300 feet above sea level. This reservoir would in turn split the nearly 2,400 square miles of the Huai Kha Khaeng–Thung Yai forest complex into three separate sections. Illegal construction of twenty-eight miles of access road through the sanctuary had already been carried out.

As of June 1987, the commander-in-chief of the Thai Army, the Thai cabinet, the National Energy Policy Committee, a subcommittee appointed by the Prime Minister's office, and the House Committee on Health and the Environment were recommending building the dam. The Prime Minister's office called opponents to the dam "gun-runners, hunters, and Communist insurgents." Government employees were fobidden to publicly criticize the project. But officials of the Thai Forestry Department, local and international environmental groups, and hundreds of Thai residents in the areas that would supposedly "benefit" from the dam, were all adamantly opposed to the project.

Proponents of the dam argued that less than 5 percent of the Thung Yai Wildlife Sanctuary would be inundated, and existing wildlife could walk or swim to higher ground. An Environmental Impact Assessment (carried out by the very company that proposed the dam in the first place) said that much of the land had already been degraded by tribal people. They insisted that with the new dam wildlife would benefit from a year-round water supply.

The opposition was gearing up for a hard fight and I was one of several "foreign experts" asked to go public with my opinions although I'd been in Thailand less than five months. No dam had ever been stopped before in Thailand, and the future of the whole region was at stake. This dam was exactly the kind of threat to Thailand's environment that I thought good scientific research could help fight against, but there was virtually no wildlife data available. Although I didn't have the resources to collect this data myself, I hoped a trip back into the sanctuary might at least give me a better feel for the issues involved.

When I told Noparat my plans, he said I should leave immediately. He estimated that we had no more than two or three weeks before heavy rains would make the main rivers impassable. I closed the traps and asked Ramesh to continue the fecal analysis. Supakit helped me plan the route, buy supplies, and choose the team.

Four days later we were in the back of the station's pickup truck on the way to our starting point, the place where I'd first seen the Hmong emerge from the forest. I had five of the best men in camp —Intah and Sombat, the youngest and strongest; Lung Galong, our interpreter for the Hmong and Karen dialects; Lung Soowan, my field assistant; and Supakit, the group's leader. We carried two shotguns, two semiautomatic rifles, and backpacks that felt heavy enough to be filled with supplies for a month instead of the planned ten to twelve days. The weight of the packs was taken up with cooking utensils, thirty pounds of rice, cans of sardines, and eight bottles of whiskey. Nothing I said would convince the men to eat noodles or some lighter food for a few meals; it had to be rice three times a day.

We were all excited. Only Lung Galong had been to all the areas we would visit, and that had been more than ten years earlier. Our first day's hike was relatively easy, seven and a half hours to the Huai Kha Khaeng, half of which was through a part of the northwestern corner of my study area which I had not yet visited. All along the way I encountered abundant feces, scrapes, and tracks of big cats.

We followed the old opium route leading out of the Dancing

Woman Mountain valley. It was still used by the hill tribe people when they ventured out of the sanctuary, and it was obviously a major thoroughfare for large cats. Track and scrape measurements indicated that the same tiger that I had tracked around camp was also traveling over the mountain and outside of the study area. The leopard we'd tracked near the monk huts seemed to reach the end of his territory a short ways out of camp. There his tracks were replaced with the tracks of a leopard I hadn't seen before. That first day our progress was slow because I made frequent stops to collect feces and measure scrapes.

By early evening we reached the river. While the men set up camp, I walked along the bank looking for cat sign. It had rained hard that day and the river was rising and starting to cover the rocks, but the damp sand made a good tracking surface and kept the spoor of animals relatively intact. I could see immediately that tigers were more abundant here than leopards. This was the opposite of what I'd been finding at Dancing Woman Mountain.

After dinner we finished off two bottles of whiskey (in order to make our packs lighter, the men said) and sat around the fire listening to the night sounds. Suddenly a rustling in the darkness followed by muffled human voices made the men grab their guns and step away from the fire. The river was a favorite site for poachers and the men were wary. But what stepped into the light of our campfire was even more unexpected—eight Border Patrol Police shouldering M-16s, a Hmong guide, and a monk!

The police, whose job is to secure the border area with Burma, were brusque and unfriendly to Supakit. They put him immediately on the defensive when he explained the reason for our presence. Then I stepped out of the darkness, and when the soldiers saw me, they became almost obsequious. They left us alone but set up camp nearby. For the rest of the evening there was a palpable tension in the air.

We broke camp early and left the Border Patrol Police far behind as we began climbing. By late morning, we had ascended above three thousand feet into a new vegetation zone, hill evergreen forest. The dampness here kept us soaked to the skin and we made frequent stops to pick off leeches. These little bloodsucking, wormlike creatures crawled up our pant legs and made open bloody wounds that healed slowly. The best way to prevent these bites was to pull the leeches off before they sank their teeth into your flesh.

The afternoon of the second day we reached Huai YuYee, the western border of the Huai Kha Khaeng Wildlife Sanctuary and the site of the former Hmong village that had been moved a year previously. Now it was a remote forest guard station manned by young boys whose guns were almost as large as they were. The first remaining Hmong settlement was a quarter of a mile beyond in the adjoining sanctuary of Thung Yai.

For the next three days we headed west, visiting one Hmong village after the other. We hired a Hmong guide, but his frequent stops for opium slowed us down. Regardless of where we were—a leech-filled forest, a muddy elephant trail, or a stream bed—our guide would suddenly come to a halt, lie down, and light up his opium pipe. These "urges" came over him three or four times a day.

At each village our first house call was always to the hut of the village headman. Lung Galong would explain who I was and ask permission to question people about cats and other wildlife in the area. The headman would then summon the heads of the families and we'd sit in council. I told Supakit in simple English what I wanted to ask, Supakit explained it to Lung Galong in Thai, and Galong translated it into the Hmong language. Then I passed around pictures of the various cat species. It was a slow process, so between questions I had time to look around and examine the smoke-filled rooms and their contents.

Most of these simple wooden houses had a packed-dirt floor and a thatched roof. They consisted of one large main room with little sleeping areas partitioned off against one wall. Along another wall was a raised platform where guests slept; above this was a storage area for baskets. In the center of the house there was a small fire pit, but cooking was done on a separate hearth against the wall. Near the cooking hearth there was always a strange-looking collection of items, mostly animal parts, sitting on a wooden stump or table against the wall. This was the family altar, used to pay respect to the various forest spirits.

Often the villagers were suspicious when they first met me, especially if they'd had recent contact with Thai soldiers. One village headman believed that I was an American drug enforcement agent. He had never met a drug enforcement agent, but he'd been told that America was behind the Thai government's harassment of opium growers. No obvious hostility was ever directed toward me, but the villagers were very suspicious of our group, and initially our questions often went unanswered. Unfortunately, the best way to break this silence was to accept the village's "hospitality," which involved sitting and smoking "tears of the poppy"—opium. This was the quickest way, I was told, to allay their fears. But after my first "opium council," I learned to be more prudent.

Several of us sat around on the dirt floor in the dark, musty-smelling Hmong hut. I watched the old man next to me as he wrapped the thick, viscous opium around a wire, set it on fire over a kerosene lamp, then jammed it through a little hole in a small clay vial with a thick wooden tube coming out of it. With his mouth over the tube, he lay on his side and sucked deeply. After going through the procedure a second time, he handed me the pipe and I sucked in the sweet-tasting smoke in short, quick bursts to avoid coughing. Several pipes were being passed around at the same time, so it was less than a minute before another pipe came along.

I had seen a few small opium fields during our hike but was told that they were harvested only during the middle of December. After the flowers drop their pretty red-and-white petals, women and children go to the fields and start cutting into the green seed pods with small curved tools made of two or three sharp blades bound together. The morning after the pods are lanced, the opium is scraped from the plants before it hardens or becomes too sticky to be extracted easily. The gum can be stored indefinitely in banana leaves or mulberry-bark paper.

On the floor of this particular little hut more packets of opium from last season's harvest were being unwrapped and the pipes kept on coming. After fifteen minutes I started feeling very relaxed as a pleasant tingle spread through my body. I tried to refuse the next pipe, but my host was insistent. Eventually my speech slurred and the questions I'd traveled several days to ask these men no longer seemed particularly important. I was more relaxed than I'd been in months. When I was certain I couldn't handle smoking another pipe I got up from the group and went into a corner of the hut to curl up with my own thoughts. Hunched over next to me was an elderly man whose emaciated frame and apathetic stare reminded me of the pictures I'd seen of concentration camp victims.

That night I sat by a stream looking off into the forest. Twice I saw elephants meandering through the trees, and once a tiger came to the stream to drink. This is how the forest should be, I thought. In the early morning hours Supakit came to sit by me, wondering if I was all right. I told him what I'd seen.

"There is nothing out there," he said. "Animals like that are not near a Hmong village. It was the opium, Alan. You see what you most want to see. You were 'chasing the dragon's tail.'"

In the morning I woke up in my hammock, fuzzy-headed and nauseous. Lung Soowan was standing over me holding a coffee cup. This is just what I need, I thought, taking a big gulp. My insides exploded.

"What the hell was that?" I choked out.

"Hmong whiskey," Soowan answered, smiling.

It was even more foul-tasting than *lao-cow*, but it did clear my head. So I steadied myself and downed the rest of the cup.

On the third day we headed farther west and arrived at two villages that had never seen a white man before. Most of the children wanted to feel my chest hair, while the women seemed most curious about my green eyes. Lung Galong kept telling them that I was a "tiger doctor" from America, which usually got him and the men invited to drink and smoke opium (our own eight bottles of whiskey were long since gone). Meanwhile I was invited to some crossbow shooting contests, and I let more people pull at my chest hair. One woman ripped a plug of hair out all at once, saying her boy was sick and she needed it for her altar.

I liked these aggressive, independent people of Sino-Tibetan stock. The women, their long hair tied back in buns, wore knee-length pleated skirts with aprons, black leggings, and a wide, usually red sash around the waist. Their clothes made them seem much older and heavier than they were. The men, with their characteristic loose-fitting black pants and short black cotton jackets, were thin and drawn-looking.

If there was no good forest for camping near a village, we'd sleep in the headman's house. This usually meant I'd be awakened in the middle of the night by someone's hacking cough or fevered moaning. I was often asked to examine people with malaria or dengue fever who, after tiring of spirit cures, were ready to take whatever medication I gave them.

In one village I took part in a soul-crossing ceremony. The local shaman decided that a sick boy's soul had left his body and had to be helped to return home. After a chicken and pig were sacrificed, each of the participants tied cotton strings around the boy's wrist, while chanting something about the soul returning. I went last and was asked to sing something special from my country. The only thing I could think of at the time was the first two lines of "I've Been Working on the Railroad." This met with a nod of approval from the shaman; then the sacrificed animals were cooked and eaten.

The next morning I woke at five o'clock to the rustling of cooking utensils. I lay there watching the twelve-year-old daughter of the headman prepare the morning food and take care of her little brother, who was already squatting to pee just outside the door. Despite her innocent, youthful features, in this culture she was already nearly a woman with adult responsibilities. But the child was still within her as she sneaked over and pinched her brother's backside, then scurried away giggling before he realized what had happened. She caught me watching, and with a guilty smile turned and went back to work.

I was worried about our timetable. We were on the move eight to nine hours a day but were not covering as much territory as I had planned. The rains had worsened, and the domestic buffalo trails between villages were now muddy quagmires in which we often sank up to our ankles. In the forest, the leeches were getting worse and we were all suffering from open, bloody bites on our legs that needed frequent tending.

However, what most bothered me was the obvious toll the drinking and opium smoking were taking on the men. One morning, Lung Galong had to be literally dragged along by Supakit after passing out face down in the mud. Another night, Lung Soowan started screaming that his tattoos were fighting each other. When I told the men to calm him, everyone insisted that such tattoos can, in fact, come alive and make you do things you wouldn't normally do. Even Intah, the one I depended on most for his strength and stamina, was disappearing in the evening and showing up wobbly the next morning.

I decided it was time to get out of the Hmong area. The men were going bonkers on me, and I was tired of sleeping packed like sardines on small wooden platforms in the villagers' houses. Supakit would often be snoring into my face on one side while Sombat made strange jittery movements on the other side. Most of all, I was tired of the groups of pigs that would follow me whenever I went out to relieve myself in the scrub around the villages, eating my excrement with relish as soon as it exited my body. The sight of endless acres of cornfields, slash-and-burn clearings, and scrubby brush was getting depressing. I was deep inside one of the biggest protected forests in this part of the world and I couldn't even hear birds singing in the morning.

We headed toward the Kwae Yai Valley, one of the areas that would be flooded by the Nam Choan Dam. I paid off our latest Hmong guide, who wanted to visit his second wife in a nearby village, then hired a new guide, who claimed to know the quickest route to the river. For a while we hiked alongside Hmong children on their way to work the fields. It was like a parade, the boys swaying as they walked, playing their bamboo mouth organs, or *gaens*, the girls following behind singing softly. Three hours after they left us, we were lost.

We had followed the wrong trail while passing through an abandoned village, then got turned around trying to locate the original trail. Eventually, our new Hmong guide gave up and lay down among a clump of trees to smoke opium. While I sat with our guide, watching his mind float away from his emaciated little body, the men fanned out in different directions to find the trail.

Intah finally got us back on the right path, and two hours later we were at the banks of the upper Kwae Yai River. This river was about a hundred and fifty feet wide and already swollen with brown muddy water. I was wondering how we'd get across when Intah's shouts directed my gaze to what looked like bamboo poles washed down from upstream. Then I realized it was a raft, about twenty-five feet long and four to five poles wide.

I squatted toward the middle of the raft while Intah, naked except for his undershorts, poled Lung Galong and me across. His tight muscular body bulged with the effort, but he was smiling as he strained against the current. Water splashed around our legs as the raft dipped below the surface. A slight tilt either way would have flipped us. On the far bank I breathed a sigh of relief. As Intah went back to pick up the other men, muffled giggles emerged from the forest behind me and I saw two little girls disappear behind a tree. We were now in the domain of the Karen.

As we entered their village it struck me immediately how different the Karen were from the Hmong. They were a more handsome people; the women were strikingly attractive in their colorful hand-woven sarongs and blouses, and the men looked strong and determined. Comprising the largest hill tribe in Thailand, the Karen are considered different, more Thai-like than the other tribal groups.

This was the fifth day of our trip and we were sore and tired. Invited by the village headman to stay as long as we liked, I decided to set up a base camp there for three days before we started our return trip by a different route. There was no whiskey or opium within a day's walk, so I knew this would be a good resting place. Several Karen villages were nearby where I could continue asking about the cats in the area.

The few days we spent with the Karen were peaceful and pleasant. Their houses were similar to those of rural Thais; wooden structures enclosed a single large room. The roofs were made of thatch or leaves, and the huts were raised off the ground. But here there were shrubs and little gardens between the houses; this was a welcome change from the large open village areas of the Hmong that had been denuded of all vegetation.

I sat on the porch of the headman's hut watching his wife weave cloth on a simple back-strap loom as she smoked a pipe and played with the baby at her feet. Young girls from neighboring huts, their mouths stained red from chewing betel nut, walked by carrying water in large bamboo canisters held to their backs by a strap of bark around their heads. A monkey skull swung gently in the breeze above the entrance to the hut. This village would also be flooded by the dam.

In the evenings, as I was hunched over my field journal, people would come and watch me write across the white pages of my note-book. They had done this in the Hmong villages as well, fascinated by my ability to write continually and quickly, filling five to ten pages in a sitting. When they asked why I wrote so much, Lung Galong responded that I "thought too much" and needed to get it all out. He made the analogy of bamboo blowing apart when the air inside was heated by fire. An old woman behind me cackled and shook her head knowingly, satisfied with his diagnosis for such behavior.

While I was visiting one of the neighboring Karen villages, the headman paraded his three daughters before me for inspection. They were lovely girls, from thirteen to fifteen years of age, with wildflowers stuck in their hair and wearing traditional white cotton gowns to signify that they were still virgins. It took me a while to understand that I was being shown the goods in case I wished to negotiate the bride-price for one of them. It would be good to have a daughter with a white man, the father explained.

On the second day, another group of Border Patrol Police came through the village and, after hearing I was there, invited me to their permanent encampment nearby. The captain was a friendly, knowledgeable man, though I sensed a callousness beneath his amiable exterior. From their outpost atop the highest hill in the area, there was a spectacular view looking down into an undisturbed forested valley between the Huai Mae Chan and the Huai Mae Klong, another area that would be flooded by the proposed dam.

We left early on the ninth day, planning to take a more direct route back to Huai YuYee. For a while as we hiked, corn and rice plantations stretched far into the distance. If I hadn't known better, I could have believed I was in the paddy fields of the central plains region instead of deep inside some of the most pristine forest left in Thailand. Among both the Karen and the Hmong, we were constantly encountering newly cut areas and new satellite settlements. Fields stretched farther and farther away from villages. This forest, as extensive as it appeared, could not keep pace with the expanding population within its borders. Deforestation was advancing at an alarming rate.

We stopped at another Hmong village before reaching Huai YuYee, then continued along the main trail directly to the Huai Kha Khaeng. It was raining hard every day now, but despite the wet clothes, chilly evenings, leech wounds, and general fatigue, we all felt strong and healthy. There was still plenty of laughter and camaraderie. I had never felt as close to a group of men.

I caught up to Intah and Sombat, who were ahead of me, and found they had stopped at a pile of rocks in a small forest clearing. The rocks marked the place where an opium trader had been ambushed and killed several years earlier. I waited as the men paid their respects, placing a cup of whiskey and a lit cigarette below a little misshapen clay figure atop the rocks. While at the shrine, we met up with two "black soldiers" coming from a Hmong village to the north. This was the second time I'd met some of these men, so named because of their all-black uniforms. They weren't real soldiers, Supakit had explained, but local Thais or Thai prisoners under the supervision of the Army. They lived in tribal villages and were supposed to help keep the peace but were generally not well liked. In addition to their reputation for bullying and taking advantage of the tribal people, they were known to be some of the worst poachers of wildlife.

We set up camp by the river, and that evening I lay in my hammock watching the men, knowing it was our last night together. Lung Galong, a lilliputian sixty-two-year-old with the body and stamina of a teenager, was in the river bathing and washing his clothes. He had smoked more opium and drunk more whiskey than anyone else on this trip, yet he was singing and splashing like he had just come back from an afternoon picnic. Supakit, spear in hand, was underwater catching our dinner, every now and then popping up along the banks to throw a fish onto shore. Sombat was building a sleeping platform from bamboo, while Intah prepared the rice and cleaned the fish. Lung Soowan was off gathering a large pile of wood for our evening fire. Whenever I tried to help, one of the men would take over what I was doing. I was the bwana. My job, they said, was to write in my notebook.

While it was still light, I pulled out my journal and tried to put into words some of the many thoughts and feelings I'd had these last eleven days. My mind kept drifting. I missed the evening ritual I'd begun in the Hmong villages of going to bathe in the stream in my short sarong while children gathered around me to stare at my hairy chest, pale skin, and green eyes. But what exactly would I tell Phairote? I asked myself. The tribal people insisted that they didn't actively hunt anymore, that they only killed the animals that bothered their plantations. But I remembered the serow carcass I'd seen over a cooking fire in a Hmong hut, the wild boar tusks and deer antlers that sat on Hmong altars, and the children who honed their hunting skills by shooting birds with their crossbows. Macaque skulls hung like talismans at the entrance to many Karen huts.

Along the trails and in the forest between villages, there had been little or no signs of any wildlife, particularly large species such as cats and elephants. Many of the plantations I'd seen were not little family plots but large cleared areas that spread far into the distance. Bears, elephants, wild pigs, and even rodents were all considered to be "pest species" by the plantation workers. Large cats that wandered close to villages were not tolerated. At first villagers would try to frighten off the cats, but if that didn't work the animals were shot. Wildlife still thrived in the forest areas that were distant from the villages, but this situation wouldn't last. A study of the village of Huai YuYee before its relocation showed that out of a population of 176 people divided into nineteen households, nearly 66 percent of the residents were under ten years old. These young people would soon be raising their own families and spreading into new, unspoiled parts of the forest.

I have heard terms such as "noble savage" and "sustainable use" used to describe simple forest peoples and their way of life. But these words have little relevance to real-life situations. It is neither noble nor savage to work, fight, and kill for your survival. Nor is this kind of lifestyle "sustainable." As long as these communities increase in size and the young people take over larger forest tracts, the wildlife will continue to disappear. In the past when village growth was much slower, and undeveloped forest patches were much larger than they are today, these villages caused a lot less damage.

Even in these remote forest communities, the tribes' way of life has been influenced by modern developments in the outside world. Opium has become a major cash crop that is now sold or traded by the Hmong outside the forest boundaries for goods such as metal cooking utensils and medicines that were never obtainable in earlier times. Numerous villages now have guns as well.

This large forest area had a good chance of regaining its natural state if the encroachment was stopped. Wildlife was abundant away from the tribal areas, and many animals, including the large cats, were already returning to places like the abandoned village we'd passed through whose residents had been relocated just a year earlier.

It was clear to me that if the forests of Huai Kha Khaeng and Thung Yai were to survive, one of the steps would have to be to relocate these tribal people outside of the sanctuary.

I gladly shared these thoughts with the government, but I wouldn't let the blame for the forest's destruction rest with the hill tribes alone. The hill tribe people were not out to destroy the forest which they considered their home. The fact that they, like the wildlife, were now restricted to the remaining forest pockets was not primarily due to their misuse of this land. It had a lot more to do with government policies and land-use practices that allowed uncontrolled conversion of surrounding forests into agricultural land, villages, and industrial projects. Even now with so little forest left, the government's current forest policy was doing virtually nothing to stop the further destruction of these areas. It was ironic that while the Thai government was busy relocating the hill tribes "to save the forest," top government officials still stood firmly behind the Nam Choan Dam, a scheme that would deal a swift, fatal blow to this same area.

The data I'd collected from the trip, though far from complete, had convinced me of one thing. Although relocating hill tribes would be important for the area's long-term survival, preventing schemes like the Nam Choan Dam was more important for the immediate future. There were good reasons why most of the poaching and tribal settlements occurred around waterways. Most animal species need these waterways and the forest habitats associated with them in order to survive. Animal behavior and distribution patterns are strongly influenced by natural waterways.

The waterways pump the lifeblood into this tropical forest. River valleys such as the Huai Kha Khaeng and the Kwae Yai are the major arteries, and damming these arteries not only would alter the forest forever but would also deal a killing blow to some of the larger, more water-dependent mammal species such as tigers, elephants, and tapirs. Important riverine habitats, which include lowland forest, are wiped out by reservoirs. The idea that a reservoir will enhance wildlife habitat is, for most species, an absurd concept. Waterways have to be protected in their natural state if the wildlife in the surrounding forests is to survive.

When we finally reached the monk huts, neither Supanyo nor the *pra-cow* was in sight. I realized how much I had missed them both. It would be good to talk with Supanyo over coffee again and to hear the *pra-cow*'s latest spirit sightings.

We all straggled into camp thirsty and tired. A soccer game was in progress, and I watched in amazement as Intah, Sombat, and Supakit dropped their packs in the grass and ran to join in. I just wanted to make it up the hill to my house.

Shortly after I collapsed on my front steps, Beng arrived to welcome me, bringing with her a thermos of hot water to make coffee. "Beng, will you divorce your husband and marry me?" I said in English, smiling. She smiled back, not understanding.

9

AUNTIE'S COFFEE SHOP

It felt good to be back at camp again. The trip had renewed my spirits, and I felt closer to the men and their way of life than I had at any time since my arrival. I'd also collected good data on the large cats and had increased my understanding of this forest. While I was gone, a small black leopard had been seen twice around camp, and the tracks of a new male leopard had appeared twenty feet away from my front door.

I decided to go after the black leopard first, this time avoiding the "ghost area" around the monk huts. I knew this cat already. It had been sighted five times within the last year. Its small body size and its distinctive two-and-a-half-inch square tracks suggested that it was a female which was occupying the central, low-lying part of the study area. We moved the large cat trap into the forest south of my house, close to where she had last been seen.

By now, I estimated that four to five leopards lived in the area. I had a hunch that only one of these leopards was black, although another black leopard, with worn canines and mangy skin, had been shot by the workers a year ago after it killed several chickens near camp. In general, black leopards, also called panthers, are relatively uncommon and were once thought to be a separate species. The gene responsible for the black leopard's coloration is recessive, making such coloration rare. How the color of an individual cat's coat affects a leopard's behavior in the wild is unknown, but some hunters claim that black leopards are "more savage, bloodthirsty, and aggressive" than spotted leopards. To some rural Thais, the black leopard is a spirit cat; some are even thought to be *seu-uh saming*, or werecats, people who turn themselves into panthers to do harm to others.

Four days after opening the new trap, a signal from a radio transmitter attached to the door indicated that the trap had been triggered. Rushing to the scene, I found the door jammed two-thirds of the way down and a dead pig in the rear of the trap.

"Damn!" I cried out, slapping my forehead. I saw immediately what had gone wrong. Having built the trap during the dry season, I hadn't taken into account the fact that the wood would swell during the rains. The door that had previously been so painstakingly measured and built to fit the trap was now worthless.

The signs around the trap were clear. We had caught the black leopard, but after realizing what she had gotten into, she had crawled out the space below the door without even taking the freshly killed bait. I was furious. Had I known then that the black leopard would never again enter another trap, I would have been even angrier.

On the way back to camp another misfortune struck. I had asked Noparat several times to repair a log bridge that had been damaged during the fires, and as I drove across this bridge, it finally gave way. I was busy thinking of a new trap-door design when I heard the wood beneath the front tires crack, plunging the truck through the bridge and embedding its front end into the muddy bank on the opposite side. My head smashed into the windshield during the fall and the steering wheel spun out of control, spraining my wrist. It was a small bridge, no more than six feet long and three feet above the creek, but in the tumble the truck's steering rods twisted and the hood and front bumper crumpled. I climbed out into the creek, then squatted down in the water next to the truck. I felt an incredible headache coming on.

I walked back to camp and, too dazed to rein in my anger, burst into Noparat's office while he was talking with some of his staff.

"I told you about the bridge and you didn't fix it," I shouted. "Now my truck is wrecked again, the bridge is wrecked, and I can't use my hand. This is how you help me?"

No one spoke. They looked at me the way they had when I had sat by the dead leopard. It wasn't the response that I'd expected. My rage suddenly deflated as I realized I was offending Noparat and being too *jy rawn* once again.

I had not been in Thailand long before I learned two of the most frequently used Thai phrases: *jy rawn*, literally meaning hot-hearted, or one who is aggressive and impatient and voices negative opinions, and *jy yen*, cold-hearted, or one who is calm and accepting and avoids overt expressions of extreme emotion. I, like most foreigners, was *jy rawn* because of my desire to get things done quickly and my tendency to react emotionally.

Buddhism teaches that there is virtue in avoiding overt expressions of emotional extremes, even those that are socially acceptable, such as love and affection. In the forest, where animistic beliefs still play a large role in people's lives, a "cool heart" has practical advantages as well. Antisocial or disruptive *jy rawn* behavior is considered offensive to the spirits, which can then take revenge for these insults on the village as a whole. The person who can't control his emotions is a threat to the group and wrong in his behavior almost regardless of the circumstances. However, although this extreme self-control creates a façade of harmony among the Thais, often their repressed feelings pour out explosively and sometimes violently.

The bridge was quickly fixed, and Supakit and Samut, the camp mechanic, helped me replace the truck's damaged parts. I brought flowers to the spirit house and tried to be deferential toward Noparat, but to no avail. The damage was done. Even the workers resented my behavior. My inability to control my temper was seen as crude.

Only the person who is serenely indifferent (*choi choi*) is respected for possessing an important virtue.

"Life is a dance," Supanyo said when I related to him what had happened. Right now it felt more like an arduous crawl. And the fallout from this incident was yet to come. Ramesh had become indispensable to me, analyzing feces and taking care of the field station while Lung Soowan and I continued tracking the cats and checking the traps. Now I was hearing rumblings that Noparat wanted Ramesh fired. When I questioned Supakit, he told me people were complaining that Ramesh was not a Thai and this was a Thai project. Noparat was also saying that Ramesh was becoming a disruptive influence in camp, by not observing proper Thai etiquette and spending too many evenings drinking with the workers.

After the black leopard escaped, I started having better luck with the small traps though I didn't initially catch what I intended. I was baiting the small traps with chickens, hoping to bring in small leopard cats. But there were many other meat-loving animals in this forest. As I bent over my first closed trap, I was met by a long black tongue snaking out at me through the metal grating. I found myself looking into the reptilian eyes of a large water monitor lizard. The next day a black eagle was captured while trying to get the bait chicken. One morning I was confronted with the handsome gray face and white eye spots of a masked palm civet. This was the first time I'd ever seen this nocturnal carnivore up close. I was curious but still disappointed. Two days later, a second civet, twice as large and not nearly as calm as the first, was in one of the traps. It was a large Indian civet whose three-foot-long, nearly twenty-pound body filled the trap as it thrust its black and white throat patches forward and hissed at me when I got near.

Although I wanted to know more about the civets, I had only five small radio collars, and if I used them on these first captures, I was afraid I might not have enough left over for the leopard cats I still hoped to trap. Yet as I set these animals free, I felt I was making a mistake. These two species had been so strikingly different from one another, and I knew that they warranted further investigation.

Over the next few days I looked into what was known about civets. Considered to be among the most primitive living carnivores on earth, this family of species originated more than 42 million years ago. Some early naturalists thought these short-legged, long-tailed animals were a type of cat, partly because of skeletal similarities, partly because they showed some similar behavior patterns. To me the civet I'd seen in my first trap, with its gray fur and ringed tail, looked more like a North American raccoon.

A survey by a Thai professor done two years earlier in Huai Kha Khaeng had listed only four civet species, and none of those listed were the two I had just captured. The workers also spoke of a small "tree civet" in the evergreen forest that remained undocumented. I realized there might be as many as seven civet species in my study area, yet almost nothing was known about civet behavior in the wild. How did so many similar species coexist around camp? What was their role in the tropical forest community? I decided it was time to take a closer look. I could always order more radio collars.

A month passed before another animal entered my traps. It was monsoon season now and heavy rains battered the camp. All my clothes and bedding became damp and moldy. Nothing was ever dry. The doors to the house warped and wouldn't close, and multicolored molds blossomed in a patchwork design on the walls. Dysentery and fever swept through camp, and only a few of the men were well enough at any one time to repair roads or go out on antipoaching patrols. I distributed all the medicine I had but it was never enough. The workers' children were continually sick and had to be brought to the local hospital whenever a truck could get into town.

It was not a cheerful time in camp, and tensions mounted. When I was repeatedly quizzed about my work over dinner, I became irritable, then morose. There was a lack of understanding on both sides. I was studying animals differently from anything most of the Thais had ever seen before. I expected them to see how it would all eventually fit together and benefit the sanctuary, but instead they saw a large investment in time, money, and resources with, as yet, no hard results. The only leopard they had seen trapped was now dead.

I found some companionship during this time from a strange source. Long before my arrival at the station, a pair of young gibbons had been confiscated from a poacher and kept in a large cage near the kitchen. This is where I first met them, and we quickly became friends. As insufficient food supplies at camp became increasingly worrisome during the rainy season, Noparat decided to open the gibbons' cage and "set them free." Of course, the gibbons, who were used to being hand-fed, wanted no part of this new situation. After attempting to go into the forest, they quickly returned and stayed near the kitchen begging or stealing scraps. Within a few days, one of the camp dogs broke the neck of the more aggressive male gibbon, killing him. The more wary female escaped the same fate, but continued to stay close to camp. She was often seen curled up with a little black-and-white domestic cat that Amporn kept around the kitchen.

Feeling sorry for the gibbon who had never learned to fend for herself, I started hoarding some of my food and slipping it to her when no one was around. Slowly, she warmed to me and started following me to my house, walking in that strange bowlegged, arm-swinging manner characteristic of apes. At first she stayed in the trees nearby or sat on the wooden beam that supported my punching bag, watching me as I exercised. In the mornings I'd hear her loud wailing call, which reminded me of a Thai folktale about a woman who, having betrayed her lover, was turned into a gibbon and forced to roam the forest forever in search of him, calling out mournfully. Actually, such vocalizations, which are sex- and species-specific, are used to define and maintain territorial boundaries.

I never tired of watching the gibbon make her long, slow swings through the trees around my house. An antomical adaptation called brachiation allows gibbons to fully extend their arms, which are more than twice the length of their bodies, overhead and to propel themselves by hand-to-hand movement. Though gibbons don't move particularly fast for primates, they can reach the ends of branches and utilize parts of trees for food that other primates avoid. Though I never saw a gibbon fall in the forest, a study of gibbon skeletons showed that 50 percent of the older animals had at least one healed bone fracture and some had as many as seven, probably from falling.

Much to Beng's chagrin, the gibbon was soon venturing inside my house when I was gone, rearranging my belongings on the floor or throwing them outside into the yard. Eventually she came inside while I was at my desk, plopping herself down on top of the maps or data sheets I was working on and putting her long, lanky arm around my shoulder. She would watch me for a while, then flip on her back and wait for me to stroke her stomach, like a spoiled child. Only when I was working with fresh tiger or leopard feces would she stay away.

One day the gibbon broke into the camp's food shed and ate the last of our vegetables while I was in the field. Noparat told the men to catch her and bring her into the forest around the Huai Ai Yo, about three miles away from camp. When I returned, I was told what had happened. Sad and angry, I told Noparat he might as well have shot her through the head and gotten it over with quickly. It was unlikely she would be accepted into an already established gibbon group, and with no knowledge of how to fend for herself she would probably starve to death.

I went several times to the area where they had released her and called out to her. Although I wouldn't be allowed to bring her back to camp, I hoped I could give her food and try to buy her some time to learn to cope on her own. But I never saw her again.

The next time Noparat made a trip into Bangkok, he asked if I would meet him for a talk at the Forestry Department. When we met, I was apologetic and conciliatory about our differences, trying to maintain an appearance of equanimity. Then he surprised me with the news that he was leaving Dancing Woman Mountain after Songkran (Thai

New Year) in April. At first I was sympathetic. I knew the decision had not been easy for him to make and went beyond our minor disagreements. But my compassion for him was quickly dispelled when I heard what he had to say next.

Noparat insisted on one final demand. When he returned to the station in a week, he wanted Ramesh gone. No explanation was given. When I asked if I could wait to fire Ramesh until I found a replacement, he refused. When I told him I'd have to give Ramesh two weeks' notice, he refused again. I had one week. It was a matter of showing who was in control. I thought of going over Noparat's head, but I knew that such an action would have made life even more difficult for me at the station. I had no choice.

Word preceded me back to camp, and everyone knew what I'd been told to do. I vented my bitterness with Supanyo.

"The very people we see as unenlightened or stupid, once we learn to accept them and our feelings about them, are our tickets to paradise," he said to me.

"Supanyo, I'm not after paradise right now. Ramesh did nothing wrong and I'm being forced to fire him. Do you think that's right?" I asked.

"You can't deny someone the freedom to be what they are, just as they must accept what we are. It's useless to correct someone's behavior, to deny them their own decisions. We are equally wrong. Giving others the freedom to be stupid is one of the most important and hardest steps to take in spiritual progress."

The day before Noparat's return, I drove Ramesh into Uthai Thani to catch a bus for Bangkok. Despite his sadness about leaving the project, he was not entirely surprised by what had happened. He was more familiar with Thai ways than I was.

We reached town by noon and, as usual, Uthai Thani was quiet and dormant in the late-morning heat. Since the town was off the beaten track, with nothing of note to attract tourists, there were few outsiders here, Thai or foreign. A week after I started working in Huai Kha Khaeng, most people in the surrounding villages knew exactly who I was.

On the single main street, nestled between the marketplace and the government offices, I had a hideaway, *lahn bah*, or Auntie's coffee shop. This was where I brought Ramesh. I had first discovered this place as I was walking through town one evening and a short, rotund Thai woman in her late fifties grabbed my arm and pulled me inside a small open-front restaurant. Thinking she must need customers pretty badly, I stayed for dinner.

After two beers I started to wonder why I was the only customer and why Auntie, as she told me to call her, spent almost all of her time on the phone. Three times she disappeared up some stairs in the far corner, returning a short time later with an attractive young girl in tow. The girls sat at a nearby table, shyly glancing over at me and giggling.

"You have beautiful daughters," I said to Auntie, causing raucous laughter.

Then Auntie sent two of the girls off on a motorcycle, and three others came down the stairs. When the motorcycle returned, another girl was sent off, then another.

"I'll be damned," I said to myself, chuckling. "This is a whore-house!"

But Auntie's was no ordinary brothel, not like any I had ever heard about anyway. It was more like a boardinghouse for girls. She would take in anyone, even the unattractive and the crippled. If a girl didn't want to be sent with men, there were other chores she could do for her keep, though her earnings were small. Most of the girls were between sixteen and eighteen years old and were from rural areas of northern Thailand. They were helping out their families by sending home money which was never questioned. None of them wallowed in self-pity, though most of them were ashamed of what they did, hoping someday to leave it behind them.

Auntie was protective of her girls, sending them out only to places or with people she knew. In turn, the girls would not tolerate a bad word about Auntie, who treated them well. Auntie's young married daughter, who had a six-year-old son, helped run the business. It was by no means a philanthropic arrangement, but in a country where women's rights are virtually nonexistent, I had seen much worse situations for vulnerable girls such as these.

After that first day I returned often. Usually I'd just sit and drink beer by myself or watch television with the girls in the back room. A few times I babysat the grandson or dropped the girls off for their weekly venereal disease checkup at the hospital. With one of the girls, I formed a temporary relationship which satisfied the physical hunger in me.

It was always a cheerful day when one of the girls left after having sent enough money home to help set up a food stall or shop. Sometimes they returned to an arranged marriage. But all too often I would see them back a month or two later. More money was needed for a brother's schooling, or a girl's past caught up with her and the embarrassment was too much for her family or her new husband. None of the girls ever talked about another's return. They all concentrated on their own escape.

We had fun that afternoon, Ramesh and I, forgetting about the research and the station. As we drank beer and joked with the girls, Ramesh missed the first bus out of town. He was about to miss the second and last bus when I realized the time. Rushing down the street to get the truck, I swung it quickly around to the shop.

My sense of distance blurred by the beer, I caught the end of the metal supports holding up a large awning over the front of the shop. There was a crash as the supports crumpled and the entire awning engulfed the truck. The girls outside screamed and scattered, and all the people from the neighboring stores came out to watch the mayhem. So much for being inconspicuous at Auntie's, I thought. Ramesh missed the last bus.

Soowan was sick with fever and chills when I returned to camp, so I tried to keep to our regular work schedule by myself. Supakit helped me until he became sick a few days later. Finally I too succumbed, waking up one morning covered in sweat and barely able to climb out of bed.

I was barely cognizant of my surroundings as I checked the traps. Every few hundred yards I leaned against a tree for support, twice doubling over and vomiting. By the time I got to the last trap I was near the spirit house and, without thinking, I walked up the hill and stood again in front of the pile of stones, feverish and shaking with chills.

"Damn you!" I shouted at the little dancing figurines.

"I've shown you respect. I've brought you flowers and incense. I've given you food offerings. I asked for your permission. What have you given me? Nothing!"

I sat down on a nearby log and put my head in my hands. I was dizzy.

"I've had it. Just leave me alone," I moaned. "I'm not coming here anymore. Leave me alone."

The next thing I knew it was morning again and I was in my bed with Soowan shaking me. He was feeling better now, he said, and could help me check the traps. The previous day seemed like a bad dream, and I realized I must have come back and collapsed, then slept through the entire day and night. My fever had broken, but I felt weak and drained. Soowan still looked pale and drawn as well. I decided to close the traps for a few days so we could both rest.

I bent over one of the small traps to feed the chicken before noticing that the door was shut. A purring jarred me out of my reverie and, shifting my gaze, I found myself looking into two green eyes. I couldn't believe it. A beautiful little spotted cat was sitting quietly inches from my face. It purred again, and I had a strong desire to just open the door and set it free. But I knew I wouldn't. Not yet.

Forgetting my fatigue, I raced back to the house to pick up the equipment. Soowan was already there waiting for me.

"We trapped a leopard cat last night," I said, grabbing his arm and smiling.

"We trapped two leopard cats last night," he said.

10

WILDLIFE
ABUSE

My lethargy vanished as I followed Soowan to his leopard cat, whom he said was agitated in the trap. As I approached the trap, I could see that this species' reputation for fierceness was definitely borne out by this individual. About the size of a domestic cat, this miniature version of the spotted leopard was hunched in a corner hissing and spitting. He charged at me when I got close enough to put a needle into his hindquarters. The chicken that had been placed in a smaller cage behind the trap was lying headless on the ground. Despite the small size of this male, I was glad there were bars between us.

I injected him and he fell asleep quickly. After recording his body and tail length (he measured a little over three feet and weighed almost eight pounds), I attached a small radio collar around the cat's neck. I could feel the musculature beneath his coat. Placing him gently back into the trap, I covered the cage with leaves and branches so that he could recover undisturbed. Then I packed up the equipment and hurried off through the forest to our next capture.

"*Jy yen yen*," Soowan called out, telling me to calm down as I left him further and further behind.

The second leopard cat was captured in a small wooden trap we had built close to the monk huts. This one was a female, slightly smaller than the male and nearly two and a half pounds lighter. She was standing quietly over the bait chicken she had partly eaten. After sedating her and attaching a radio collar, I ran my hands through her tawny-colored fur, checking for external parasites. This was my first chance to take a close look at one of these smallest and most common wild cats of southern Asia.

Called *chin-ch'ien mao*, or the "money cat," by the Chinese, who think its spots resemble Chinese coins, this species ranges from the cold, dry environments of the Himalayas to the tropical rain forests of Borneo. Although it is generally a solitary forest animal, it can live in disturbed areas close to humans. These cats eat everything from snakes and lizards to small deer. Its small size belies its energy and ferocity. As with the civets, virtually nothing is known about leopard cat movements in the wild.

Suddenly the cat's body trembled, as in a passing bad dream, and I lifted her onto my lap. She was such a little thing; she had barely even jumped when I injected the tranquilizer. Just before she fell asleep, she had gazed at me with a look of fear, and distrust.

I knew this little cat would open the door to a new mystery for me. I would be the first to follow these secretive little carnivores through their daily lives. But it was hard to push aside the sadness that always followed the elation of a capture and the excitement of touching these wild animals. I often felt that my interference was soiling something beautfiul.

As I watched the cat to make sure she was sleeping quietly, my thoughts turned to a gangly, slightly crippled sixteen-year-old girl who was named Nit, or "Little One," a new arrival at Auntie's. When I had met her two weeks ago she was sitting alone trying to teach herself English while the other girls watched television. She was studying to become a teacher back in her village she said. I hoped that because she limped and was unattractive, she might be spared, but Auntie told me that her innocence and vulnerability made her appealing. She was much in demand by the men.

The cat stirred again as the drug wore off. I made a bed of leaves and grass in the trap and placed her back onto it. According to Thai tradition, a baby officially becomes a "person" and no longer belongs to the spirit world after its name is chosen and entered into the village's records.

"You are now Nit," I said, writing her name at the top of my data sheet. "And if there really are spirits around, maybe they can help you both."

Several days later I returned alone to the spirit house. None of the men knew what had gone on there in my delirium and I wasn't sure myself. I unpacked the pieces of chicken and whiskey I'd brought and laid them on the rocks. There were things I'd planned to say, but I felt suddenly uncomfortable in front of this little wooden house now that I was alone there with my senses intact. I lit incense and candles, and then busied myself by pulling weeds from around the rock pile and replacing some stones that had fallen. Then I sat on a log and watched the smoke from the incense spiral upward and disappear among the trees. Soowan's wooden penis was still where he'd placed it. Fifteen minutes later I left.

I felt that it was time for a break. I'd been in Thailand for nearly nine months now, and I needed to talk with friends and get some of my perspective back. I decided to return to New York for a few weeks.

I made my decision quickly, before something could change my mind. I closed the traps and briefed Soowan on tracking the leopard cats with the radio equipment. Beng and Supakit agreed to watch over the house, and I put Anant in charge of the gym.

As I settled in by the window on an express bus to Bangkok, a Chinese kung-fu video dubbed in Thai played on a television at the front. The driver raced along at full speed, often in the wrong lane, passing every vehicle that couldn't keep up. His eyes continually shifted between the road and the video. I tried to put the frequent reports of bus crashes out of my mind by looking out the window.

The scene spreading before me outside the bus was one I never tired of, a sea of green stretching to the horizon—the central plains region, the heartland of Thailand, the rice bowl of Asia. This area has been the traditional source of Thailand's wealth for more than seven hundred years. It is the domain of *mae pasop*, the Rice Mother, whom the Thais say is hard at work becoming "pregnant" again at this time of year as the rice plants begin to seed.

I rarely enjoy looking at land devoid of trees; I usually find it lifeless. But this scene was full of life. The crops were a deep, rich green that could have been painted on the sky. When a breeze swept over the plains, the plants swayed in unison, and the rice danced to the soundless crooning of the "mother."

This seemingly endless, smooth green sea was broken only by small islands of palms and bamboo which partially hid little houses, set high on poles above the household pigs and chickens. Occasionally I'd catch the flash of a glittering Buddhist temple in the distance. In spite of all the modern intrusions of Bangkok, this area seemed timeless. The simple Thai farmers here lived as they had for generations.

I thought of the day I took one of the workers to his family's home outside of Lan Sak. Sitting in one of those little island pockets on a bamboo mat outside the house, I gazed out at eye level with the fields. Before eating our meal of rice, dried fish, and fruit, his father put some rice to the side for the insects and birds, so that they could share in a bounty that was not seen by these farmers as being entirely their own. As each family member finished his meal, he gave a quick *wai*, or bow, over his plate, to show respect to the Rice Mother. Later, we walked to the temple compound, where I was shown the new roof that the village was putting on one of the temple's buildings.

This little Thai community was like thousands of others around the countryside, the end product of millennia of tradition. The farmers' homes were simple wood or bamboo structures and the villages were self-governing units. The temple was the focal point of the community and often served as the school, the hospital, the community center, and a refuge for the poor, the aged, and the mentally disturbed all at the same time. Until 1921, these temples were the only places for children to get a basic education in Thailand. These small villages represented Thai life at its purest, nearly undiluted by outside cultural influences. In a place like this, I could believe in magic and spirits.

At different times of the year, the scenes and colors of the central plains change. Around May, toward the end of the dry season, the farmers and water buffalo labor at trying to till the brown parched ground for the next crop. Up before dawn and working the fields by first light, they don't return home until dusk. This is also the month of Visakha Puja, Thailand's greatest religious holiday, commemorating the Buddha's birth, enlightenment, and death. Even those who have been out all day in the fields go to the temple at dusk and join the procession, circling the chapel three times with flowers, a candle, and three incense sticks representing the Buddha, the dharma (his teachings), and the Sangha (the monastic order).

When the monsoons arrive a month or so later, water inundates the paddy and the young, green rice plants start to emerge. As the plants seed, and the fields become "pregnant," a spirit ceremony is held to strengthen the plants through this period of weakness and vulnerability. By early November, when the rains cease, the grain turns golden. In late November or early December, harvest time arrives. The work continues now well into the night. The fields are lit by lamplight, and some villagers sleep among their crops in makeshift shelters. During the harvest, the paddies are filled with women and children, their wide-brimmed straw hats hiding their faces, their voices occasionally drifting through the hot, still air.

This system of paddy growing, called *sawah* agriculture, is practiced throughout Asia's most populated areas. Because these irrigated paddies often produce similar or increased yields from the same land for centuries, this type of agriculture is capable of absorbing and feeding expanding populations in a way other forms such as "swidden" or slash-and-burn agriculture cannot.

But rice is more than just a commodity to the Thai people. Symbolically, it represents a gift to be respected and shared. Rice grains are not to be intentionally thrown on the floor and, if seen on the ground, should not be stepped over. The Thai words "to eat," *geen cow*, literally mean "to eat rice." Eight out of every ten Thais are rice farmers. As of 1986, more than twenty million tons of rice were produced a year. Over a quarter of this yield was for export; Thailand is the only developing country in the world that is a net food exporter.

Yet the irony is that as Thailand's wealth increases and the number of Mercedeses and skyscrapers in Bangkok mushrooms, the Thai rice farmer finds himself plummeting to the bottom of the Thai economic pyramid. The farmer, who is often merely a tenant on the land, is a frequent victim of usury. Sometimes the farmer is forced to sell even his most cherished belonging, his water buffalo, just to survive. A 1987 survey estimated that 80 percent of Thailand's villages were in debt. The enormous sums owed averaged over $80,000 per village. This economic instability causes chronic hardship that often results in landlessness, poverty, and the collapse of family units.

Before leaving for New York, I had hoped to spend a few relaxing days in Bangkok. But during my first two days there, what started as a pleasant shopping excursion turned into something quite different.

The morning after I reached Bangkok, I went to visit the famous Chatuchak Weekend Market, an intricate maze of over five thousand vendors which spreads over twenty-eight acres. It's like a massive flea market and Thai-style county fair rolled into one. There were stalls selling everything from wild boar meat to human skulls. If shopping became tiresome, you could go watch a cockfight in progress.

I'd seen some of these Thai oddities before. There were scores

∴ M̶y three-room house in the forest at Dancing Woman Mountain.

∴ B̶eng, my housekeeper, bringing water up from the stream for my evening bath.

∴ A̶ scrape mark with feces left by a male leopard outside my front door, shortly after I set up house in the forest.

∴ My first field assistant, sixty-year-old Lung Galong, putting on his best face for my camera.

∴ A wild male gaur I encountered at a mineral lick in the forest. (PHOTO BY TERREPAT PRAYURASIDDHI.)

∴ Supakit holding the sedated male leopard that we snared over his sambar deer kill.

∴ The station chief, Noparat, giving the forest monks their daily meal of rice. The German monk, Supanyo, is second from the left.

∴ **L**ung Galong at the spirit house, asking the mother spirit of Dancing Woman Mountain to grant me permission to carry on my research.

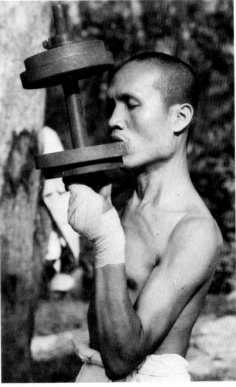

∴ **T**he "pra-cow" performing his own exercise rituals with my dumbbells.

∴ A young Hmong child standing alone behind her house in the early morning light.

∴ A Hmong woman looking me over, just after ripping a plug of hair from my chest to put atop her spirit altar.

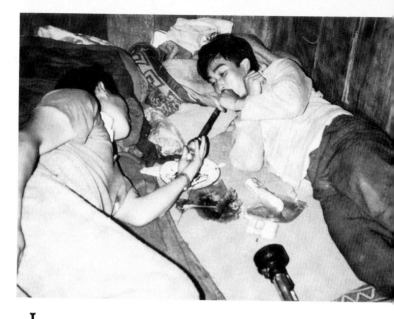

∴ **I**ntah, one of my strongest workers, smoking opium one evening at the Hmong huts.

∴ **T**he three virgin daughters of a Karen village headman being offered to me for the "bride price" of about $200 apiece. Jangair is in the center.

∴ A newly destroyed area of forest within the sanctuary cut and burned by the tribal people.

∴ A large monitor lizard captured in one of my small carnivore traps.

∴ The tame female gibbon after she was set free. She stayed around camp and became good friends with a domestic female cat that was kept at the kitchen.

∴ **S**etting a large wooden trap to catch leopards and tigers in the forest. (PHOTO BY SUSAN WALKER.)

∴ **T**he female leopard cat, Nit, captured in one of the wooden traps.

∴ **T**eaching my field assistant, Lung Soowan, how to locate the collared cats with the radio-telemetry equipment. (PHOTO BY SUSAN WALKER.)

of open-air shops in Bangkok selling stuffed cobras, or caiman and crocodile handbags and wallets by the hundreds. On all the major streets, stalls hawked up-country jewelry alongside cases upon cases of beautifully mounted butterflies, scorpions, and bats. Many of these species, which are so abundant on the street, are rare in the wild.

Anyone looking for something more exotic can visit the numerous leather shops selling boots and handbags made from the skins of snakes, turtles, sharks, lizards, crocodiles, and elephants. On one pair of cobra-skin boots, I saw the snake's heads were still attached hissing at me from the toes. Or there were numerous stores with bear, tiger, and leopard teeth and claws, all beautifully mounted in gold and silver settings. Twice, I was offered the skins and heads of the animals that went with these accoutrements.

When I got to the wildlife section of the Weekend Market, I was stunned at the variety of animals that could be bought openly and cheaply. There were hundreds of cages filled with wild jungle fowl, beautiful little pittas, hill mynas, pheasants, hawks, eagles, falcons, macaws, and parrots. The harder-to-obtain or illegal species were sold in darker, more hidden areas of this part of the market. One cage housed both a baby gibbon and a baby langur, the animals clinging to the wire of their cage. Their mothers were most likely killed to get them. Another cage held a python, and still another contained two leopard cats.

But the most pitiful sight was the squirrels—one of the more popular "pet" items at the market. Burmese striped tree squirrels, Indochinese ground squirrels, grey squirrels, and white-bellied flying squirrels were all tied by little strings around their necks to the top of a table, with no food or water nearby. The sun found its way through rents in the awning and beat down on the more unfortunate ones. Nails were clipped, sharp teeth were filed, tails were fluffed, all in order to make them cuter playthings.

I watched Thai children pass by with their parents, poking here and there, trying to play with the cute furry balls. When one young boy went to pet a white-bellied flying squirrel, its stiff body simply shifted space. A look of puzzlement flashed across the child's face, and the vendor quickly replaced the dead animal with a young golden-colored ground squirrel. The boy smiled and giggled as the new little squirrel snuggled against his finger. The sale was made.

What struck me most was that there was no conscious maliciousness on the part of the vendors. These animals were commodities to be bought and sold like anything else. I looked at the body of the dead squirrel that had dropped to the floor. How many in a day? I wondered.

The next morning, while jogging in Lumpini Park in the middle of Bangkok, I was attracted to an area on the perimeter of the park where groups of people were milling about. As I approached, I saw cages of snakes, and then a curtained-off area where a live king cobra hanging from a hook was being slit open for its warm blood and gallbladder. At a table nearby, joggers, the majority of whom were Chinese, finished up their runs with a cocktail made of cognac, cobra or Russell's viper blood and gall. There were several of these stands open six days a week, except Monday, when the streets were cleaned.

At this point, I was thoroughly disgusted by all I had seen and I decided to spend the next few days in Bangkok talking with people, following leads, and looking through old newspaper files. I wanted to try to understand how extensive the illegal wildlife trade situation here was because it directly reflected on the government's true attitude toward protecting what wilderness was left in Thailand.

Thailand's only Wild Animal Preservation and Protection Act was enacted in 1960. This was the first major attempt by the Thai government to protect its increasingly depleted wildlife populations. This legislation created two categories: reserved wild animals, which are not permitted to be captured, hunted, or kept in possession, under any circumstances, and protected wild animals, species which can be captured and sometimes killed but only with a special permit. Nine species, considered to be Thailand's rarest and most endangered wildlife, were placed in the reserve category:

Javan rhinoceros	Schomburgk's deer	hog deer
serow	goral	Sumatran rhinoceros
kouprey	wild water buffalo	Eld's deer

· Today, four of these species are considered extinct in the wild in Thailand. Two more species, Eld's deer and the hog deer, if any still exist, are close to extinction. The goral and the wild water buffalo exist only in small numbers in a few restricted pockets. The serow, or goat-antelope, is still holding out—only because it makes its home on steep limestone mountains and cliffs which are relatively inaccessible.

In January 1983, because of increasing international pressure, Thailand finally ratified the Convention for International Trade in Endangered Species (CITES), the most widely accepted conservation agreement in the world. Thailand signed the bill initially ten years earlier. But it was not until 1983 that the Thai government actually agreed to pass legislation to implement the convention, which would enforce protection for species classified by CITES signatory nations, now numbering nearly a hundred. But to this day, none of this new legislation has been enacted in Thailand and endangered species from other countries are still openly and legally bought and sold.

The results of a 1984 internationally funded survey called Operation Tooth and Claw found that 95 percent of the jewelry stores in Thailand that cater to tourists still carried large-cat products. The average store carried fifteen large-cat claws and seven large-cat teeth. That same year, Bangkok was denounced by the Associated Press International as a major regional market for wildlife souvenirs.

In 1985, one of Thailand's biggest exporters of wildlife, Suchino Corporation, was openly distributing a shopping list which included thirty-three species of mammals and seventy-five species of birds for sale. The more expensive items included:

| Baby Asiatic elephant | $19,500 |
| Baby Malayan tapir | $ 5,500 |

Young clouded leopard	$ 5,000
Eld's deer	$ 2,000
Douc langur	$ 1,200
Great hornbill	$ 250

During this same year, TRAFFIC, an organization set up to monitor illegal animal trade activities, documented that a large number of the thousands of pangolin and python skins which had arrived in Japan had originated in Thailand. In addition, countless numbers of birds and mammals were discovered in the luggage of people traveling between Bangkok and Tokyo. Most of these animals died en route.

In 1987 (just months after an official from the Thai Forestry Department was quoted at the biannual meeting of all CITES signatory countries as saying: "Thailand will cooperate to control trade in some of the over 5,000 endangered species of fauna and flora listed in the CITES . . ."), the "Eating Out" section of the *Bangkok and Beyond* newspaper favorably reviewed two new restaurants. Their delicacies included snake flesh, tiger penis in whiskey, snake blood cocktails, sea turtle, black monkey, and black dog.

As the wildlife trade became publicized internationally and it became more difficult to get certain species out of Bangkok, animal exporters started shipping from Vientiane, the capital city of Laos, a country that had not signed CITES. In the 1987 listing of wildlife, Suchino Corporation now had an addendum: ". . . our company has [an] Export License for live animals in Appendix I and II (CITES) from Laos. We can supply [these] to you legally by official texts. [For] the animals in Appendix I and II (CITES) and species out of stock, please give us more time." Appendix I species are animals considered to be in danger of extinction; Appendix II contains species that could be threatened with extinction if trade is not controlled.

Suddenly, in August 1987, Laos arrested three of the largest Thai wildlife dealers on wildlife-smuggling charges and sentenced them from one to three years in prison. Two months later, a Thai government official flew to Laos and convinced the Supreme Court to set them free. "After all," the Thai official said, "through the nature of their work, the men had earned a large amount of foreign exchange for Laos."

In 1987–88, a survey of the bird and mammal trade of the Chatuchak Weekend Market listed 225 native bird species, 51 exotic bird species, and 24 native mammal species. Of the native birds, 78 percent were protected, and less than 3 percent could be legally sold through the market. The offices of the Thai Forestry Department and the Wildlife Conservation Division are less than two miles away from this marketplace.

After a few days of research I knew I had only scratched the surface of this enormous problem, so I decided to talk with some of the officials whose job it was to protect Thailand's wildlife.

"You have only been here a short time; things have gotten better," was a common response from Forestry Department officials.

"Our hands are tied," one man told me. "We patrol these areas, but wildlife officials don't even know what is protected and what is not."

"There are too many ways around the law," another said. "People can legally possess two of any protected species as long as they don't capture or sell them."

"The police are corrupt and don't care. They hinder all our efforts."

All these statements were, to some degree, true. But I was bothered by a feeling that had been plaguing me at Dancing Woman Mountain. It seemed that much of the sentiment expressed in Thailand, the constant assurance that "things have gotten better," was all just a façade to keep up appearances both for the international community and for Thais themselves. The reality was that the wildlife was being exploited more than ever before. I was starting to believe that the poorest villager cared more about conservation than the highest-ranking officials.

Symbolically the forests and wildlife represent many things to the Thai people: life forces to be protected and nurtured, the spirit world, fear and power, beauty and strength. However, in day-to-day practices, animals and trees represent resources to be tapped and land to be utilized. Wildlife is to be used: strong animals are put to work, beautiful animals are worn, dangerous animals are eaten to gain power, and anything can be caged or chained for man's entertainment. Three hundred years ago there was a thriving trade in rhino parts between Thailand and its neighbors. Now that the rhino is extinct, other species have taken its place.

Even Buddhist practices in Thailand have been severely corrupted. I was especially offended by the Thai tradition of buying little containers or cages containing birds, fish, and turtles, then setting them free during special occasions such as festivals or birthdays. Through this beneficent act the buyer gains "merit" for his next life. Yet it is obvious that the sale of such animals, captured for just this purpose, is a thriving business in death and torture which contradicts the most fundamental Buddhist beliefs. Most of these animals soon die or are quickly recaptured after their release. One vendor told me that she addicted her birds to opium so they'd return to her. Now, she bemoaned, opium was too expensive.

I stopped counting the gibbons and macaques I saw chained by the neck at Buddhist temples. Monks accepted such gifts freely from the people, sometimes believing they were doing the animal a service by caring for it. Often, however, the monks knew the value of such animals to their temple. Sometimes the abbot of a temple requested certain species of animals because they brought in tourists and increased the temple's donations. Many temples had little zoos. One temple compound in Uthai Thani kept a leopard cat, a civet, a Javan mongoose, and numerous forest birds in pitifully cramped little cages to attract the townspeople. The monks fed them what little remained from their own meals. The water dishes in most of the cages were bone dry.

Then there were the buckets of frogs in the marketplace. I watched as women skinned them alive, then severed the legs from their bodies to sell. With eyes bulging, the still living naked torso was thrown into a separate pail to be discarded.

"Why don't you kill the frogs before you dismember them?" I asked repeatedly.

"It is not right for Buddhists to kill," I was told.

Once I arrived in New York, I stayed several weeks and made contact with Sue, a very special friend. I had first met Sue while I was finishing my dissertation at the University of Tennessee and she was in her last year of her bachelor's degree in anthropology. Her quiet, self-contained demeanor masked a sharp intelligence that attracted me immediately. After a first date hiking in the mountains, a romance quickly blossomed. It was the beginning of a turbulent on-and-off relationship that was to linger for seven years.

Sue had worked with me for nearly six months in Belize, after my initial survey capturing and studying jaguars in the rain forest turned into a full-blown project. Although the pressures of living and working together eventually became an intolerable strain on our relationship, Sue had been an excellent field assistant. Her tall slender body possessed an inexhaustible amount of energy and moved easily through the dense jungle foliage. Within a short time, she could track and capture jaguars as well as myself.

I had not seen Sue for over a year now and she was involved with someone else. As we talked on the phone, our conversation was friendly but dispassionate. Still, I could hear the familiar quiver creep into her voice as she strained to hold her emotions in check. Finally, she told me she was restless and wanted to get back into the field and work with animals again. I told her I needed a field assistant badly. We were both quiet for a few moments, remembering the past.

If Sue had been a less special person, I would never have considered asking her to work with me again. Neither of us harbored any more illusions about a long-term romantic involvement, but we were still attracted to one another. I had strong doubts about whether we could maintain just a working relationship. Furthermore, it had taken me such a long time to be accepted and feel at home at Dancing Woman Mountain. Despite my loneliness and frustration, I still felt selfish about sharing this place with anyone. But as the barriers came down and we talked and laughed together, I realized again how much Sue and I had gone through and how well she knew me. Introducing Sue to the Dancing Woman might be a good thing. We agreed to give it a try. She would come in February.

On the plane back to Thailand, I thought about Supanyo. He would have left Dancing Woman Mountain before I got back. The rainy-season retreat had ended a week after I'd left and he was to return to his temple for Thot Kathin, the annual ceremony at which monks are presented with robes, utensils, and anything else necessary for their upkeep during the forthcoming year. When I had asked if we'd meet again, he had said that he didn't know what the future held. He would continue his "flight of a dust particle, from wonder into wonder."

I opened the note that he'd left for me the morning of my departure, and reread what he called his "final reflection of a deluded monk."

> Try to be mindful and let things take their natural course. Then your mind will become still in any surrounding, like a clear forest pool. All kinds of wonderful rare animals will come to drink at the pool and you will clearly see the nature of all things. You will see many strange and wonderful things come and go, but you will be still. This is the place of knowing. This is the dance of the universe. Very graceful. No owner! I will meet you there.

I folded the note carefully, feeling that these were the last words I would ever hear from that joyful *farang* monk. They were beautfiul, gentle words, and they calmed me as his words had done so many times before. But this time he had also helped strengthen my resolve to continue my work regardless of the circumstances. And he had given me a place to meet him when I needed to.

11

TIGER
TRACKING

It was wintertime at Dancing Woman Mountain. December and January were the coldest, driest months of the year. Temperatures often dropped down as low as the forties during the night. In the evenings and early mornings, families huddled around large fires outside their shacks. Unmarried men slept by the fires, which they preferred to the cold, dark solitude of their huts.

Except for sporadic showers, there was no significant rainfall during these months. Many of the smaller streams dried up and even the Huai Chang Tai ebbed down to a trickle, causing water shortages in camp. As water also became scarce in the forest, the movement and distribution patterns of many animals changed.

Monsoon-season illnesses were replaced by the more minor ailments of the cold season. A lack of warm clothes and blankets caused colds and fevers and the men were still frequently too sick to go on patrol. During early December, a third civet was captured. This species, called the small Indian civet, was different from the first two that had been released. This time the seven-and-a-half-pound male was fitted with one of several new radio collars I had brought back from New York.

I was radio-tracking two leopard cats and a civet now. The male leopard cat I named Li Po, after a famous Chinese poet born in the eighth century, whose poems were among my favorites. Both he and Nit were doing well. After the civet was collared, I put together a large, ten-element antenna that I had not yet used and attached it to a sixty-foot bamboo pole that was mounted beside my house. The base was sunk into a hole in the ground; a wooden crosspiece allowed full rotation of the pole. Now I could hear the cats' radio collars from a much greater distance.

Lung Soowan came up one morning and told me that a truck filled with monks had just arrived and that the driver had seen a tiger just two miles from the station. When we went to take a look, the tiger's tracks were still distinct in the shaded areas of soft dirt along the roadside. It was an adult male, whose tracks and feces I'd been seeing regularly. This was the third sighting within the last year.

Male tigers have tracks that are generally more square and less angular than those of females. Hunters claim that with older cats the tracks splay more, becoming even wider in proportion to their length. This was a wide track with a lot of space between the toes and lines clearly showing on its pad imprint. It was likely this tiger was well past his prime.

Soowan started calling the animal Payak, literally meaning large tiger, but also implying strength and power. We followed the tracks, noting changes in gait. Both tigers and leopards typically leave double tracks, the smaller hind foot leading the larger front foot—in this case, by two to three inches. Species other than cats often leave single track sets, or tracks that overlap when they walk. There is some speculation that when the tracks of big cats overlap, this means the animals are old or wounded; possibly their joints are stiff or injured and the cats are incapable of bringing their hind legs as far forward as they normally would.

As we walked along the road, the gaps between the tracks increased. Payak had started a fast walk or trot, possibly after he had become aware of the truck. Soon afterward, he veered off into the forest. Once in the underbrush, I lost all sign of him. Tracking carnivores in the forest is difficult for even the best of trackers. The pads of cats leave few signs and, unless they're dragging prey, there is often no clear trail to follow. Yet Lung Soowan could read the cat's movements as if it were loping along in front of us. Whenever I was convinced that he was just guessing, he'd show me where leaves had been displaced or point out a tiny patch of matted grass.

We came to a gap in the forest, and as we entered the clearing, we heard a high-pitched bark followed by a sudden crash in the undergrowth. There was a flash of a white rump as a barking deer resting nearby bounded off. This alarm cry, followed by a conspicuous flash of coloration, is usually given when a dangerous predator is approaching. The sudden burst of sound surprises the predator just long enough for the deer to escape. It also alerts other deer in the area.

We were in a clearing about twenty feet in diameter, and the ground looked like someone had been digging for buried treasure in wet dirt. It was a mineral lick. Big-cat tracks dotted the area; some belonged to Payak, others were from previous visits by tigers and leopards. The soft, moist dirt of the lick made a good tracking surface that told many stories to anyone who could interpret the various scratches and diggings. The presence of the barking deer meant that Payak was not around, but this was obviously a place he regularly visited.

Noparat and his men had already found at least twenty-two mineral licks within my study area. Because visitation to these licks by deer, wild cattle, and other prey species influences the movements of the large cats, I periodically visited these areas to see what was going on. Sometimes, tracks showed that a leopard had come just to the edge of the lick, circling it but remaining under cover. Occasionally, cats bedded down on the periphery.

. . .

During this time I put Soowan to work building a new and larger trap along the main road, where Payak's tracks were seen most often. When the trap was nearly finished, he came to my house carrying a cardboard box and sporting one of his strange grins.

"Now we'll catch cats!" he stated emphatically.

I was wondering if he'd carved another wooden penis when I heard a whining from inside the box. The lid flipped up and a light-colored pug-faced puppy popped its head out.

Ever since we had opened my first trap, the men in camp had insisted that I use young dogs to catch big cats. Dogs were afraid of the forest at night, they said, and their crying would attract a cat's attention, pigs remained quiet and inconspicuous. More importantly, puppies could be had for nothing at almost any village. Small pigs cost almost forty dollars each.

I told the men that I would never use a dog. I didn't even like to use live animals as bait, but since it was necessary, I used animals that would have been killed and eaten anyway. It was true that the pigs were quiet in the traps and that a cat had to walk right by the entrance to know it was there. Still, I refused to cultivate the terror of one animal to trap and study another.

This made no sense to the men. I either wanted to trap cats or I didn't, and why should I buy something when I could use a better alternative for free? It was another reason to doubt both my intelligence and my ability. Soowan, with the best of intentions, had decided to take matters into his own hands.

"The men named her Chai Lai, meaning beautiful one," he said, smiling. "We can put her in the trap tomorrow."

I laughed in amazement. I couldn't believe they gave this name to an animal that they were sending to be terrorized before its death.

"We'll see," I said to Soowan, as Chai Lai licked my hand and cried softly. I couldn't tell him what I was really thinking. I still felt that I had somehow failed the female gibbon. I was determined that I wouldn't fail Chai Lai.

Toward the middle of December, a new monk arrived in camp. He planned to hike into Thung Yai and the tribal areas, but asked permission to rest at the station for a few days beforehand. Since the rains had ended, numerous monks had come and gone, but I hadn't interacted much with any of them. For the first time since Supanyo left, something about this diminutive, humble monk pricked my curiosity. That same afternoon I jogged out to the huts and found him sitting on the coffee-drinking platform looking off into the forest.

What I had taken for a very young face from afar aged as I got closer and I noticed the sprinkling of gray fuzz at his temples and the deeply set wrinkles around his eyes. We had difficulty speaking together at first because his Thai was different and more formal than what I had learned in camp. But when he simplified the conversation, we were able to talk easily.

His given monk name was Boonchuay, meaning "to be supported by the merit of the people," and he had been a monk for seventeen years, having entered the monkhood at eighteen. He had no desire to do anything else.

From that day onward, I reestablished the schedule I had maintained with Supanyo and spent part of almost every day at the monk huts. Boonchuay's few days of rest lengthened into three weeks. As I drove by the monk huts every morning at six-thirty to check the traps, I'd find him sitting on the raised platform like a little gnome, hunched over in his orange robes and orange knitted ski cap, looking off into the forest. Then on my way back, he would stand by the trail as if waiting for a bus. I would stop the truck and he'd climb into the passenger seat for our morning exchange while I checked two more small traps. The ride itself wasn't important to him; he just wanted to talk. Boonchuay was not the teacher that Supanyo had been, but I didn't need that now. Instead he guided me by example, in a way that was revealed slowly.

Half a mile from camp before the trail intersected the main road, I would stop and let him out. It didn't look good for a monk to come driving in for his morning food alms, he said. After I'd drive away, he'd come humbly walking in, his little five-foot-four-inch frame bent over as if deep in meditation.

During the second week, I captured another leopard cat. Boonchuay was with me and watched as I drugged and collared this new eight-pound male. Like the first male leopard cat, he was a fierce fighter. He struggled before giving in to the two doses of drugs I injected into him—more than enough to put a much larger animal to sleep. Despite his years in the forest, Boonchuay had never seen this secretive little cat before. As I finished attaching the radio collar, Boonchuay leaned over and gently stroked the cat's fur, then cradled its head in his hands. For the first time, he remained silent right up until the time I dropped him off near camp. Afterward Boonchuay never spoke of the capture. I named this leopard cat Tu Fu, after another Chinese poet, who had been a friend and admirer of Li Po.

At the end of the month, I went to Bangkok to pick up George Schaller. He was visiting me on his way to Vietnam, where he was going to conduct wildlife surveys in areas that hadn't been visited by Western biologists since the Vietnam War. I brought him back into my study area, eager to spend time alone with him in the forest.

For several days we hiked and checked traps. In the evenings we'd sit outside, talk, and listen to the sounds of the forest together. Our friendship grew during this time, and because of George's years in the field, I could share thoughts and feelings with him that few people would understand. He liked Dancing Woman Mountain, but pointed out what he considered the paucity of large mammals compared with similar habitats where he had worked in India.

I was surprised by his observations. The poaching in parts of Huai Kha Khaeng was intense, but I hadn't thought it was bad enough around my study area to have drastically altered the structure of the wildlife community and the densities of large mammals. This was an area considered to be one of the richest pockets of wildlife left in Thailand and possibly the entire region. What, then, was the difference here?

Often comparisons between the rich wildlife spectacles of the African plains or the mixed grasslands in India and the fauna of forested areas such as Huai Kha Khaeng are not valid. Because of the abundance of food in the form of grasses and edible leaves for the big herbivores, the highest diversity of large mammals in the world occurs in protected areas of mixed grasslands and alluvial plains. When forest cover is mostly continuous such as in Huai Kha Khaeng, patches of edible vegetation are sparse and the area naturally supports a lower density of large ground-dwelling herbivores. In such a case, most of the mammal biomass comes from only a few species. Both the large herbivores and their predators are forced to lead more solitary lifestyles or form smaller groups than when they live in more open areas.

But there were also other factors that I hadn't considered until now. The areas in India that George referred to not only contained larger grassland components, but their diverse and abundant wildlife had been protected longer than equivalent areas in Thailand. Until 1960, Thailand had no wildlife laws, national parks, or wildlife sanctuaries, and it was not until the 1970s and 1980s that many of the best remaining natural areas became legally protected. By this time the rich lowland areas had become cities, towns, and rice fields, and many of the hoofed species, or ungulates, were in serious trouble. Schombugk's deer was extinct, while Eld's deer, hog deer, Fea's barking deer, and Sumatran and Javan rhino species were already close to extinction.

I also underestimated the extent of the damage that years of hunting inflicted throughout this forest. Until the 1970s and 1980s, few Thais lived within fifty miles of what is now the Huai Kha Khaeng Wildlife Sanctuary. But within a few years, timber concessions and dam construction brought thousands of people into the province of Uthai Thani. An extensive trade in wildlife was established and the area became known for its availability of game meat. Within the sanctuary, the few lowland grass meadows which attract the larger herbivores were occupied and hunted regularly by tribal villagers. Even around Dancing Woman Mountain, the poached carcasses of gaur, banteng, and deer were still regularly discovered at the salt licks. George's comments brought home the reality of the situation here. This extensive forested region was relatively rich in wildlife in comparison with the damaged areas outside its boundaries, but it was still a poor representation of what it and other areas of Thailand had once been.

In 1869, an adventurer-explorer named John Bradley camped on the bank of Thailand's Chao Phraya River, not far from Nakhon Sawan, now a city just north of Uthai Thani. He wrote in his diary what he saw that night:

> During the night we were greatly disturbed by the wild animals, which came down to the river to drink and bathe. The moon was about full, and the light it gave was so brilliant that we could distinctly see elephants, rhinoceroses, buffaloes, and other animals sporting in the water. There were many hundreds of the various species and it was rather dangerous work to approach so large a number. Each species kept to itself in the water, but they were very close together and we witnessed a fight between a bull buffalo and a rhinoceros, in which, however, neither seemed to be much hurt.

Before I brought Schaller back to Bangkok, I took him to meet Boonchuay. Two other monks had recently come to stay at the huts and Boonchuay felt it had become too crowded. He was leaving for Thung Yai the next day to finish the walk he'd started nearly a month earlier. He planned to return in a few weeks.

Boonchuay motioned George to sit next to him on the platform and fold his legs in the lotus position.

"He has a good face," Boonchuay said to me after George contorted his body as best he could.

I looked at George, who was at home in these surroundings, sipping the sweet coffee.

"He has been many places and helped many animals," I told Boonchuay. "He is a famous zoologist in the United States."

Boonchuay nodded, turned toward George, and smiled. He motioned for him to readjust his legs to correct his lotus posture.

"Tell him I can't bend both legs that way," George said.

But Boonchuay was already concentrating on fixing himself another cup of coffee. "Yes, a good face, a strong face," Boonchuay repeated, adding a second spoonful of sugar.

By the time I saw George off in Bangkok and returned to the forest station, I'd been gone nearly a week. I knew there was something wrong when I greeted Lung Soowan and he didn't ask me what I'd brought him from town. After I told him that we'd reopen the traps in the morning, he mumbled something I didn't understand and walked away. I asked Beng what was going on.

Evidently, while I was in Bangkok, Supakit, with Noparat's approval, had appropriated six of my seven bait chickens and fed them to a group of Thai university students that had arrived unannounced at the station. The truck had been back to town twice since then, but my chickens hadn't been replaced. Now I had no animals to use as bait for the small traps.

Despite my resolution to be *jy yen*, I lost my cool again.

"We will get you more chickens," Supakit said, taken aback by my anger. "You were not here. Why do you need chickens if you are not here? The animals will still be in the forest to catch."

The next day I drove my truck into Lan Sak to buy more chickens.

My anger was assuaged somewhat when, only a few days after I reopened the traps, two more civets were captured and collared. Now I was tracking three different civet species. The two new animals, a common palm civet and a masked palm civet, both had different appearances and habits from the civets I had captured earlier.

The small and large Indian civets which I had captured were known as "true civets." These species have highly developed perineal glands which secret a thick, yellowish musky substance known at "civet," often used for making perfumes. They are the most terrestrial of the civets. They walk on their toes, the rear part of their foot raised up off the ground. The new civets I captured were called "palm civets," species with less developed musk glands which spend more time up in trees. They generally walk on the soles of their feet, heels touching the ground.

I had been least lucky with the tiger trap along the main road. It remained empty. I had heard that tigers are more intelligent and wary, and less tolerant of human presence than leopards. Stories abound of tigers passing up tied bait or taking bait only when they know a situation is not dangerous for them. Though I assumed that Payak had never seen a trap like mine before, he still avoided walking near the trap when it was open with a pig inside.

I decided to try taking the pig out of the trap and tying him along a creek nearby. Within four days, Payak took him. When I tied a second pig to the front of the trap, Payak took him on the second day. Now I was convinced Payak had overcome his wariness. I tied a third pig back inside the trap, no more than four feet from the last one. A week later, Payak's tracks showed him walking up to the front door, looking in at the pig, and walking away. He never came back while the pig was inside the trap.

One night, while listening to the signals from the leopard cats and civets, I decided to stay up all night and do a twenty-four-hour monitoring session, assessing whether each animal was active or not every fifteen minutes and determining the animal's location every thirty minutes. This was easy to do with the leopard cats, Li Po and Nit, who were close to camp; to locate the civets, I had to walk farther into the forest.

About 2 A.M., the camp dogs started barking and fighting in the distance. Thirty minutes afterward Li Po's signal went inactive and stayed that way until sunrise. I had that bad feeling in the pit of my stomach again. When Soowan came to relieve me at 7 A.M., I took off to find Li Po. If something had happened, I wanted to see it first and get a clear picture of the circumstances.

His signal led me directly to the back of the workers' houses and into a stream bed that had been made into a vegetable garden during the dry season. The workers, seeing me with my radio-tracking gear, watched from their houses. It took only minutes to find Li Po, lying in some tangled brush a little beyond where the garden met the forest. Bending over him, I saw canine tooth marks in his neck. Realizing I'd been listening as the dogs got him, it struck me how horribly impersonal these radios were. The only indication of his death I'd received was when the signal had changed from fast to slow beeps.

I could feel the workers watching me as I lifted the cat and carried him through camp on my way back to my house. This time I was determined not to let my face give me away. If they wanted me to be more like a Thai, then I would.

Later that day, a rumor circulated around camp that the radio collar had killed the cat. I couldn't believe it. I had purposely shown the workers the bite marks on Li Po's neck. They had seen the evidence and they had heard the commotion created by the dogs during the night. But they stuck to their own opinions despite the evidence.

"The dogs never caught and killed a leopard cat before," they said to me.

The fact that the dogs were all known killers of macaques, langurs, bamboo rats, and porcupines around camp didn't seem to count for much. The fact that Li Po had worn that collar for a month without dropping dead didn't seem to make much of an impression either. I knew what they were thinking. They had seen a dead radio-collared leopard cat in my arms, just as they had seen the dead radio-collared leopard some months earlier.

12

LEOPARDS
AND
LEOPARD CATS

Sue arrived the first week in February. After the first few hours together, all my fears about us working together as partners which had resurfaced since my return to Thailand were put aside. We had grown apart in the year since we had last been together, but our initial discomfort with each other was quickly dispelled. Sue looked at Thailand with a fresh eye, and she could see how the project was affecting me.

As I knew she would, Sue loved Dancing Woman Mountain and fit in immediately, as though she had lived there for years. Although it had taken the people at the station a long time to overcome their fears and shyness with me, they took to Sue immediately. Beng, not quite understanding the situation, was thrilled that I had found a woman to take care of me. Even Noparat liked Sue and there were no new complaints about my hiring a foreign assistant. But it was the puppy, Chai Lai, that derived the greatest pleasure from Sue's arrival. She found in Sue the mother she had lost.

It was the end of the cold season, and many of the trees were shedding their leaves as the dryness continued. Nearly every evening there were short bursts of rain, known as "mango rains," which broke the monotony of the dry heat and synchronized with the blooming of the mango trees.

The morning of the second day after Sue's arrival, signals from the mast antenna indicated that the door to one of the large cat traps had closed. There were now two big traps open, and the one that had been triggered was in the evergreen forest, nearly three miles from camp. There had been two earlier false alarms from this trap already when the pig had triggered the door release with his snout. Assuming this had happened again, I sent Soowan off to reset the trap and fix the pig's harness. Then I started working on the previous day's data while Sue practiced taking the radio locations of the animals that could be heard from the house. An hour later Soowan came charging in. It was no false alarm this time. There was a leopard in the trap!

The equipment was ready to go. I grabbed the pack and told Sue to follow behind with Soowan, who was already tired from the run back. I took off running—the adrenaline pumping through my system like high-grade gasoline.

I desperately hoped this would be a "clean" capture, no injuries and no escape. Leopards had been known to dig their way out of traps. I turned and ran up a dry stream bed, hopping onto the larger rocks and skirting the small ones, cutting minutes off of the regular trail route. I'd been over this old elephant trail so many times, I could walk it in my sleep.

This trail beneath the closed canopy of the evergreen forest was my favorite. Usually, I'd let myself be distracted by gibbons calling overhead or I'd stand and watch jungle fowl scurrying around in the underbrush. Now, my heart pumping strongly, I imagined myself the hunter. The three-foot-long jab stick I carried in my right hand was my spear. As I listened to myself grunt in response to the cramping in my leg muscles, I felt a primal surge of well-being. I heard a rustling, followed by a flash of color, as a wreathed hornbill took off in the canopy. It distracted me for a moment, and a rock caught my foot, sending me stumbling into the trunk of a sharp-thorned tree. My shirt ripped above the elbow and blood began trickling down my arm, but I pulled away and started running again.

I was running down into another dry stream bed and up the other side of the rise when a growl pierced the air and brought me up short. I had almost run past the trap without realizing it, but the leopard heard me coming. Although I couldn't see him yet, a shiver of fear and anticipation went through me.

I crept up quietly to look through the bars of the cage, the only place I could see into the trap. The wooden doors had been replaced with iron after the escape of the black leopard. As I leaned around the corner of the trap to peek inside, I found myself staring right into the face of the leopard, its head pressed against the bars. It roared and slammed its front paw against the bars, claws protruding. I hollered and fell backward.

The leopard looked small, small enough to be a young adult. I had expected the larger male I knew was around here. The cat's presence explained the slightly smaller tracks I'd seen in this area, the ones that Galong had insisted were from a clouded leopard. I was loading the syringe with a sedative when I heard a noise behind me. Soowan and Sue were watching from a distance, looking past me to the cat's face, peering out from behind the bars.

"Go over to the right side of the trap and make noise so I can drug it," I called to Soowan.

Soowan went up to the trap halfheartedly, but when the leopard threw itself against the front bars again, he backed away. He wouldn't go closer.

"Sue, you do it," I yelled to her.

She grabbed a long stick off the ground and pushed it through the bars. The leopard swung at her, snapping the stick with its paw. As its haunches came into view, I jabbed it. Then we backed out of sight and waited.

After ten minutes I pulled the leopard from the trap. It was an adult female measuring six feet from head to tail and weighing fifty pounds. She was on the small side but within the normal size range of female leopards from this region. Her worn, discolored canines and brown nipples suggested she was at least four or five years old. The pig lay dead in the back of the trap, uneaten.

After attaching a radio collar and examining her for wounds and parasites, I opened her jaws again so that Sue and Soowan could get a closer look. I showed them why cats were the ultimate carnivores. Besides the musculature that gives their large canines their killing power, their jaw structure precludes the possibility of grinding and is built strictly for up-and-down scissorlike shearing of meat and bone. There is only one pair of upper molars, very small and often lost. The only lower molars have two bladelike cusps that form cutting shears.

We placed her back in the trap and propped the door open to leave a foot of open space at the bottom. It isn't safe to allow a semi-drugged cat to wake up in the open while other large cats are around. A tiger or leopard might injure or kill another cat that can't fully defend itself. The small opening beneath the door, which we covered with brush, gave the cat an escape route once it was fully awake. I named her Jangair, after my favorite of the three Karen daughters who had been offered to me by the village headman during our hike into Thung Yai.

"Not bad for your second day here," I said to Sue as we started back toward camp.

"Alan, why is your arm bleeding?" she asked, reminding me of the wound I had received when I fell into the tree.

"A tribesman's spear," I said. "Don't worry, it's only a nick." I took Sue's hand and squeezed it gently.

I brought the pig back to camp to examine it more closely. It seemed strange to me that two leopards had killed the bait pigs but not eaten them. This female had been in the trap for at least three hours with the dead pig. I wondered if her hunger had been forgotten in the face of the terror she experienced when she suddenly realized that her freedom had been taken away. I thought about the male leopard who had let us chase him from his kill twice, and the black leopard who had never reentered a trap after his first narrow escape. Anyone who believed that these animals lacked the ability to think and feel was mistaken.

The pig had large canine puncture wounds above its eyes, where the leopard's teeth had penetrated the skull. Only large cats kill in this way, using a deep puncture bite instead of the shallow slashing bite used by many canids and smaller cats. When I was through looking at the pig, I gave it to Beng to divide among the families.

Temperatures went up into the sixties and seventies during February and, despite an increase in rain, the dryness continued. Sue worked closely with Soowan and me, analyzing feces and radio signals and studying the tracks and scrapes of the different cats around camp. I took Sue along the network of roads and elephant trails, and showed her how these paths formed important components of the animal community.

During the day, hundreds of small burrows which dot the roads suddenly came alive with beautifully colored butterfly lizards, who peek their heads out carefully before racing off into the grass after food. Ground-dwelling green snakes often lie in wait, hidden in the grass or coiled beside these holes, ready to snatch the lizards as they emerge. The crested serpent-eating eagles watch from the trees, swooping down after the snakes once they spot them from the air. Some days, there were fresh tracks along the road left by a dhole that had come by in the early-morning hours hunting rodents, snakes, or jungle fowl. Larger packs of these wild dogs hunted together for larger prey, such as barking deer and wild pigs.

In the hours after sunset, the roads fill with cryptically colored great-eared nightjars, which sit quietly on the grassy edges of the road until they suddenly burst into flight after insects. The Indian civets come out along the roads and trails at this time as well, along with an occasional leopard cat or Asiatic jackal. As the night wears on, the bigger predators emerge, the tigers and the leopards, who often leave feces, scents, and scrapes—prominent signs of their passing.

Only the big cats commonly leave their distinctive marks in the form of single or double paw scrapes. Usually this behavior precedes urination or follows defecation, but the exact reason for it is unknown. It may be both an olfactory and a visual signal, which marks the ground with secretions from special glands in the cat's feet.

The small leopard cats, which are more populous than other cat species in the area, left these kinds of marks only infrequently along trails. This paucity of markings made sense. Obviously the leopard cat didn't want to announce its presence to larger predators.

Although information is exchanged through these markings, the exact meaning conveyed by different kinds of marking behavior is not clearly understood. My research with jaguars, and much of what we were seeing here, indicated that feces, which were often spaced at frequent and regular intervals along roads or trails, left the longest-lasting visual mark. They probably help the large cats delineate the boundaries of their individual territories. Fresh scrapes, often combined with feces, urine, and/or anal gland secretions, were often found in highly trafficked areas that were being marked by more than one cat at the same time. These more transient marks might impart information that helps a cat to find available mates and avoid aggressive encounters in the vicinity. It is possible that the same mark can transmit different information to different animals. Research on animals' olfactory signals shows that mammals' odors consist of complex chemical mixtures that elicit different responses. This response can vary according to the context in which it is received, the animal's prior experiences, and the age and status of the individual relative to its peers.

I was explaining all this to Sue one night as we sat in front of the house. When I caught her eyes gazing off into the forest, I knew her thoughts were not on what I was saying. I stopped talking and sat there with her in the darkness.

"Can you give me a hug, Alan?" she asked, after we were both quiet for a while.

I slid over and put my arms around her.

"Sue, I've been wanting to touch you every day since you've been here," I said, my face close to hers. "But I've been scared. I swore I wouldn't let Belize happen again."

"I don't want Belize again either, Alan," she said.

We hugged for a while and then we kissed each other gently, tasting our own long-forgotten scents. Eventually the generator in camp went off and we were enveloped in a warm, dark silence.

Toward the end of February the fires started again. They were early, coming on the tail of an especially dry year. The little water that Beng could find and haul to the house was brown and it left spots of dirt after bathing. The men cut and cleared firebreaks around camp, then set them ablaze. This protected the camp but spread fires into the forest. The trap from which the black leopard had escaped burned to the ground. This ended our efforts to catch that cat.

Something was going on with the leopard cat Tu Fu. For more than a month, he'd concentrated his activities within a single square mile of deciduous and evergreen forest. Suddenly he moved to the periphery of his range. Then overnight, his signal disappeared. We couldn't find him anywhere.

It was now early April and the height of the hot, dry season. Temperatures averaged about eighty-two degrees, and the smoke from the many fires burning both inside and outside the sanctuary turned the sky a hazy gray. Sue discovered that Chai Lai was pregnant, possibly by as much as four to five weeks, although her lanky frame hid nearly all signs of her condition.

Then suddenly, two weeks after we had lost his signal, we found Tu Fu again. But it was by chance, in an area where I had never thought to look for him. Tu Fu had moved nearly three miles from his old range into an adjoining valley that was burning extensively. I followed him closely for the next four weeks while he wandered over nearly two square miles. Finally he confined his movements to an area less than a third of a square mile along the banks of a stream. I couldn't understand it. There was no obvious reason for this cat to leave a seemingly safe refuge in the wetter and leafier forest to move into a dry area that was burning. Had he been forced out? I wondered. Attempts to walk in on him proved fruitless. Whenever I'd get close, he'd move away.

In early April, a second leopard was captured in the same trap as the female leopard, Jangair. Weighing 132 pounds and measuring six and a half feet, this was a big, healthy adult male, the one I'd been after in that spot all along. It was captured and collared by Sue and Soowan while I was out of the study area. Once again, the pig was killed but not eaten.

Ten days later, the now collared leopard walked back into the same trap, and I got to see him for myself. He was waiting calmly and quietly, watching me from a low crouch. As I approached, he snarled and moved into the darker recesses of the trap. Sue said he had behaved the same way when he was first captured. He looked to be about three or four years old. His youth and nonaggressive behavior indicated that he was still unfamiliar with people.

I crouched in a position similar to his and started crawling toward the trap on my hands and knees, making my movements as unthreatening as possible. A low, slow growl came from the darkness. Finally I reached the bars and peered in. All I saw at first was its eyes. For just an instant, my monk friend Supanyo's face flashed in front of me.

I put the jab stick slowly through the bars and injected him with just enough of the drug to make him groggy. I had to sedate him so that we could safely open the trap and let him escape later by himself. The dead pig was still intact—except, this time, the ears had been eaten. Definitely a gourmet Thai leopard, I thought, choosing to eat pig ears and leave the meat.

I sat there looking into his eyes, wanting to reach out and stroke him. But he was still semi-conscious and I was afraid. I noticed a distinct difference between his facial spots and those of the female leopard. The spots on a leopard's muzzle and the patterns around the forehead and eyes can vary from individual to individual and they can be used to distinguish between different cats. I grabbed the data sheet to make some notes. On the top of the sheet where it said "Animal Identification," I wrote "Supanyo," and smiled. My friend was back.

Soon after we captured Supanyo, I went in search of Tu Fu, whose signal had been inactive for a day and a half. He was not hard to find. The radio signal traveled easily through the open forest since the fires had stripped away much of the underbrush. He was lying within a burned bamboo thicket, but only his skeleton remained.

It was an eerie sight; smoke rose from the charred ground, and the radio collar still circled the upper vertebrae, just below the skull. Examination of his skull showed that he'd lost his upper left canine sometime after his capture. The edges of the missing tooth's socket were already calcified.

Tooth breakage is not uncommon in carnivores, particularly among cats, who often use their teeth to puncture and chew the bone parts of their prey. The most commonly broken teeth are the canines, and the cost of losing these teeth is relatively high, since they are used to hunt and eat. The canines are also used to display aggression. When two cats snarl at each other, the baring of teeth helps one cat establish dominance over another.

Cats with broken canines are often forced to hunt smaller or more easily caught prey. Research on three of the largest cats—tigers, jaguars, and leopards—shows that mouth injuries, whether they occur naturally or as a result of gunshot wounds, contribute to these cats becoming livestock killers and, in some cases, man-eaters. To a small carnivore like the leopard cat, which is already forced to feed on small prey within a limited area, such injuries cause almost certain death.

The fires must have played a role in Tu Fu's death as well. Why he had been forced to move here in the first place, I'd never know, but food was scarce in newly burned areas. Something, possibly his canine injury, had made Tu Fu weak and vulnerable. The fire helped do the rest.

. . .

The first steady rains came in May, soaking the ground and slowly filling the streams. Chai Lai had her puppies, four pug-faced little mutts, with Sue helping her through the trauma of her first motherhood. I had to leave on a three-week trip to Taiwan, where I was to meet up with Schaller again. The trip was to be the culmination of more than a year's involvement with this country.

Working with a few dedicated Chinese biologists, I had helped coordinate the research that had led to the designation of the Tawu Mountain Nature Reserve, the largest wildlife sanctuary in Taiwan. Like Huai Kha Khaeng, the new Tawu Reserve was one of the last strongholds for many of the existing species of wildlife on this island. Schaller and I were returning to Taiwan to meet government officials there and praise their conservation efforts.

Toward the end of our trip, we met with Taiwan's president, Lee Teng-Hui. I was skeptical before the meeting. Few politicians have more than a vague understanding of the true importance of conservation research. But President Lee was different. A handsome, vibrant man in his sixties, who was considered a young, almost boyish president, he had a doctorate in agricultural economics from Cornell University. He was well aware of the benefits of environmental conservation and he wanted to seriously discuss them.

Our allocated fifteen minutes turned into nearly an hour, as President Lee unwound and we discussed the future of wildlife and conservation in Taiwan. He appeared to be a man of action, and though nothing moved quickly through the bureaucratic tangle of Taiwanese politics, both George and I left feeling hopeful. If there were more men like President Lee in high political positions, conservation would not be nearly as difficult as it has been.

Toward the end of my stay in Taiwan, a letter from Sue arrived:

Five days of diarrhea, eating tetracycline. One of the men saw the black leopard again. Chai Lai snapped at Lung Galong while I was gone. The men decided she was dangerous, so Supakit shot her. The puppies are not weaned yet. Lung Galong roasted and ate her. Walked in on the masked palm civet and saw him! Could you please bring me some of that hair gel I like? Mine will run out by the time you get back. I hope you are well.

I read the letter twice. The wording shocked me almost as much as the contents. Our dog, Chai Lai, a gentle, scrawny new mother, shot by a man who had been my best friend in camp, and eaten by another who had worked with me and shared my home. Then Sue asks me to buy her hair gel! Did she realize that life in Thailand was changing her as much as it was changing me?

Over the next few days my emotions swung between rage and laughter at the bizarreness of my life at Dancing Woman Mountain. Rage was futile, so eventually laughter tinged with sadness was what surfaced. I was convinced that my previous outbursts with Noparat and Supakit were partly to blame for the death of Chai Lai. It was the men's way of showing me who was in control, and that I was the outsider. After nearly a year and a half in Thailand, I understood the Thais' way of reasoning less than ever.

When I returned to camp, everyone seemed happy to see me. It was as if nothing had happened. I expected to see some traces of guilt on some of their faces, but I was disappointed. Sue had been out of the sanctuary when Chai Lai was killed and by the time she returned she knew there was nothing she could do. The Thais respected her for such levelheadedness.

That night some of the men wandered up to my house to see if I had brought back any whiskey. Supakit didn't come. As the men sat around drinking and joking, I eventually shifted the conversation to where I wanted it.

"I sure miss Chai Lai a lot," I said, pouring another round.

No one paid much attention, continuing their conversation about a certain kind of edible mushroom they were now finding in the forest.

"Chai Lai was such a pretty little dog," I continued. "She had such cute puppies. Sue and I really liked her."

"Chai Lai was not good. Dangerous," Muuk said about this scrawny dog which had cringed for the first two months I'd had her whenever anyone tried to pet her. Sometimes she cried so badly in her sleep that we had to wake her. "She tried to bite Lung Galong."

"What will you do with the puppies?" Riap asked. "They're pretty. I want one for my brother-in-law."

"Where did she bite you, Lung?" I asked, ignoring Riap's request and turning to Galong. "I'll give you medicine for it."

"She missed me," Galong said, "but she tried."

"Why did you eat such a scrawny little thing?" I asked, no longer caring about being circumspect. "She never hurt anybody. She had babies to care for." Sue got up and left the room, her eyes moist.

Galong smiled but was silent, too drunk now to know which way to go with my question.

"Why did you eat her, Lung?" I asked. "You should have eaten the puppies also. It would have made a bigger meal."

"I didn't eat her," he said to me, straight-faced.

"Everyone said you ate her," I said evenly, the smile gone from my face.

"I didn't eat her," he replied.

"Then I'm sorry, Lung," I said. "People in camp lied. They told me you and Supakit caught and shot her, then you ate her. Now I feel bad. Muuk, why did you lie to me?" I turned to Muuk and everyone was silent.

"She didn't taste good anyway," Galong suddenly said. "Too skinny." Then he started to cackle. The other men joined him in his laughter, breaking the tension in the room.

The party continued well into the evening, but I retired shortly afterward. I had nothing to celebrate.

13

POACHERS

Noparat finally left Dancing Woman Mountain. His replacement, Ong-art, was a Thai-Chinese who understood very little about wildlife research. Ong-art had previously been chief of one of Thailand's captive breeding centers. He believed that a research stations' purpose was to create a more "useful" forest where animals could be readily and easily observed. After our first conversation, I wished Noparat had stayed.

"I know of your problems here," Ong-art said to me, his voice dropping to a conspiratorial whisper. "But don't worry. Most people do not understand that animals must die for research."

I stared at him speechless. I knew he was referring to the leopard that had died over a year ago.

"I have heard you spend a lot of time at the monk huts," he continued. "*Farangs* are always interested in our Buddhism here. Have you learned anything about it yet?"

"No," I said sarcastically, "nothing. It is too difficult for me to understand how Buddhism says one thing and Thais do another."

"Yes, it's hard for you to understand," he answered, oblivious to the sarcasm. "Buddhism is the Thai way of life. We study it as children." Then his expression changed. "But, you know, monks do not belong in the forest," he said emphatically. "They belong in temples. The forest is not a temple."

With Ong-art's permission, some of the workers helped me build a small thatched cooking area next to my house. Now that Sue and I were always in the field, our eating schedule had become so erratic that we were rarely around when food was prepared for the rest of the staff. Ong-art was happy to be absolved of the responsibility of feeding us and, unlike Noparat, he had no desire to be continually informed about what we were doing. He had gone into the field with us once, and after that he declined all further invitations. An occasional present of a bottle of whiskey kept me in his good graces.

I doubled Beng's salary to 2,000 baht ($80 U.S.) a month, and she enthusiastically took on her new role as cook. By the time we sat down to our first meal, we had the latest in rural Thai kitchenware: wok, aluminum pot, kettle, large glazed water urn, stone mortar and pestle, small charcoal stove, and a sharpening stone. Along the food shelves sat our first few meals: four live breeding chickens in a cardboard box, a bamboo basket filled with glutinous rice, green papaya, a bag of small green and red chilies, a basket of vegetables, and a jar of fermented fish that smelled like it had come from a rotting animal carcass. It was a while before Beng learned to prepare anything other than spicy northeastern food, but our independence from the station's kitchen was worth the increased trips to the bathroom.

In the same unexpected manner in which he had left, Saksit suddenly reappeared at my door, ready to start work again. This time, he brought a friend with him, Suwat, another recent forestry graduate, whose lively, energetic personality I took to immediately. By now I'd learned never to question good fortune, so I acted like I'd been expecting them. Saksit agreed to stay until he compiled sufficient data for his master's thesis. Suwat was hired on a one-month trial basis. Both would get salaries, live at the station, and take their meals with us.

"Why didn't you tell me you had two more workers coming?" Sue asked me quietly that night as we all sat down to dinner.

"I didn't know," I whispered back.

With the new kitchen came an alarm clock. Every morning at five-thirty Beng arrived and started banging around preparing our morning food. When I wasn't in any rush to get going, I'd sit on my bed and peek out the window at her lovely face glowing in the light of the coals as she huddled close to the little stove.

Having my own kitchen made me notice two activities around the station that I'd never given much thought to before. One was where the charcoal used for cooking came from. Small hardwood trees were cut in the forest and sectioned into pieces about three feet long. Then the logs were partially burned in makeshift dirt ovens. This practice, which is common throughout Thailand, explained the many small stumps I had seen around camp.

An even more potentially harmful practice in this "protected forest" was the making of a resin known as *kee dty*. This dark, viscous liquid, obtained by tapping certain large tree species (called *yaang* trees), was used primarily to light charcoal cooking fires. Since my arrival at the sanctuary, I had noticed that many of the largest trees had up to three fist-sized holes in their trunks which penetrated nearly a foot into the tree's heartwood at breast height. These holes, which were made by boring into the tree and then starting a small fire inside, caused *kee dty* to collect in the newly bored space. The resin was harvested by the workers and, after some was set aside for personal use, it was sold in town for 20 baht (80 cents) per liter. A large tree could be tapped for several years without dying.

This explained something that had been puzzling me. After a fire season, I constantly encountered big, healthy trees that had toppled or were teetering on half their original bases. Yet I knew that these dipterocarp tree species were more fire-adapted than others; the heat from the annual fires doesn't penetrate below the bark of a large healthy tree. Now a closer look revealed that each of the trees that had mysteriously fallen had old *kee dty* tap holes. Through these holes, the fires were able to burn right into the heart of these trees. Over the course of a fire season, numerous big trees fall, opening large gaps in the forest.

As the ordeal of another dry season passed, and the rains brought a spattering of new young shoots, the night's silence was often disturbed by the sound of poachers' guns. Some seemed frighteningly close to camp. The recently burned forest was now more open and accessible and the poachers knew to go into the areas where new vegetation attracted large mammals. Patrols of forest guards were occasionally sent out with their old weapons, but there was little they could do.

There were different kinds of poachers in the forest, some more dangerous than others. Most of the hunters were hill tribe people and local villagers who were after meat for their own tables, but would kill anything they could sell. Their weapons were often homemade rifles which used lead balls and black powder. Though this limited the kinds of animals they could easily kill, the sum total of their destruction was significant. At one time Noparat estimated that at least thirty poachers a day were in the sanctuary; the workers believed there were easily twice that number.

A second level of poaching involved what locals called "outsiders": police, soldiers, and city people. They were better armed and were often after items such as bear paws, cat skins, claws, and teeth; baby gibbons and monkeys. They often used the villagers as guides or put in orders with villagers for the species and body parts they wanted. Some paid villagers to herd their cattle into the sanctuary, so they could follow behind and shoot the deer and wild cattle that inevitably tried to join up with the domestic stock.

Noparat once met a truckload of policemen with automatic weapons on the road to our station. They were just "looking around," they said, but told him to forget having seen them. Local hunters regularly spoke of policemen who wanted to buy gaur and sambar deer horn for several hundred baht, baby gibbons and leaf monkeys for two to three hundred baht, and bear bile for up to several thousand baht. If the price a policeman offered was turned down, the hunter was threatened with arrest.

It was the waste and cruelty that left me stunned. A year earlier, the carcass of a female gaur in the process of giving birth was found by the workers. The head and front legs of the fetus were protruding from between the mother's legs. The baby's new, tender skin was already baked hard from the sun. The female's head had been brutally hacked off and lay fifteen feet downstream in a little side pool, the nostrils flapping in the current. Only the horns were missing.

The most dangerous and in many ways the most destructive of the forest intruders were the tree poachers, who were after illegal timber but who also occasionally killed wildlife when they encountered it. These people destroyed large areas of protected forest. Sometimes just individual large trees were cut and taken out piecemeal while other times sizeable lots were totally removed. Although villagers and tribal people played a role in this destruction, the most extensive and systematic devastation came from organized, well-armed groups who were backed by businessmen and corrupt government officials. Because there were large profits to be made, these schemes were often given legal cover by officials who called them "timber concessions," "reforestation projects," "tree plantations," or "rural development." The boundary lines between protected forest and areas authorized for "legal" exploitation were often ignored. Interference by forest guards or officials who were trying to do their jobs was not tolerated for long. One substation chief in Huai Kha Khaeng who had energetically pursued forest encroachers while I was there was ambushed and shot to death.

Despite my growing frustration with the dangerous and complex poaching situation in Huai Kha Khaeng, I knew catching poachers was beyond the boundaries of what I had come here to do. My job was research; preventing crimes was beyond my capacity. But as the sound of gunshots kept me awake at night, I wondered when one of my radio-collared animals would be next, or if a hunter might stumble upon an animal in one of my traps before I got there.

A few weeks later the poaching problem hit closer to home. Saksit was alone on Khaeo Khieo Mountain radio-tracking the leopard Supanyo, whose range extended over into the next valley. As he hiked along the ridge he almost walked right into a poaching party that had stopped to rest along the elephant trail. He hid in the undergrowth for almost an hour until they left. The incident left Saksit badly shaken and he refused to go into the forest alone again.

Three days afterward while I was checking a trap along the Huai Ai Yo, I heard a loud splashing in the stream and sneaked over to see what animal was making the ruckus. Peering out from behind a tree, I saw two hunters walking in the water, rifles over their shoulders. I reacted before I had time to think.

"Hey, you!" I screamed in English, forgetting that I was alone and that they had guns.

"What the hell are you doing here?" I started crashing through the forest toward them.

They started as if they had seen a ghost, one of them dropping his rifle in the water. Then they took off running and I chased them into the forest. After going about a hundred feet I stopped suddenly, realizing I could no longer see them. The forest was quiet around me. They could have been pointing their guns right at me. I backed up to the stream and made a beeline for camp.

A patrol was sent out, but nothing came of it. That night in camp the story of how I had chased two armed hunters was told and retold. I laughed along with the men, but inside of me a new feeling had arisen, fear. Now the gunshots in the forest had faces attached to them. I could no longer separate my research from the violence. I would never again feel completely at ease in this forest.

Poaching's toll on the wildlife in the sanctuary was far greater than I'd imagined. Another incident soon reminded me of its often brutal results. Soowan found the body of a magnificent big-horned male gaur, maybe fifteen hundred pounds, with its head jammed beneath a large fallen tree. He'd been shot through the jaw, the bullet exiting through his shoulder. The carcass was still warm.

The gaur must have escaped or chased off its pursuers, and then wandered for miles, perhaps days, his useless broken jaw dangling from his head, unable to feed. Maggots found their way into the leaking wounds, and when his strength finally gave out, he collapsed in front of the tree where he now lay. Half of the gaur's head was buried beneath the fallen tree. Galong and Soowan both believed that, in his agony, the gaur pushed his head into the ground until he died.

Several days later Anant came running to my house.

"We need some rope," he cried. "We need to tie a man up." He explained that some of the workers had captured a poacher and were holding him at the kitchen.

"Did he have anything?" I asked, rummaging among my equipment for the rope.

"Bear teeth," Anant said.

I followed Anant back down to the kitchen, still angered over the earlier incidents, and hoping I could help put a scare into this man or at least gloat over his capture. My spite vanished once I reached the kitchen and saw the "poacher." He was a young seventeen-year-old village boy, with torn clothes, a dirty face, and disheveled hair. He looked like he should have been out playing baseball.

It didn't take any coercion to get his story. He was the youngest of a group of five who had been in the forest several days, staking out salt licks and traveling along the waterways. The men had stayed at one salt lick for several nights, waiting quietly in a tree blind, urinating in bamboo containers and burying their feces in a hole in the ground at the base of the tree so that the animals nearby wouldn't catch their scent. They were after barking deer, which was considered the best meat by hunters. Deer were the easiest animals to kill as well. If they were lucky, they might shoot a wild boar, one of the hardest animals to kill.

When the patrol confronted them, they had killed six squirrels, a macaque, and, just that morning, a bear. Only the young boy was captured. He had tripped over a tree root. His face showed neither fear nor defiance as he answered our questions quietly. He was resigned to his fate and I felt only pity for him.

But my anger resurfaced when the boy's story led us to the remains of a Malayan sun bear not two miles from camp. The smallest bear in the world, this species measures only three to five feet long and weighs about sixty to a hundred pounds. Still, many Thais fear this bear as one of the most dangerous animals in the forest. Hunters tell of its ferocity when it attacks, using its powerful jaws and sharp canines to bite while slashing with its razor-sharp claws. This carcass in front of me was the closest I'd come to seeing one in the wild. Only the canines had been taken.

I wasn't angry at the young boy, or even the older hunters who had been with him. I was angry at the faces I would never see who bought and resold these trophies in Bangkok, the men who would proudly wear bears' teeth around their necks, thinking, with some warped sense of logic, that they now possessed the power of the dead animal. Most of all, I was growing increasingly resentful of the government officials who busily spewed out rhetoric about protecting the forest while they sat at their desks in Bangkok and did nothing.

When I later asked the men about the confiscated canines, no one knew what had happened to them. I wasn't surprised. The line separating the workers from the poachers was very fine. Some of the workers had once been poachers, and all of them knew poachers who were friends or family members from their local villages. The canines would still end up at their originally intended destination. I couldn't blame these men for taking the teeth. They had families to feed on salaries of $60 a month.

After these incidents, I spent more time befriending and talking with the hunters in surrounding villages. I wanted to know how these men, who were often gentle by nature, reconciled the killing of wildlife and the stealing of certain animals' babies with their Buddhist philosophy and their belief in guardian forest spirits. Expecting contradiitions, I was surprised to find that the men had a clear framework of belief and guidelines that, in their minds, absolved them from guilt and protected them from potentially bad karma.

The "old ways" had to be followed, they said, even by the younger hunters, who claimed they no longer believed in magic and spirits. Most importantly, the forest spirits had to be pacified. This was usually accomplished by placing offerings of rice and whiskey at the base of a large tree. Rice was the food of life, and whiskey was the food of pleasure; both should be shared with the spirits. Some hunters continued this practice every day while in the forest. At night, they avoided sleeping beneath large trees which were known to house spirits. Since certain behaviors were offensive to these spirits, such as urinating on or close to a tree, it was best to camp along a stream.

Any animal could be killed, but if a particular animal's cries warned you of potential danger, such as an approaching bear or tiger, the species that had alerted you should not be killed that day. When an animal was killed, some hunters dipped the end of their gun into the blood of the wound for good luck. If a pregnant woman was seen while a kill was being divided, she was given twice the portion of meat that the others were given. No one knew the exact reasons for this, but the hunters spoke of feelings that related to maintaining and strengthening the "clan," since any woman in the area would likely be a member of their village or extended family. If no misfortunes or visitations by evil spirits occurred while the men were hunting, then it was assumed that the forest spirits did not disapprove of any of their actions in the forest.

The hunters also saw no contradiction between their Buddhist beliefs and the taking of animals' lives. There was a clear understanding by all the hunters that what they did was not in strict accordance with the Buddha's teachings, but being merely men, not monks, they had to live as best they could. The villagers also drew a distinction between killing in general and the killing of forest animals which were viewed as having been created for man's use. Buddhism allowed for these kinds of discrepancies, the men said, by neither condoning nor condemning an individual's actions. Still, the hunters observed special rules in the forest to indicate their respect for the Buddha.

Certain days of every week are called *wahn pra*, or Buddha days, and on these days you do not go into the forest to hunt. During other days when you are in the forest, you cannot discuss anything that involves the Buddha or monks, and you cannot sit in the lotus position. Most of the hunters agree that the best thing to talk about in the forest is women, because forest spirits like such talk. When animals are killed or captured, sometimes a young one is given to the local temple for merit or, at the very least, some of the best cuts of meat are put in the monks' bowls on their daily food rounds.

In spite of the poachers, our research went on, usually in teams of two for increased safety. Suwat agreed to continue working for me as long as Saksit stayed. Soowan started carrying his gun more often. Meanwhile we captured another male leopard cat and two more civets and I was able to show Saksit and Suwat how to drug the animals and attach radio collars. I named the new cat after the Japanese poet Basho.

Eventually, Boonchuay, after several sojourns deep in the forest, decided it was time to move on for good. Now that Ong-art was in charge, the monks were no longer as welcome as they had been under Noparat. Also, three younger monks had come to stay for several weeks. This made the camp too crowded for Boonchuay. It was from these young monks that I first learned about the reputation of my quiet, little monk friend.

Apparently, Boonchuay was a well-known wandering ascetic among the forest monk community, a monk who followed the true traditions of Buddhism and was considered to be on his way toward enlightenment. I was surprised by the younger monks' awe of him; to me he seemed to be simply what a monk should be. When I told Boochuay how much the younger monks respected him, he shook his head. It was a pity that adherence to Buddhist teachings should be seen as special, he said.

"It is time for me to go," Boonchuay quietly told me one evening. He had spent much more time at Dancing Woman Mountain than he had planned.

"I have learned much from you," he said. "I have walked the forests of Thailand for many years now. But I have been unaware of many things. It is good to know what I share with the forest. It is important."

I said nothing, flattered by his statement and thinking of the day when he held the sleeping leopard cat in his hands. I felt lucky to have shared these times with him.

"Come walking with me," he said. "We can see many things together."

"You usually go alone," I said, feelings tugging every which way inside. "I would like to walk in the forest with you, Boonchuay. There is nothing I would rather do, but I can't. I have to finish my work."

"Your work is inside too," he said.

I smiled. "I know. But right now the outside work must come first."

Then he smiled with his whole body. He reached into his little orange pouch and extended his cupped hand to me. When I put both of my hands out in the traditional Thai fashion, he placed a small gold amulet in them.

"This was my teacher, Luang Boo [Grandfather] Waan." He pointed to a face engraved on the front. "He was a great man. He was loved by the king and all who knew him. You can wear it."

"But I'm not a Buddhist."

"It shows respect. Respect for me and respect for the goodness and compassion of my teacher. When we meet again, I will know you," he said with a glint in his eye.

The next morning he was gone.

The night after Boonchuay left, I told Sue I'd monitor the radio-collared animals from a second mast antenna we'd set up on a hill near the Huai Ai Yo. I wanted to be alone. I couldn't shake the feeling that I had made a mistake by not going with Boonchuay. Gunshots in the distance brought my attention back to the present.

During the night, the signal from Jangair, the female leopard, went inactive and stayed that way until morning. Two days later, after we had picked up only a few brief surges in activity, Sue and Soowan went off to search for her. They returned late that afternoon, unable to isolate the signal. I set off with Soowan again the next morning.

It was a long, torturous process to walk in on this particular signal. Jangair's territory encompassed a rugged hilly area several miles west of camp, and it was easy to get turned around or lose the signal when we dropped behind a mountain or hiked through a ravine. After seven hours, I was about ready to give up.

I played one last hunch and went off at right angles to the direction the signal was coming from. The hollow we were in might be channeling the signal and throwing me off. Sure enough, I soon realized that we'd been going in the wrong direction. From a higher vantage point I easily located the signal as coming from a hill not far away. The collar lay in the middle of a bushy thicket atop the hill.

There was no obvious evidence that the female leopard had ever been there. There were no tracks, no carcass, no signs of a bed or of a den. I thought of all the gunshots we had heard over the last month. I picked up the collar and examined it closely. It wasn't cut, and there was no blood on it.

Mulling over the different possibilities, I was stymied. The collar had been fitted to the leopard's neck in such a way that it was unlikely that she had pulled it over her head. But there was nothing to indicate that she had died or had been killed by hunters in the area either. If hunters had killed her, they would have had to cut off the cat's head, then carried the collar here, knowing it would mislead me. I wondered if we had been tracking a poacher when we heard those strange random bursts of activity. I remembered the local villagers proudly telling me that they knew all about what I was doing.

A week later, we lost the signal from the new male leopard

cat, Basho. The chance of radio failure after only a month of use was unlikely. We searched for him over a large area in case he had shifted his territory the way Tu Fu had done, but we never found him again.

"They got him too," Soowan said to me. He had no doubts about the fate of either Basho or Jangair.

After the loss of the leopard cat and the female leopard, I fell into a depression that was hard to break. Hitting the punching bag, running through the forest, talking with Sue—nothing helped. I became very irritable with everyone around me.

"Damn you! Why do you insist on doing this to yourself and to the people who care about you?" Sue asked me one night after I blew up over something inconsequential.

"You deliberately work in areas where you have nothing but problems, where you often have to deal with the people more than the animals. You want challenges and danger, but it eats you up inside. Then you let loose at me and everyone else for any stupid reason. The men are afraid of you and I hate you sometimes."

"You're right. I'm sorry," I said contritely.

"Maybe you're sorry, maybe you're not," she said. "It's not just now. You go too far sometimes. You push too hard. What are you so angry about?"

"I'm angry about everything," I said, sitting on the edge of my bed. Outside the window I could see Beng fixing dinner. "I'm angry because things aren't the way they should be. I'm angry at the poachers, who are just trying to survive. I'm angry at the forest workers who would as soon sell a skin as protect the forest. I'm angry at the government officials who brag about how many new protected areas they have on paper but don't give a damn about what's really happening out here. I'm angry at the monks who chain and cage animals at their temples for their own pleasure. It's all bullshit! And I'm angry at myself for continuing this charade when I wonder who I'm really doing it for—the animals or me."

There was silence between us and I turned back toward the window, tightening the muscles in my face.

"You're worried you'll fail, aren't you?" she said, softer this time. "This isn't like your preserve in Belize, or the wildlife sanctuary in Taiwan. Here it's all different."

"I knew it was different from the beginning," I mumbled. "That's why I came here."

"But were you prepared for this?" She waved her arm as if to encompass all of Thailand. I could see the top of Dancing Woman Mountain in the distance.

"Maybe not," I said. "No."

That week I received an unexpected letter with no return address. I recognized the handwriting immediately. It was from Supanyo. I tore it open eagerly, hoping it would say something to cheer me up.

Just some lines from the far north of Thailand. How liberating it is that this dance is without owner. For me it's just flow, very joyful. Emptiness isn't the black hole, it's joyfulness. That is so important, to live this contradiction, that is life itself. Alms round to a village of Karen. People don't call me *farang*, but *chik-ko*, meaning beatnik monk. And how are you doing? Think of you. Maybe will meet you sometime for fun over a cup of German ginger. Life, that fleeting show. Dancing Woman Mountain, that funky show, is forgotten, into the cool north. All part of death row. This night some meditation. Sending you good vibrations. Hope they meet you. Only love.

I looked up at the leopard's collar hanging above my desk. Tears streamed down my face.

14

ANIMALS
IN
CAGES

Despite the loss of the female leopard Jangair and the male leopard cats Li Po, Tu Fu, and Basho, we had our hands full. There were still radios on the male leopard Supanyo, the female leopard cat Nit, and five civets. We were tracking the spoor of the tiger Payak, the black leopard, and another uncollared male spotted leopard. Saksit and Suwat spent much of their time working with the civets, and Sue started a mark-recapture study on rodents.

Sue's rodent study was a new addition to the research. We'd documented twenty-one carnivore species in the study area, and we knew that at least 75 percent of them were eating rodents. The feces we collected told us what rodents were being eaten, but I wanted to know how abundant the different rodent species were in the area and how they reacted to seasonal climatic changes. Knowing the distribution of such a major food source would help me better understand what was going on within the carnivore community. While two hundred rodent box traps were being built in Uthai Thani, Sue and I worked out the techniques necessary to study these little animals.

By clipping hair from different areas on the rodents' bodies, individual marks could be made on captured animals that would last several months. Soowan started cutting a system of trails to delineate trapping grids for us in two different forest habitats.

Whatever else happened in the maelstrom of events surrounding the project, Nit the animal and Nit the person both became important focal points for me. Whenever I was in town, I'd stop by Auntie's to visit the young girl Nit and bring her a book or a writing pad for her studies. She had changed since I first met her—she was a little less shy now and a little tougher on the outside. I knew what these changes meant. Sometimes a call would come in while I was there and she had to "go out."

At first I waited for her to return, but she would rush past me, eyes downcast, and not come out again until I was gone. Once I saw bruises on her arms, but she refused to talk about them. When she wasn't working, we could both pretend she was still the same innocent up-country girl who would one day become a teacher. She would read to me in English while I'd sit and drink beer, helping her with her pronunciation and explaining what certain words meant.

Nit the leopard cat was the smallest animal I had captured, and she had been with me the longest. Her movements kept her close to the station. Sometimes I'd just listen to the beeps of her radio and watch her run in my mind's eye.

The secretive lives of these little leopard cats were less of a mystery to me now. Data from Li Po, Tu Fu, Basho, and Nit showed that during most times of the year these cats ranged over areas of about half a square mile. But since their movements varied with seasonal changes in weather and food availability, the total amount of forest that a leopard cat traveled over in the course of a full year was much larger than this. Tu Fu had ranged over three square miles in less than four months. Nit used a total area of two and a half square miles over eighteen months.

. . .

When the leopard cats were resting, we often tried to follow the radio signals right to the animals. Usually the cats were on the ground and would run off before we could see or hear them. Their activity patterns were erratic, and there was no telling when one of these cats would be up and about, hunting for food. Survival was tough for these small carnivores, and though they ate mostly medium-sized rats, they were also constantly on the lookout for lizards, snakes, birds, squirrels, tree shrews, porcupines, and even hog badgers.

My suspicion that there were fewer tigers than leopards around Dancing Woman Mountain was now proven clearly to be true. There were four resident leopards (two males and two females) and only one resident male tiger in my forty-square-mile study area. At least two other leopards and one other tiger had territories that occasionally included portions of the study area.

The movements of the resident male leopards overlapped to some extent, but they maintained distinctive territories. The female leopards moved freely within the areas of the males. Payak, our resident tiger, was using thirteen square miles of the study area, sharing his range with both a male leopard and the black female leopard.

Tigers are dominant to leopards and coexistence between these two species is not a general rule. In areas where tigers are relatively abundant, leopards will travel mostly at night and stay away from the roads used by the tigers. But it seemed that the low tiger density at Dancing Woman Mountain made Payak's influence minimal. Here, leopards were active day and night and traveled on the roads frequently, except when Payak or another tiger was in the area.

Leopards are believed to be more solitary than tigers. Except when cats are mating, tracks of more than one leopard together usually imply a female with her young. Female leopards can have up to four cubs, but the most frequent sightings are of only one or two cubs per female in the wild. The young stay with their mother up to two years and are close to adult size before they go off on their own. I had seen tracks of a young leopard with its mother twice along the Huai Ai Yo, but the female's tracks were not those of Jangair or the black female leopard.

Most of the time, the leopards and the tiger used areas less than half the size of their overall range, usually close to the Huai Chang Tai or the Huai Ai Yo. These were the cats' "core areas," places which contained refuges and dependable food sources. Waterways were a key component of these core areas, probably due to the abundance and diversity of prey there. There were so few tigers in the study area because they are much more dependent on good water sources than leopards and they prefer large prey species, usually over a hundred pounds. As Schaller pointed out, the larger herbivores, such as sambar deer, wild boar, and wild cattle, were sparse in the area, particularly during the dry season; they were much more plentiful in the Huai Kha Khaeng Valley.

By this time we had analyzed several hundred feces samples and realized that the big cats were eating at least nineteen different mammal species as well as birds, crabs, lizards, and snakes. The omnipresent barking deer was the prey species most frequently eaten, although wild boar, sambar deer, porcupine, and hog badger were also popular food items. Leaf monkeys and macaques were favored by leopards but not by tigers.

The presence of at least five big cats at any one time made other medium-sized carnivores in the area more wary. Dholes and jackals were at least twice as abundant as leopards but rarely used the roads and trails. The three other cat species in the area—the forty-pound clouded leopard, the thirty-pound golden-colored Temminck's cat, and the ten-pound jungle cat—were all uncommon, presumably because so many other carnivores were sharing their same prey base. Such a large number of carnivore species in the area made it difficult for any one species to be abundant.

All the data we collected pointed to the importance of waterways. These riverine habitats supported the greatest diversity and abundance of wildlife, and their richness allowed many species to use adjacent areas of degraded or marginal forest. In order to protect the forest community, it is vital to maintain the natural network of these streams and rivers.

In April, a ray of light was shed upon an otherwise gloomy environmental picture. The government, in response to the largest outpouring of national resistance over an environmental issue to date, shelved the Nam Choan Dam project. This action set an important precedent in the battle between private interest groups and Thailand's budding environmental movement. A potential ecological disaster for the Huai Kha Khaeng—Thung Yai Sanctuary complex was averted. But less obvious threats continued to eat away at the country's remaining forests and wildlife.

"Alan, did you see the baby banteng yet?" Soowan asked me as we were getting ready to go into the field.

"What banteng?" I asked, thinking a herd of wild cattle had wandered close to camp.

"By the kitchen. The men caught it near the bridge when its mother ran off. Terrepat wants to study it."

The day before, Terrepat, the assistant chief, had seen a young banteng crossing the road with its mother near the entrance to the station. The mother bolted into the forest, but the calf, confused and frightened, had frozen in the road. It was leashed and taken back to camp.

The banteng stood no taller than my shoulders, with two little knobs of horn sticking out from his head. As I came up to his pen, the banteng ran to the far side, frantically looking for a way out. Eventually, he lay his head between the two wooden poles of the corral, facing the forest.

"Bastards," I said to myself. "How could Terrepat do this?"

Terrepat had a master's degree in wildlife and appeared to be one of the few Thais I'd met who really respected the animals. He was working hard to curtail the poaching problem around the station. Now I didn't know what to think of him.

After a month, Terrepat's "research," which consisted of watching the banteng acclimate to captivity, ended. Since this was a rare and endangered species in Thailand, the banteng was sent to one of the Forestry Department's "nature education centers." These centers, administered by the Wildlife Conservation Division, are little more than poorly maintained zoos, situated close to sanctuaries and reserves from which they often get their animals. Ostensibly meant to educate the public, these centers exemplify how little the Thai government truly cares about the rights of animals and their preservation in the wild.

In addition to numerous "nature education centers" scattered throughout the country, there are also nine captive breeding centers which are controlled by the Conservation Division. Their stated purpose is "to provide captive stocks for commercial exploitation, to help alleviate hunting and trapping pressures in the wild, and to contribute to the eventual restocking of wild habitats." But these centers are little more than wildlife farms. They provide no comprehensive management of captive populations and no follow-up programs to reintroduce the young to the wild. Some captive animals, particularly the more valuable species, end up in small zoos and private collections. Ong-art had formerly been chief at one of these centers.

Unfortunately, the difference between breeding in captivity and captive breeding as a conservation tool is frequently misunderstood. Often the term "captive breeding" is intentionally misused by owners of personal animal collections or commercial wildlife farms. And even when captive breeding is seriously employed to help save species that might not otherwise survive, the proper techniques of reintroduction are rarely used.

Most attempts at captive breeding don't even get to first base. The primary objective of this technique is to establish self-sustaining and healthy animal populations in captivity that can then hopefully be reintroduced to the wild in the future. In order to do this, sizable numbers of animals are needed and extensive records must be maintained so that active management of the genetic makeup of the population can be carried out. The cost of this work alone can be prohibitive. Dr. William Conway, general director of the New York Zoological Society, estimated some of these costs (based on 1984 maintenance costs at his facilities): the Siberian tiger, more than $500,000 a year; the striped grass mouse, approximately $130,000 a year; and for a particular species of bullfrog, $40,000 a year.

In order for these captive-bred species to be reintroduced into the wild, first a suitable habitat must be found, preferably at a location where the species once existed but is no longer present. The factors that originally caused the decline of that species must be eliminated, and then the captive-bred animals must be trained to survive naturally in the wild. Finally, the animals need to be monitored after their release to determine if the reintroduction was successful.

Unfortunately, the reintroduction of captive species, particularly mammals, is often not feasible due to the high costs and the logistical difficulties involved. In the past, only a few species have been successfully reintroduced to the wild. This is not to say that captive breeding and reintroduction is not worth the effort and expense. No price can be put on saving even a single species that might otherwise have been lost. However, a halfhearted or haphazard and incorrect approach is both a waste of resources and a source of potential harm to the animals involved.

Toward the end of May, Sue went to Bangkok to renew her visa, and I gave Saksit and Suwat time off to go with her. Two days later, Soowan's wife got sick and he had to return to his village. Except for Beng, I was alone at the house for the first time in almost a year.

I had forgotten how much I missed the stillness of the house at night, and also how lonely it could be. I kept the traps open, waking before sunrise so that I could check them and be back for breakfast before eight o'clock. The third morning I awoke late, then rushed along the trap line, my thoughts intently focused on my empty stomach. Saving the farthest but most scenic trap site for last, I parked my motorcycle by the river, then hiked the half mile through a beautiful stand of tall evergreen forest to the trap. As usual, the pig squealed when he heard me coming. He was hungry too.

While I was pouring food and water through the top of the trap, I saw that the pig's harness was caught on the nail that held his food bucket in place, so I crawled into the trap to untangle the pig. When my hand brushed the string triggering mechanism, I jerked it back immediately. But it was too late. The nearly fifty-pound iron trap door was already sliding down. I threw my left leg backward out the trap's entrance, and braced for the impact. The pain was more than I expected. I felt a bone crack.

I lay on the floor of the trap for half a minute with my face in the dirt. Then I picked my head up and looked at the pig. He was munching contentedly at his food, unfazed by my predicament.

"You think this is poetic justice, I bet," I said to him. He snorted and continued eating.

I turned over, grimacing with the pain, then sat up and lifted the door from my leg while I slid out underneath it. The trap was equipped with an external locking mechanism which prevented a large cat from lifting the door with his mouth once it had been shut. If the door had closed completely, I would have been trapped inside. No one in camp knew where I was, and I couldn't have broken out of the trap with my bare hands.

I shuddered at the thought of being locked inside that enclosed dark box, not knowing when or if I'd get out. This is what a trapped animal must feel, I realized. Only they had no idea what was happening to them. No wonder they didn't eat the pig.

I crawled over to a tree and tried to stand, but found I couldn't put any weight on my left leg. I picked out another tree, about fifteen feet away, and hopped over to it. Then I did the same thing with the next tree and the next. I tried using a stick as a crutch, but it made walking more difficult. Finally I reached the small hill that led down to the stream. I was breathing hard and was drenched in sweat. As I hopped down the incline, I lost my balance and fell into the water, my injured leg hitting a rock. Bile rose into my throat.

Because it was still the dry season, the stream was low, so I slithered along the rocks on my belly, letting my left leg dangle. When the current banged it against a rock; I gritted my teeth. Once across, I hopped over to my motorcycle and climbed on.

After kicking the engine over with my right leg, I forced my left foot upward, switching the gear lever into first. Shooting pains went up my leg. Then I drove slowly back to camp, walking the motorcycle across the log bridges by balancing the entire weight of myself and the bike on my right leg. After the third bridge I was exhausted, but the more difficult crossings were still to come. I knew that if I fell before reaching camp, it would take more strength than I had to get up again.

15

CIVET
SOCIETY

I had broken my fibula close to the ankle joint. Fortunately the tensed muscles in my calf had absorbed much of the impact, so there was almost no bone displacement. After looking at the X rays, a doctor in Uthai Thani said that a cast was not necessary; I could use a brace and crutches. I cursed my carelessness. Now there would be more work for everyone else.

At first I occupied myself with catching up on all the data analysis that I hadn't had time for earlier. But as the weather turned gloomy and the rains made even limited movements on crutches difficult, I became ill-tempered. Supakit lightened my mood a bit by carving a beautiful bamboo cane for me to replace my crutches. We were spending more time together again, as his dissatisfaction with the new chief, Ong-art, grew.

Ong-art was not well liked by the workers. He was not at the station often, and when he was there, he preferred staying in the office to going into the field. The men had no respect for this behavior and their loyalties remained with Noparat. They believed Noparat would come back and be chief again once he realized how much he missed the place. I knew he'd never come back.

Just as Sue and the others started adjusting to the additional work caused by my injury, another disaster struck.

"Alan, come quickly!" Beng came screaming to my door one morning, forgetting that "quickly" was not presently an option for me. I knew it was serious when she burst into my room while I was lying half naked in bed, reading.

"Lung Soowan, motorcycle, bridge," were the only words I caught as she spoke rapidly in her native dialect. Her face told me something bad had happened. Soowan had left to check the traps over two hours earlier and should have returned by now.

"The first bridge," she said as I hobbled outside. A few hundred feet from my house was a bridge twenty feet long and a little more than ten feet above the Huai Chang Tai stream. There were deep grooves between the bridge's logs, and a steep downgrade preceded the bridge from the forest side. When the dirt road was wet, it was hard to slow the motorcycle down before it hit the slick, rounded surface of the logs. It had rained hard the night before.

I hopped as fast as I could, and found most of the camp already milling around the bridge. The motorcycle lay in the stream, and Soowan, pale and only semi-coherent, was sitting along the road. His leg was twisted at an awkward angle in front of him, and he was having trouble breathing. Blood trickled out the right side of his mouth. The men had already administered their usual first aid, giving him nearly half a bottle of whiskey to kill the pain.

"No more whiskey," I said. "Supakit, go get the truck over here. We need to get him out to the hospital now!"

We loaded Soowan into the back of the pickup, and four workers went along to support him during the bumpy ride out. I didn't think my leg could stand the ride, so I stayed behind, after instructing Supakit to get him the best care possible. After the truck left, two of the men pulled my motorcycle out of the stream.

Later, Soowan told me that after coming down the last slope, the bike's front tire had caught between two logs of the bridge. Soowan lost his balance and slid under the bike as they both went over the side of the bridge and landed in the rocky stream bed below. After his fall, he had crawled up the bank and along the road until his screams for help were heard by the wife of one of the workers.

The next day we radioed Uthai Thani and learned that Soowan's injuries were worse than we'd thought. He had broken two leg bones, four ribs, and his shoulder. One of the ribs had partly punctured a lung, and his tibia was badly broken and needed surgery. When I realized the seriousness of the situation, I asked Supakit to drive me into town immediately.

After talking with the doctor, I made arrangements for an orthopedic surgeon to attach a stainless-steel rod to Soowan's broken tibia. This would make recovery faster than if the bone was reset, and the leg would be as strong as before. Soowan was tickled by the thought that part of his leg would be made of metal. His only concern was that I'd replace him on the project.

"You're still working for me," I told him. "Everything's taken care of and you're still on salary."

"I'll be back soon," he insisted.

Supakit glanced over at me, but I smiled at Soowan and nodded. We both knew that the project would be finished before Soowan's injuries fully healed.

I took Supakit to Auntie's coffee shop, wanting to forget about Dancing Woman Mountain for a while. I partly blamed myself for what had happened to Soowan, knowing that my relentless drive for data shaped everything about this project. Right now I was in no mood to return to camp.

Several of the girls came by to sit and talk. I told them about Soowan's injury and made small talk about a new store in town. But the one face I wanted to see wasn't there.

"Where's Nit?" I finally asked a girl named Jiap, who was sitting with me.

"She's gone," Jiap said, her eyes riveted on the television.

"Gone where? Is she working already?" I asked.

"No," she answered. "Don't know where."

"Did she go back to her village? Where?"

"She left here," Auntie hollered in her raspy voice from the chair by the phone. "I think she teaches English now."

I knew Auntie was lying to me and her voice signaled the girls to say no more. The girls weren't interested in talking about it anyway. In their eyes, you were there or you were gone.

"We have some new ones," Auntie said, nodding her head at two young girls coming down the stairs.

"Did Nit say goodbye to anybody?" I was afraid to ask if she had left word for me.

"She said goodbye," Auntie said. "You want me to send over one of these new girls?"

I took the black shiny rock I'd brought from the forest for Nit and laid it on Auntie's desk.

"No, I'll just have another beer," I said.

After a while, Supakit told the girls sitting with us to go away, then he turned and put a hand on my shoulder.

"The men say the mother is angry with you again," he said.

I looked up from my beer, wondering what the hell he was talking about.

"They say you didn't give her the presents you promised. That's why so many bad things have happened at camp."

I gulped down some beer, thinking back to that day when Lung Galong told me to make a list of everything I promised to the mother and to make sure I followed it exactly.

"Every time I captured an animal, I brought things to her," I said, knowing I hadn't brought exactly what I'd promised.

Supakit shrugged, to tell me it wasn't him saying such things.

"Some of the men also asked if you spoke in English with her?"

"Of course." I thought he was joking.

"Maybe that's it, then." Supakit looked thoughtful. "I think the mother only understands Thai."

. . .

The active field team was now down to three people. We closed all the traps and made sure that the movement and location data of the radio-collared animals were still regularly monitored. Sue continued the small-mammal trapping, while Saksit and Suwat stayed with the civets.

The civets were proving to be interesting. We had five animals of four different species radio-collared now: a five-and-a-half- and a nine-pound common palm civet, a seven-pound masked palm civet, a seven-and-a-half-pound small Indian civet, and a nineteen-pound large Indian civet. They were active only at night, and all shared a common range of foods that included fruits, rodents, lizards, birds, frogs, and insects. But each species seemed very different in both appearance and behavior when they were in the traps. Although it wasn't possible to do this with the leopard cats, with the civets we could walk in on some of their radio signals and see them sleeping up in the trees. I still wondered how they were sharing limited food resources among themselves and with other carnivores.

As my leg got stronger, I took slow, careful walks into the forest using my cane for support. I'd usually leave the trail at the same spot every day and cut through the forest to a little ravine where the Huai Chang Tai cascaded over a short rocky drop. It was cool and peaceful there and it was an area where the ranges of all the resident large cats overlapped. On almost any day I could find fresh tracks from the tiger or the leopards or put my nose into a scrape and smell the pungent scent of urine or anal gland secretion. Usually I'd find a comfortable seat on a rock or on the trunk of a fallen tree and just wait to see what came by.

During one of my first excursions, I heard a rustling overhead and looked up to see a furry little tawny-colored ball balancing on a limb and staring down at me. When I tried to move closer it grasped a branch nearby with its long tail and swerved around, moving swiftly off into the forest canopy. I had finally met the small-toothed palm civet, the mysterious tree civet I had long heard about. I watched this four-pound arboreal species disappear from sight, thinking how rare this once common inhabitant of tall, dense forests had now become in many areas.

But usually it was the smaller visitors that I spent most of my time watching and listening to—the Burmese striped tree squirrels scurrying along branches, emitting their birdlike chirps, a giant black squirrel building its nest high in the canopy, red-capped woodpeckers hammering away as they moved upside down and sideways looking for food. If I waited long enough, I'd see the gibbons that lived in the area, sometimes even a mother gibbon with a little one clinging tightly to her belly. Once, a leopard cat emerged close to where I sat and, unaware of my presence, went about its business hunting rodents in the undergrowth.

One afternoon, a large twenty- to thirty-pound hog badger, a member of the weasel family, came out from the hollowed base of a tree and walked directly toward where I was standing. The hog badger staggered suddenly and fell, long curved claws flailing the air for several seconds before it regained its feet. Its eyes were glassy and its piglike snout dripped with mucus. I made a clicking sound, warning him I was close, but he took no notice. He walked directly into my legs, then fell over again. It was so unexpected that I remained perfectly still. He arched his back, hairs bristling, then he rubbed his head against my leg like a house cat wanting to be petted, before ambling off into the forest. Twice he stumbled while I watched. A sadness welled up inside of me. This is how many wild animals in the forest meet their end, I thought. It seemed terribly lonely.

Hobbling back to camp, I heard splashing from behind a large rock and sneaked over to take a peek at what was causing the noise. Not knowing what to expect, I was caught off guard by the large hairy creature I found growling and hissing menacingly near my face. I jumped up—forgetting my injury and fell immediately on my backside into the water. Half expecting to see it leap on me from its perch on the rock above, I looked up in time to catch a flash of white atop its hairy ears as it vanished with a bearlike shuffle into the undergrowth. It was a binturong, known as the bear cat by the locals.

This large, black, shaggy-haired animal, often weighing over forty pounds, is the largest of all civets, and the only other civet species in the area besides the tiny small-toothed palm civet that we never captured. Like its smaller relative, the binturong is mostly arboreal and is one of only two carnivores in the world with a completely prehensile tail. I wondered how many members of this secretive species were left in the forest. I had already found binturong hair in several leopard feces samples.

As I sat on the bank, wet and a bit shaken, it struck me that I was now no more than thirty feet from where I had first seen the tiny small-toothed palm civet. The masked palm civet was captured less than two hundred yards from here, and the large Indian civet regularly moved through this area. Suddenly, all the months of research came together. Why hadn't I seen it before? I started back to camp immediately to take a closer look at the data and confirm what I'd just realized.

Despite the apparent overlap in their ranging movements, the civets were, in fact, clearly partitioning their forest home into individual habitats and avoiding competition with each other. The arboreal civets used trees exclusively; the semi-arboreal palm civets alternated between the trees and the ground; and the Indian civets were mainly terrestrial. And these different species also used different forest habitats. The small Indian civet preferred the more open, grassy forest while the binturong and small-toothed palm civets were restricted to the thicker, closed-canopy evergreen forests. The more terrestrial civets moved over larger areas and ate mostly animal prey such as rodents, while the arboreal and semi-arboreal civets fed more frequently upon fruits within smaller areas.

Sue's rodent study and Saksit's tree surveys were showing that the abundance of rodents and fruits could vary greatly by season and between the different forest types. This explained why the various civet species reacted to seasonal changes differently. The abundance and location of fruits had a greater affect on arboreal and semi-arboreal species, while dry-season fires had a large impact on the movements of the terrestrial civet species, who preyed more on rodents for food. Now I knew how all these closely related civets lived together.

I had also begun to think more about the diverse array of fruits that our civets were eating. Civets' role as important seed-dispersal agents for trees had never been clearly defined before. Because their movements were often more wide-ranging than other fruit-eaters, such as gibbons and monkeys, they could deposit seeds in areas where the seeds might not otherwise be spread. During the rainy season some civets moved over a mile in a day, leaving fresh feces loaded with fruit tree seeds in their wake. Most of the fruit trees were found in the mixed deciduous and evergreen forest. Seed dispersal by civets was probably helping to counterbalance some of the damage done to these particular habitats by seasonal fires.

The civet research had started almost as a whim to satisfy my scientific curiosity about this little-known group of animals. Now I realized that these cute furry mammals were helping to maintain both the biological diversity and the structural complexity of the forest itself. I was struck once again by the most essential element of natural systems: every form of life is interrelated and interdependent. In this case, civets were intricately connected to both the wildlife and forest communities.

What worried me was that civets, like many species, were suffering their own "tragedy of the commons." Because some civet species breed easily in captivity and are often found near human habitation, conservation schemes frequently overlook them in favor of the less common but more glamorous species such as big cats. But the ecological needs and behaviors of all animals must be considered if a diverse natural system is to be maintained. Otherwise, more species will disappear.

After two months I was walking without a cane and the leg brace had been replaced with Ace bandages. I still couldn't shift the clutch pedal on the truck without pain, but I could drive the motorcycle. When an early-morning radio message said there was a package for

Sue at headquarters, I decided to take the motorcycle and pick it up. It was my first trip out of camp alone since the accident, and the sun and wind against my face made me feel more carefree than I had felt in months. I made the ten miles to headquarters in little over an hour.

Proud of my success, I decided to continue into Lan Sak. It was still early in the day and we needed brake parts for the Landcruiser. If I could pick them up, it would save us the trouble of bringing the truck into town.

Once I left headquarters, I exited the sanctuary and was passing through the more heavily settled forest reserve. A recent plan by Phairote to make the area part of the sanctuary or at least an uninhabited "buffer zone" was meeting with resistance. Illegal settlement in the reserve was increasing. Many of the illegal tree cutters and animal poachers made their homes in these settlements, and there were more and more conflicts between these people and local forestry officials.

The first six miles were easy. Then I was stopped by a massive tree fall that must have happened that morning. Usually I would have chopped a path through it, but I didn't want to risk twisting my leg. I remembered passing a small dirt track a few hundred yards back that probably led to one of the illegal settlements. There were likely to be trails there that cut back to the main road.

After turning back and taking the side road I met some people walking out. They directed me to a little trail that went to their fields, but then forked, the left path going out to the main road in front of the tree fall. It was narrow and a little overgrown, they said, but wide enough for the bike.

The trail was easier than I expected and soon I could see the road through the trees. Just then, a large, pointed rock in the middle of the trail made me swerve left into the grassy undergrowth. Before I knew what had happened, I was thrown from the motorcycle, and heard myself screaming. Piercing pain shot through my left leg. Thinking I had rebroken the fibula, I sat up and looked down at my foot. I couldn't believe what I saw.

A bamboo stake was sticking out of my sneaker like a spear. It had entered the top of my foot at about a thirty-degree angle and had almost gone entirely through. I felt my blood starting to pool inside the shoe.

I gritted my teeth and pulled the stake out. As blood started gushing out, I cut off the sneaker with my knife, then grabbed the foot in both hands, pressing down hard to slow the bleeding. Already I was feeling cold and clammy and my breath was coming in short gasps. I still had no idea what the hell had happened. Had the villagers purposely sent me into this trap? Or was it just bad luck? I knew what the men at camp would say among themselves—it was the mother spirit.

The front gate to the reserve was still three miles down the road. I knew I had to get back onto the motorcycle and get help. I took my hands away from my foot and saw that a chunk of flesh was missing and I could see the bones of three of my toes. I tried wriggling my toes, but they wouldn't move. More blood started coming out, so I tore off a piece of shirt and stuffed it in the hole to slow the bleeding. Then I crawled over to the motorcycle, which had fallen a few feet away.

The bike started up immediately. I tensed my body against the expected pain, and pushed my foot against the gear lever. The cloth had fallen off and I heard a "squish" as the metal of the lever sank into the wound and touched my bones. The metal stuck to the mess of blood and skin and, with a quick jerk, I tore it away. I was close to passing out.

All I remember next was seeing the gate ahead and the smiling face of Somchai, the gatekeeper, coming out of his little hut to greet me as he always did. Then I passed out.

16

CITY
OF
ILLUSION

I ended up at the hospital in Lan Sak, a place I definitely would have avoided had there been a choice. It was late afternoon when we got there and a nurse's assistant was the only one on hand. He searched for the keys to unlock the medicine cabinets while some ambulatory patients wandered in from the adjoining room. By the time a bottle of antiseptic and suture material were rounded up, five strangers were peering into my wound, speculating on the extent of the damage.

Already exhausted from the ordeal, I barely felt the medic trying to stitch the gaping wound. It looked better when the foot was wrapped in nice white bandages.

"We have no room for you to stay here," the medic said apologetically, handing me two small plastic bags of aspirin and tetracycline. "A radio message was sent to the sanctuary. A truck is coming to take you back."

"This should be all I need, thank you," I said holding up the bags of pills and smiling at the faces around me. I'll walk back rather than spend the night in this place, I thought.

Eventually Supakit and two of the workers arrived. With a typical display of equanimity, they showed no surprise at my latest predicament. When I told them the story about the bamboo spike, Supakit shrugged.

"It was probably meant for us," he said.

It was nearly midnight by the time we got back to camp, but Sue was waiting up. She was furious. She knew the accident wasn't my fault, but she considered me selfish and reckless for having taken the motorcycle into Lan Sak before my broken bone healed. I looked at her face and saw how tired and drained she was.

I let Sue talk as I unwrapped and changed the bandage on my foot. As soon as she saw the wound, her expression changed. The large black jagged stitching looked like it had been sewn with a knitting needle, and even I was taken aback by how swollen and inflamed the wound was. She was immediately more sympathetic.

By morning, I had a fever and the foot was grossly swollen, making the stitching painfully tight. Three days later, the swelling hadn't gone down and the area around the stitches was dark red. Sue suggested we drive into Bangkok, but I decided to wait a few more days. If we both left the project, most of the work would stop. I doubled the dose of tetracycline, but by the fifth day there was no change. The pain was nearly unbearable and a red streak now ran up the inside of my leg. We left Saksit and Suwat to keep things going and drove directly to a hospital in Bangkok.

When the doctor on duty saw my foot, he hospitalized me immediately and called in a surgeon that night. I had septicemia, or blood poisoning, the surgeon said, after he reprimanded me for having waited so long to come in. I was put on a twenty-four-hour antibiotic drip in each arm, and for the first few days nurses woke me every four hours to inject additional medication.

After five days the infection stabilized and the surgeon seemed visibly relieved. That day, he came in to talk with me at length for the first time. As it turned out, he had completed his residency in New York City and his English was excellent. I also learned that he had spent a year in the Thai-Cambodian border camps during the

Vietnam War. Finally he got around to telling me that he wanted to schedule me for surgery the next morning.

"You have tissue and nerve damage in there," he said. "The wound was badly infected and I have to go back in and scrape the dead tissue out. It's no big operation. There'll probably be no permanent damage."

"Permanent damage?" I repeated.

"You're lucky," he said. "I haven't seen a wound like this since the war, when these bamboo punji stick traps were used all the time. Then the tips of the bamboo stakes were often rubbed with animal or human excrement. This caused serious infections that were hard to treat. Sometimes I had to take off feet and legs." He grimaced as if the words conjured up bad memories.

"When I first saw you, I was worried," he said. "I wasn't sure about the foot. But we have stronger drugs now."

"I'm glad you didn't tell me this before." I managed a smile.

"Well, we're not finished yet," he said.

In the operating room, he gave me an injection that numbed the lower part of my body, and he talked to me as he worked. I heard him scrape bone but felt nothing as he calmly described what he was doing. He'd make the scar as small as possible, he said. That was the least of my concerns. Ten days later I was told I could go home.

"The foot looks good," he said during his last bedside visit. "You should eventually get the feeling back in your toes but you've got to stay off your feet and keep the wound clean. Don't go back to the forest for a while."

I settled into an apartment near the hospital in the northern section of Bangkok. Sue had stayed with me the entire time, and now we both agreed that she needed to get back and run the project. As she lay beside me that night, we talked of feelings that needed airing.

Things between Sue and me were not working out well. We had long since given in to our passions, both thinking that this time we could distance ourselves from any unrealistic expectations. But then when I'd catch the hope once again flickering in Sue's eyes, or find myself inextricably drawn into a whirlpool of emotion, I'd pull back from her, becoming cold and distant. Months of riding an emotional seesaw had caused continual anguish and stress for both of us. I was closer to Sue than to any other woman I'd ever known, but still inside of me was a deep, personal need to continue my life alone.

At first, I was almost totally bedridden because the circulation in my foot was impaired. If I lowered my leg for more than a minute at a time, the blood would pool and cause intense pain. I relied on my Thai neighbors for most of my needs and simply resigned myself to a period of sleeping and reading. Though I tried not to think about the forest, I still woke at sunrise every morning expecting to see Beng nearby.

After two weeks, when I could once again get around on crutches, I became restless. But initial attempts at exploring the neighborhood proved more difficult than I'd expected. Bangkok is not a city built for handicapped pedestrians, and as the cars whizzed by, the stares and comments from curious onlookers made me uncomfortable. A Westerner was unusual enough in this part of town, but one hobbling around back streets on crutches was a strange sight to behold.

I changed my tactics and started going outside at 5 A.M. Bangkok was a different city at this time, a quiet and peaceful place, and I could meander along the nearby canal or explore the side streets without any problems. My neighborhood was a clear example of the multiple contrasts in Thai life. Behind my apartment, there were lavish compounds, their high protective walls topped with pieces of broken glass or barbed wire. These were the homes of *poo yi*, Thais of high status and wealth, who often held positions in the government and police department. Just outside the walls were the simple wooden dwellings of the common laborers, taxi drivers, maids, and shop owners, the Thai people who made up the life of this city.

I watched the bar girls and nightclub singers return home in their gaudy, glittering outfits, so incongruous in the setting of the simple dwellings that were their homes. Along the grated sewers, middle-aged women in their sarongs and bras squatted as they washed vegetables for the opening of their food stalls. Some women were already tending to the large steaming bamboo baskets that held the day's first batch of sticky rice.

By six o'clock I would arrive at the little stand where I bought my breakfast, a ten-baht bag of *bah dton go*, or fried flour cakes. Sitting and eating my cakes, I watched the early shift leave for work carrying their day's food in little tins. Taxi and *tuk-tuk* drivers, coming off a night shift or just getting started after another night of drinking, swung by to pick up flour cakes or a five-baht bag of sticky rice. Nearby a woman sat stringing together fragrant jasmine buds into small garlands. Traditionally this practice originated in the royal court when the ladies of the court were expected to master various elegant skills such as flower arrangement. Today it's a cottage industry seen throughout Thailand, and these garlands are bought to place on Buddha statues, in spirit houses, or around the rearview mirror of cars.

About this time of day the monks came by on their morning rounds. Young boys, who were cared for by the temple, walked behind the monks, collecting the offerings in large plastic buckets to be distributed among the occupants of that monk's particular temple. People waited patiently along the monks' route, gently placing fresh food and lotus flowers in their bowls, then kneeling to show their respect. For those who wanted to make merit but didn't have the time or desire to prepare special food in advance, there were stalls along major alms routes selling "merit food to go"—prepared plates of rice, vegetables, and fruits. Merit came cheap at ten baht a plate.

These urban monks were different from the ones I'd met in the forest. I could see the difference in their eyes and their movements as they went about their morning rounds. I was reminded of my first visit to Bangkok, when I'd seen some of these monks in department stores, wearing sunglasses and checking prices on televisions. Supanyo had told me there were temples in Bangkok with restaurant food, televisions, and videos. Recently, several scandals involving swindles, profiteering, and sexual relationships among monks had greatly offended the Thai people. Now many Thais gave only to monks or temples they knew well.

I was surprised how comfortable I felt on the streets and how far I'd come since those first days in Bangkok when everything seemed so incomprehensible to me. I was slowly learning to accept what I didn't understand, and I had a greater appreciation of the day-to-day struggles that made up the lives of these people.

By eight o'clock modern Bangkok emerged. Mercedeses and BMWs appeared from behind the compound gates, their darkened, closed windows isolating the car's occupants from the streets outside just as effectively as the glass-studded walls around their homes did. They merged into the flow of the nearly two million other cars estimated to be in the city. The early-morning chatter of the street people was quickly eclipsed by the blaring of traffic horns. Faces that smiled in the predawn darkness were now hidden under bamboo hats or hunched intently over sewing machines and cooking pots.

Eventually I was back to my cane and could explore further afield. Wherever I went I was struck by the incongruities that develop when an old traditional culture is squeezed out by the demands of the modern world. One day I chanced upon, of all things, an elephant standing in a weed-choked lot overshadowed by a large government building. Two men nearby were talking with a well-dressed Thai woman on her way to work. A second woman waited in the passenger seat of a red Peugeot nearby. One of the men waved me over when he saw me watching.

"Only seven baht," he called out to me.

"Seven baht for what?" I asked, limping closer.

"The elephant. It's good luck to pass under an elephant," he said.

I must have looked confused as I glanced over at the woman.

"She's pregnant," he said. "If she walks under the elephant, she will have very little pain during birth."

I watched as she ducked under the belly of the shackled beast. She paid her money, got back into the Peugeot with her friend, and drove off.

"What are you doing with an elephant here in Bangkok?" I asked. I could tell from their clothes and accent that they were from the north.

"Not much demand for elephants anymore," one of them said wistfully. "I have to feed her. In Bangkok, I can make fifty or sixty baht a day. Feeds her and us."

I struck up a friendship with a *tuk-tuk* driver named Peechai, who bought fried flour cakes at the same stand as I did every morning. When Peechai didn't want to work, he'd come by my apartment and take me cruising through the intricate maze of the narrow, hidden back streets of Bangkok. Usually we'd end up in his friend's little shanty along the Chao Phraya River, the country's most important waterway. This 230-mile stretch of river is said to have played as important a role in Thai history as the Nile has played in Egypt's. Called the country's "main artery," the Chao Phraya has also become Thailand's biggest sewer; thousands of tons of waste are dumped into it daily.

Peechai was born in Bangkok, in an area called Klong Toey, the poorest, most depressed part of the city. It was through Peechai's eyes that I was able to see Bangkok's darker side. I'd already had dinners in the fancy hotels and restaurants, walked through the ornate temples, watched stage shows depicting Thai culture in all its splendor, and shopped for the wonderfully inexpensive clothes and handicrafts that were available everywhere. Now I visited shops and small factories where girls were locked inside over their sewing machines while they worked, then packed into a small room on an upper floor to sleep. I ate with workers and their families in little box shanties that were their homes on expensive construction sites. I watched a grossly deformed leper being injected with heroin before being sent back out on the street to beg. I sat in a bar and watched a young Mongoloid girl making unintelligible scrawls on a piece of paper, then listened to the bar's owner charge a customer three hundred baht to take her for the night. The owner was her mother. The good life in this city carried a big price tag.

For the first time in over a year, I could follow national and international events in the English-speaking newspapers published in Bangkok. I wasn't surprised to see that Thai Forestry Department scandals were regular daily copy. Some days there were stories about illegal logs and sawmills seized in reserve forest areas. Other days, articles spoke of high-ranking government officials being investigated or arrested for their role in resort development schemes and illegal forest encroachment. Finally, the director general of the Forestry Department, Chumni Boonyophas, was relieved of duty and faced with arrest for events related to illegal logging in forest reserves.

Thailand had gone from being 57 percent covered by forest in 1961 to 30 percent covered in 1981. Now, in 1989, it was estimated that no more than 10 to 13 percent of the country's natural forest was left. Publicly, the Forestry Department was touting massive reforestation programs and intensified forest and wildlife protection, but in reality all their talk amounted to very little. The press was referring to the Forestry Department as "the Department of Stumps" and one newspaper called it "an inefficient and bloated bureaucracy with a large financial stake in the timber industry." I almost wished I hadn't started reading the newspapers again.

I'd already seen examples of reforestation projects outside of Huai Kha Khaeng. With Forestry Department approval, some natural forest areas were actually being cut down and "reforested" because there was more money per acre available for government-sponsored replanting than there was for the protection and maintenance of an already existing forest. Reforestation was also often being used as an excuse to give control of forest reserve land to private commercial interests for tree plantations.

One day I read a news item that hit much closer to home. The Thai Plywood Company, a state-owned enterprise, was given permission by the Forestry Department to reactivate old logging concessions in the Huai Kha Khaeng Wildlife Sanctuary. This was the result of a new government ruling which stated that old timber concession agreements must prevail, even in wildlife sanctuaries, until they are legally revoked. This ruling made a mockery of the 1960 Wildlife Act, which states that the government may declare any area to be a wildlife sanctuary by Royal Decree when it is deemed appropriate, and that no person can destroy the wildlife or the forest within that area. In Uthai Thani, there was a public outcry. Although the Forestry Department had the power to simply revoke the concession and end the controversy, they wouldn't do it.

Some of the facts uncovered were never widely publicized. On the board of directors of the Thai Plywood Company sat a majority consisting of the permanent secretary and a former permanent secretary of the Ministry of Agriculture, two deputy permanent secretaries of the same ministry, and the director general and a deputy director general of the Royal Thai Forestry Department. More than one of these men had supported my research in Huai Kha Khaeng in order to "help save it for the future."

While the current Minister of Agriculture continued to cooperate with international conservation groups to propose both Huai Kha Khaeng and Thung Yai sanctuaries as "a world heritage site of outstanding universal value," the Forestry Department under this same minister was publicly proclaiming how difficult it was to cancel Thai Plywood's rights to log in Huai Kha Khaeng. This was all on the tail of the government's five-year-plan policy for 1987–91, in which they aimed to reestablish 40 percent overall forest cover through reforestation, and to protect 15 percent of the forest for parks and sanctuaries. Disgusted by what I was learning, I felt tricked by the people who had invited me to Thailand. Even worse, I felt that the Thai people were being deceived as their government raped the last of the country's forests.

I wondered why international funding agencies weren't doing more about the obvious environmental damage that was clearly taking place in Thailand. There is no shortage of agency offices or foreign consultants in Bangkok claiming to be addressing these issues. I spoke with people from the United States Agency for International Development (USAID), the World Wildlife Fund (WWF), the International Union for the Conservation of Nature (IUCN), the United Nations Environment Program (UNEP), the Food and Agriculture Organization (FAO), the National Park Service (NPS), and the United States Fish and Wildlife Service (USFWS). Frequently their assessment was that, despite the problems, Thailand was doing its best and things were improving. It takes time, I was told repeatedly. While representatives of these agencies continued submitting management strategies and filing policy documents, trucks filled with illegal logs increased their nightly runs in the countryside, the sounds of poachers' guns filled the air, and each day there were fewer animals with less space in which to live.

"I want to show you something that does work," my British friend Belinda said to me after seeing my despondency. "They've been wanting to meet you anyway."

I felt like I was in a spy novel as Belinda brought me to an old building which housed a Turkish bath and coffee shop. We climbed three flights up a dark narrow stairway. Then she opened a door into a small cluttered office that buzzed with activity. This was the headquarters for the Project for Ecological Recovery, a small group of mostly young Thai volunteers who were trying to help the Thai people understand and fight the ecological battles that were becoming more and more pervasive in their lives. They worked behind the scenes, at the village level, and were now gearing up to stop the logging in Huai Kha Khaeng.

I was introduced to Witoon, a dynamic twenty-nine-year-old who was the group's director. As I learned more about their organization, I realized how pivotal this small group had already been in structuring the environmental movement in Thailand. They understood that the environmental situation in Thailand was bleak. But to these young Thais, the forests were all they had, and the many difficulties they faced just meant they needed to fight harder to save the wildlife that was left. I had been so depressed when I'd learned that no substantial progress was being made by the larger, better-known organizations that I'd forgotten how much effective conservation can occur behind the scenes, in little dingy rooms such as these. It gave me hope.

When my foot healed enough for me to walk without a cane, I started spending my afternoons at a gym, trying to strengthen my body again. Afterward, I'd go to Blu Jeans, a little bar hidden in the middle of Patpong. It was a hangout for foreign correspondents, aging Vietnam vets, and expatriates who have been in Thailand longer than they usually cared to talk about. Jean, the owner, had come to Asia during the Vietnam War and never went home again. He'd feed me from his private stock of chili or shrimp gumbo, then sit and talk with me about animals or the latest political intrigues of the Thai government. It was my hideaway, a Bangkok version of Auntie's coffee shop, and when it became too sedate, I just stepped outside into the glittering craziness of Patpong.

The day my stitches were removed, Peechai took me to celebrate. We went to a "cocktail lounge" that was just a darker and noisier version of other bars he'd taken me to. My hand still stuck to the dried beer on the table. Young up-country girls came over and sat down, asking for a glass of watered-down green soda that cost fifty baht, from which they made twenty-five baht. For a few more baht, the girls would accompany you to one of the upstairs bedrooms.

Even the youngest of these girls appeared old for their age— many had glassy, vacant stares that often meant an addiction to sniffing glue. Peechai was already in deep conversation with the girl next to him. I sat alone over my drink, not inviting anyone to join me. The bar was dark, the only light coming from little dim candles on the tables. Then the flame from a cigarette lighter caught my attention at a table nearby and a face flickered in the light for just an instant.

"What's wrong?" Peechai asked, seeing the change in my expression.

"That girl, I want to talk to her," I said, pointing into the darkness. "The one at that table over there."

"She's with someone," the girl with Peechai said. "I'll bring you my friend."

"No," I said. "I want her. Tell her someone wants to buy her a drink."

Peechai whispered to his girl and she went off, returning moments later with the girl I wanted. They both looked at Peechai as if he was the one who had summoned them.

"Hello, Nit," I said, moving into the light of the candle so she could see me better.

There was a flicker of recognition in her face, but nothing more. Her eyes went dead. I don't know what I expected from her, but it wasn't that. The voice of a drunk Thai called out to her.

"I'm with somebody," she said. "I must go back. Why are you here?"

"I hurt my leg," I said. "How is your English coming? Are you still studying to be a teacher?"

"No," she said. There was not even a show of pretense. "I must go back." She remained standing there.

"Nit, stay and talk with me for a while. You don't have to go back there." I motioned toward the table she had come from.

"Why? You want to take me home instead?" she asked. "And what about tomorrow?"

I didn't answer. I was staring at the needle marks on her arm. After she turned and walked away, I paid the bill and left.

At seven o'clock the next morning, the phone rang.

"I am calling for a monk named Boonchuay," the woman's voice said, straining to speak English. "He is near Nakhon Pathom with our son, who is a novice. He asks to see you. We can take you there."

I smiled into the phone. I didn't know how Boonchuay had found me but it didn't matter. I was to see my friend again.

I was picked up the next day by the nephew of the woman I'd spoken with. After a two-hour drive we reached Nakhon Pathom, one of the earliest settlements in Thailand, dating back to the fourth century B.C. As we passed through town I glimpsed one of Thailand's landmarks, the famous golden *chedi*, or Buddhist relic mound, rising four hundred feet into the air, the largest in the Buddhist world. It is here where the teachings of the Buddha were thought to have been first brought to Thailand from India, more than two thousand years ago.

We continued on into the countryside, eventually taking a dirt road that wound its way up a little forested hill surrounded by rice fields. I saw no sign of any temple nearby. Finally we pulled off and parked in front of a tall white smokestack, standing like a monument among the trees. It was an old crematorium.

The young novice was nearby, sweeping the dirt just as I had seen forest monks do so often at Dancing Woman Mountain. When he saw us, he came over and invited us for tea. Boonchuay was meditating in a little thatched hut among the trees, he said. I waited quietly, enjoying the tranquillity of the place.

"Do many people come here?" I asked the novice. I'd seen no houses nearby and this was the only patch of trees in the area.

"Nobody comes here," he said. "Too many ghosts."

Boonchuay came out a few minutes later and took my hand in a gentle squeeze.

"When you can't stay in the forest, you find a patch of trees among the ghosts," I said jokingly. He smiled.

"Sometimes it is good people believe in ghosts," he said. "It gives me a quiet place to rest. I see you are wearing the amulet I gave you," he said, looking at my neck.

"It reminds me about kindness and compassion," I said, reiterating the words he'd used to describe his teacher whose face was on the amulet.

We spent the day together, wandering among the small patch of trees and looking out over the rice fields. I told Boonchuay all that had transpired since his departure from Dancing Woman Mountain, and he told me about his travels and the animals he had seen. By late afternoon my driver was anxious to return to Bangkok, and I felt it was time to leave.

"I had a dream about you," he said to me as we walked back to where the others waited. "You were an insect flying over water and the wind tried forcing you down. You were flapping your wings hard against the wind. Finally you went down into the water. As the stream carried you, you were still flapping, trying to break from the water."

I said nothing, wondering what he was trying to tell me.

"It is only a dream," Boonchuay said, smiling. "Stay a while longer." He meant days, not hours.

"My leg is much better. I have to go back to the forest. Boonchuay ..." I struggled for the Thai words that would tell him how much his friendship meant to me, how the amulet kept him close to me.

"I'll wait for you in the forest," I said.

"I think we will not see each other again," he said.

17

FLOODS

When I finally got back to camp after more than a month of convalescence, everything had the damp, dreary look of the rainy season. The southwest monsoons had come early and brought more rain than usual, causing a greater incidence of illness in camp. Otherwise little had changed—except that the Thai Plywood Company had started logging in the southern part of the sanctuary, home of the last population of wild water buffalo in Thailand.

With the onset of the rains, the fruit-loving civet species started to stay in restricted areas as fruit became readily available again. The tiger, leopards, and leopard cats, on the other hand, increased their movements now that their major food items, rodents and ungulates, were once again uniformly available throughout a widespread area.

Toward the middle of September, we received the worst rains of the year; the precipitation eventually totaled twenty-seven inches for the month. Some of the lowland areas became flooded, making the roads often impassable or at the very least dangerous for vehicles. Everyone was working hard to maintain the data collection, but it was taking its toll. Sue was often lethargic and weak; she had never gotten her full energy back after catching scrub typhus during the dry season. Caused by a microbial organism and transmitted by chiggers (mite larva), this disease had given Sue a rash, fever, chills, and headaches for nearly a week. Her lymph nodes were swollen for a month before antibiotics brought the illness under control.

Saksit had started to lose his appetite and become feverish as well. At first we thought nothing of it, until his eyes turned yellow and he complained of pains in his liver. Then I immediately sent him off to Bangkok, where he was treated for hepatitis. He returned four weeks later, but was still debilitated for months afterward. Only Suwat remained as healthy and cheerful as ever.

Toward the end of the month, it rained nonstop for four days. The Huai Chang Tai overflowed its banks and the lower section of the station was submerged. Part of our rodent trap line and most of the bridges around camp washed away. Without the bridges we were stranded at camp, and soon everyone's food supplies ran low. By the time the rains finally stopped we were out of nearly everything except rice. As Beng opened up one of our last cans of sardines for lunch, the workers scoured the forest for edible plants.

"The Thais say the tiger got its stripes during rains like this," I said to Sue one rainy day as we played cards in an effort to pass the time. She humored me with a smile.

"They had solid-gold coats before. But if you don't want to hear the scientific facts behind why they now have stripes, fine," I said.

"Okay, Alan, enlighten me." She smiled.

"Well, it was a period of incredible rains and flooding. No one could remember a season that wet. The people were safe in their houses, but they couldn't go out for food. The animals had to climb trees or move to higher ground and they couldn't hunt. Finally, the people prayed to the guardian spirits and the rain stopped.

"There was one old man who lived right on the edge of the jungle. He was so hungry by this time that as soon as the rain stopped, he went into the forest to collect bundles of rattan to trade for food. But while he was collecting the rattan, a huge paw caught him by the neck. It was the golden tiger, who was just as hungry as the old man. The man knew he'd soon be dead if he didn't think of something quick, so he said to the tiger, 'You can eat me, but you'll be dead by morning too!'

" 'What are you talking about?' roared the tiger." And I roared like a tiger, grabbing Sue behind the neck. She had been looking down at her cards instead of paying enough attention to me. She jumped and yelped.

" 'Haven't you heard?' the old man said to the tiger. 'The floods are not over. The biggest flood is coming tonight. Everyone in the village is building a raft to save himself. That's why I'm collecting rattan. If you let me go, I'll build a raft big enough for both of us and tie us both onto it. Then you'll be safe too.'

"So the tiger let the old man go and watched over him as he built a big raft right there in the forest, using the rattan to lash together the large bamboo poles. As evening came, the man, looking up at the sky, said, 'Quick, the sky's getting dark. The rains are almost here. Get on the raft and I'll tie you on first.' Since the tiger wasn't too smart, he let the old man tie him securely to the raft with the rattan. 'Make it tight,' the tiger said. Once the tiger was tied on, the old man said he was returning to his house for his belongings and would be right back. Of course, he never returned.

"After two days, the tiger finally realized he'd been tricked, and he wriggled and twisted trying to break free. But the more he fought, the more the rattan cut into his golden coat. Finally, by the third day, he broke free. But by then his coat was ripped and slashed from the rattan. Well, the tiger learned to be less trustful of men, but his coat never fully recovered. From that day on, the tigers of Thailand wore golden coats with the obvious black scars of their encounter with man."

Once the water level of the Huai Chang Tai dropped enough, the men fixed the main bridge out of camp so that the truck could go out for supplies. But the truck never even made it the four and a half miles to the next substation. Nearly all the log bridges between our station and headquarters were wiped out or badly damaged, and large sections of the road were gone entirely. The largest bridge, crossing the river at the sanctuary's headquarters, had collapsed along with several others in the adjacent forest reserve. With all the crews of workers mobilized, it would be at least another week before any vehicle could get out.

An arrangement was made to bring in basic necessities—namely, rice, cans of sardines, and whiskey—from Lan Sak. The supplies were driven in as far as possible, then carried by villagers to the river boundary. While the water was still high, a line was rigged to ferry the food across into headquarters. But since we still couldn't get to headquarters ourselves, I told Beng to kill what remained of my bait animals, a pig and two chickens, and distribute the meat among the families.

By the end of the week, the smaller bridges and much of the road had been fixed or rebuilt. In some areas the men had to cut new roads through the forest; in one area they constructed a log roadway on top of an impassable morass of mud that couldn't be circumvented. The workers viewed each obstacle with aplomb, never doubting there was a way to overcome it.

Ten days after the flood, we tried to get out again. Ong-art and I took both trucks in tandem, filled with workers, chains, shovels, and axes. We repaired parts of the road and cleared fallen trees as we went along; logs on newly built bridges were chained together to enable them to take the weight of the vehicles without separating. When Ong-art's pickup slid down muddy embankments, my heavier and more powerful Landcruiser pulled him back up. After two hours, we reached headquarters muddy and exhausted. But the main bridge out of the sanctuary was still not fixed.

We stood on the embankment and looked at the collapsed bridge, slanted to one side and lying a foot below the white swirling water. Though still intact, the bridge was no longer connected with the far embankment, where the road had been washed away.

"It's no problem. We can fix it," Intah said. I thought he was joking.

"The trucks can pass over most of it. It's only the connection we have to fix," he said, as if it was as simple as changing batteries in a flashlight.

The men talked among themselves for a minute then started spreading out at different tasks. When I realized what they were doing, I waded into the river and helped collect large rocks, carrying them to where the road had washed away between the bridge and the bank. Other men, using picks and shovels, broke down the far embankment and sculpted it into a road that rose forty-five degrees from the water.

Several hours later we were finished and my foot was throbbing. But we successfully crossed the river into the forest reserve—only to be stopped three miles down the road at the site of another large bridge that had washed away. Most of the workers from headquarters were sitting around nearby, still assessing the damage. The only one working was an elephant that had been confiscated from poachers several months earlier. He was hauling newly cut trees to the bridge site.

The stream was narrow, so an area was cleared where we could drive the trucks down the embankment and ford it. I went first, but immediately got bogged down in the soft mud. None of the men's efforts could budge the truck.

"Wait," the mahout, or elephant driver, called out to us as the elephant emerged from the forest pulling another log. He unhooked the chain dragline and brought the elephant over.

"Stay away from him," the mahout warned us. "He's dangerous."

At the mahout's prodding, the elephant put his forehead against the rear window of my truck and pushed it through the stream. I could see one of his eyes in my rearview mirror, bloodshot and tiny against his massive gray head. Then the elephant was hooked to Ong-art's truck; he pulled it across with as much effort as a child uses to pull a wagon.

The rest of the trip was uneventful. After racing around to pick up supplies in Lan Sak, we got back to the bridge a little after six o'clock. The mahout had promised to wait until dark.

It had been a hard day for the elephant. As he stood with his eyes half closed, getting hooked up to my truck, he looked dead on his feet. Still, he pulled my truck across the stream easily, although he moved more slowly than before and his labored breathing was clearly audible. Ong-art's truck was next, but as it reached the far side of the stream, the rear wheels jammed on something under the water and the truck tilted sideways. The mahout urged the elephant on, gently slapping him on his rump.

The elephant tugged and tugged, and just as the truck started moving, it jammed again. Groaning, the elephant dropped to his knees. The mahout continued to urge him on, so the elephant kept pulling, still on his knees, his head now bent into the dirt. When the truck finally broke free, the elephant crawled forward until the truck cleared the water. Finally, he stopped, and stayed hunched over on the ground for a few seconds before slowly rising.

Forgetting the mahout's earlier warning, I walked over to the elephant. His eyes were closed, but they opened a bit as I stood beneath his head.

"What the hell have they done to you?" I whispered. I reached up and touched his jaw.

"Stop! Get away from him!" the mahout shouted as he looked over from where he was talking with Ong-art. I jumped back, startled, and the elephant spooked, running a few steps toward the forest. For an instant, I thought he'd keep on going—back to where he belonged. But at the forest edge, he stopped and stood still again. The mahout rushed over and secured him with leg shackles, glaring at me angrily. As we drove off, I looked back at the elephant still standing there, eyes closed.

On the night of the birth of the Buddha, an elephant entered the dreams of Queen Mahamaya, his mother, imbuing Gautama Buddha with patience, strength, and meekness. Later, while seeking solitude in the forest, the Buddha was attended by an elephant who provided him with fruits and warm water for bathing. The elephant held a special place in the heart of the Buddha, for he himself had been an elephant in an earlier life. It was a hunter who had first told me the myth of the Buddha and the elephant. He then explained to me that these animals are usually safe from hunters' guns because their weapons are not powerful enough to kill them easily. Most of the valuable large-tusked elephants were killed some time ago anyway, he said.

The elephant is a creature of Thai royalty, and "white" or albino elephants are automatically the property of the king, representing signs of the monarch's greatness and a supernatural omen of divine favor. Elephants are also religious symbols to the Thai people, and their likenesses are displayed in thousands of temples, carvings, and decorations throughout the land. In *A Cry from the Forest*, a Thai publication meant to combine Buddhism with conservation education in Thailand, it is noted that "elephants stand in a special place for the concern of Buddhists. In normal circumstances, elephants would be loved and well protected." But everyday reality apparently does not constitute "normal circumstances," and in real life elephants are not truly loved and protected. In fact, Thailand has a long history of mercilessly exploiting its elephants.

In 1921, elephants became the first species of wild animals to be protected by law in Thailand. They were granted this special status in order to conserve their numbers for use in warfare and for logging and heavy transport. At the beginning of this century, there were believed to be tens of thousands of domesticated elephants in Thailand. Today, only an estimated two thousand elephants survive in the wild here. And those that survive do so partly because Mother Nature was inadvertently kinder to the Asian elephant than to its African counterpart. She made the Asian females without tusks and the males with relatively short tusks, some not even visible beyond the lips. While this has helped save the lives of many elephants, man's ingenuity has sought out other uses for this species.

On November 11, 1987, an article in the *Bangkok Post* described the discovery of nearly a dozen elephant carcasses in the forests of Kanchanaburi, a province adjacent to the Burmese border. Their penises had all been cut off. Elephant penises, which can weigh nearly forty-five pounds, are worth nine to ten dollars a pound on the black market, and are purchased by the Chinese as an aphrodisiac.

During October, the rains let up only slightly. Another eighteen inches fell that month. Our trucks were constantly getting bogged down despite continuous repair work on the roads and bridges. The flooding caused most of the radio-collared animals to stay in areas of high ground within their ranges. Those that had no high ground available shifted into adjoining areas. Nit, the female leopard cat, was moving around more than usual. I checked up on her regularly just to make sure she was okay. Every time I listened to her signal, I saw Nit's face in the bar that night. For some reason, I felt that if anything happened to this little cat, there was no hope for that girl back in Bangkok.

One day I took two workers with me and drove into Uthai Thani to drop off Sue and pick up Saksit. Sue was leaving to get a medical checkup in Bangkok, and Saksit was returning from one. It had been raining all day and we got stuck twice on our way into town. During the return trip, the truck bogged down again, and it was almost dark by the time we dug it out. Shortly afterward, I missed circumventing another bad mud hole and the front differential sank in and grounded.

We were less than a mile from the sanctuary's headquarters at this point, so I sent Saksit and a friend he had brought with him back there for the night with instructions to bring help in the morning. Because the truck was filled with food and equipment, the men and I stayed behind, sharing a bottle of Mekong and trying to sleep in our wet, mud-encrusted clothes while the mosquitoes feasted on us. It took me a long time to fall asleep in the sweltering confines of the truck. Even the whiskey didn't help. The sharp, raspy call of a gecko, or *too-kay*, pierced the darkness, and I thought it strange to hear one at this time of year. The Chinese consider these large multicolored lizards to be good luck. The Thais, however, feel they are bearers of ill tidings.

By ten o'clock the next morning Saksit still hadn't returned. I was ready to go to headquarters myself when we heard a truck approaching from the direction of Dancing Woman Mountain. Ong-art's truck came into view and I wondered why help was coming from the wrong direction. Then I saw that all the workers were carrying guns. Something was clearly wrong.

The previous night, shortly after Saksit and his friend had left, eight forest guards from the sanctuary's headquarters were ambushed and shot while returning from a party at a local village across the river. Now they were in the hospital in Uthai Thani, two of them seriously wounded in the stomach. The men from our station were going in to help fortify the area around headquarters.

In the days that followed, the story behind the events of that night got more and more muddled. The ambush had been well planned and took place when the guards were unarmed and officially out of the sanctuary. But nobody seemed to know why. Some said that the forest guards had been cracking down too hard on illegal timbering and encroachment in the area, confiscating cattle and other equipment. Then I heard that the bullet wounds were not from black-powder weapons but from pistols and shotguns, firearms not typically owned by the local villagers. After this incident, work details were sent out with armed guards and no one went anywhere without a weapon. Suddenly I was working in a war zone instead of a wildlife sanctuary.

When I went into town to meet Sue's bus from Bangkok, I stopped at the hospital to visit the injured guards. They were not men I knew well, but they had helped me dig my truck out on several occasions and I had shared food and drink with them. They confirmed what I already knew of the ambush and asked me to relay messages back to their families. I was shocked to learn that, in the four days since the incident, not one police or government official had visited them. The doctor asked *me* what was going on!

A few days later I left Sue in charge and returned to Bangkok for a checkup on my foot. At the first opportunity I called on the Forestry Department. I was shocked to learn that most of the officials I knew at the department claimed to know nothing about the shooting incident; others clearly didn't want to talk about it. I was angry. Eight forest guards had been injured, two of them critically, and nobody seemed particularly concerned.

I decided to extend my stay in Bangkok and call the newspapers. After I related the details of the ambush as I knew them, I was told they'd get back to me after checking it out. The next day there was a knock on my door. Someone from the Forestry Department had come to pay me a visit for the first time since I'd been in Thailand.

"The newspapers called the department yesterday," he said after ten minutes of small talk. "You called them about the shooting. They spoke to the chief of the Wildlife Conservation Division. I was asked to come see you."

"By the chief of the division?" I asked.

"No, higher," he said. "There are things you do not understand. But anyway, they are of no concern to you. You are here for research. It's what you have a visa and a permit for."

"You're right, I don't understand," I said. "Why shouldn't you want the newspapers to print this? Your men were shot because they were trying to protect the forest. People should hear about it."

"We are not sure of the details of what happened," he said.

I was quiet, unable to absorb all that was going on.

"Are there higher officials involved somehow?" I asked. "Is that why you're here?"

"Everyone says you work very hard. Don't be concerned with other things. Is your work finished yet?" he asked.

I smiled tightly. He was as subtle as a sledgehammer.

"No. You know I am not yet finished," I said.

He stood up to go and smiled, saying we should meet for dinner soon and discuss the progress of my research. I agreed, though we both knew we never would. It was the polite way to end a game that he had just won. The research project was too important for me to jeopardize it now, and he knew I wouldn't pursue this matter further.

The story was never printed. When the local police tried to investigate, they were turned away by the chief of the sanctuary, who was transferred not long afterward. One official version of the incident was that the forest guards got drunk and shot each other.

18

WILD
ELEPHANTS

I was in Uthai Thani for the Auk Pansa Ceremony, signifying the end-of-rains retreat for the monks. Atop the highest hill overlooking the town, scores of monks gathered at Wat Sangkat Ratina Khiri, a beautiful old temple housing a thirteenth-century bronze Buddha. On this day, a procession of seven hundred monks led by five Brahman priests would descend en masse from the hilltop. The festival marks the Lord Buddha's descent from the heavens, allowing beings in hell, the world, and the heavens to see each other, as part of his teachings.

This was the first time I'd seen Brahman priests. Their white robes and conical hats made a strange contrast to the deep-orange robes of the Buddhist monks. These priests were part of many of the formalized rituals of Thai Buddhism. Traditional Thai weddings are Brahman in origin, and Brahmans still preside over various royal Thai court rituals. Buddhism originally took hold in India as a reaction against the strict rituals of Brahmanism (later Hinduism).

Hundreds of people waited below to give offerings of food and flowers to the monks. For the people, the end of the rains signified the high point of the year, the beginning of the rice harvest; for the monks, it was the end of a period of studious training and study. Now the monks were again free to wander the countryside and be among the people.

The path the monks would walk upon after descending the mountain was already lined with people. Politicians and Thais of high status were in a special cordoned-off section at the base of the mountain so that they could make merit first. Wealthier, well-dressed families came next. Everyone else waited toward the rear.

Before the monks began their descent, Sue and I sat among a group of local children who would help carry the monks' food, thereby earning a meal for themselves. As I told them stories about the animals in the forest, imitating a tiger's growl and a leopard cat's snarling and spitting, they laughed at my antics. Just as I was about to act out the charge of a wild boar, one of them motioned behind me and they all scattered. I turned to see Ong-art standing there with an older, well-dressed Thai man.

"The governor of the province wants to meet you," Ong-art said. "He has heard much about you."

I had heard about him too. This was the man who had publicly said that he wouldn't tolerate opposition to the Thai Plywood Company's logging in Huai Kha Khaeng. I greeted him with the traditional *wai*, or bow of respect, and told him how pleased I was to be there. He spoke in English, asking me the typical questions I'd been asked dozens of times before: what were my impressions of Thailand, could I eat Thai food, wasn't I impressed with the gentle beauty of the Thai people? Before I could give my rote answers, he excused himself and left.

"Friendly guy," I said to Ong-art sarcastically. "I'd vote for him."

"The governor told me to tell you not to sit with those children," Ong-art said to me. "It's not proper. This is a special Buddhist ceremony." So that was it.

"Poor children are not part of Buddhist ceremonies?" I asked, smiling.

"I told him you wouldn't understand," Ong-art replied.

Just then a murmur went through the crowd. The monks had started their descent. Ong-art took that as an opportune time to make his exit.

It was all over rather quickly. Once the monks had passed and the offerings were made, the crowd started to disperse. Now several women appeared carrying dozens of little wooden cages with birds inside. Here was an additional opportunity to gain merit by setting free a captive bird for only ten baht. The governor was one of the first to set one free.

The worst monsoon season of the last five years in Huai Kha Khaeng finally passed, but the damage was extensive. Several miles of the entrance road through the forest reserve had to be permanently abandoned while small village paths and cattle trails were widened and patched together to make a new access road. Nearly all the station's workers were on road-repair detail for the next month. There was no time for antipoaching patrols.

Supakit and his wife, Amporn, left the sanctuary. Supakit couldn't work with Ong-art any longer and finally requested a transfer to a national park near Amporn's village in the north. I was sad to see them go. We'd become good friends again, although the shooting of Chai Lai always remained between us. As I watched the truck take them out to town for the last time, I thought of how Supakit had befriended me during my first weeks at Dancing Woman Mountain, while Amporn had helped me with my Thai and saved me extra portions of food. Only later did the other things interfere. For an instant, I wished I had told them that those other things didn't matter. But they did.

After I found fresh tracks of Payak's close to camp one day, Muuk and I set out to try to find him. Although I had never trapped him, I now had a good feel for this tiger's movements, and I never missed an opportunity to see if fresh spoor would lead me to one of his kills or to Payak himself. I was hunched over, measuring the length of the cat's stride, when a large clump of bamboo to my right suddenly shuddered, and then was swung aside. There was a loud snort as a big bull elephant stepped into view about thirty feet away from me.

This was the closest I'd ever been to a wild elephant, and in the dark, quiet greenery of the surrounding forest, I felt very vulnerable. He was unaware of us squatting near the ground, and continued making a beeline through the trees. How different this elephant was from the broken-spirited animal who had dropped to his knees while pulling our truck.

"Let's follow him," I said to Muuk.

"It's dangerous," he said. "And your leg is still not good."

I was walking almost normally by now, but there was still occasional swelling.

"He can't be far ahead. I want to see him again." I started after the elephant without giving Muuk a choice.

Though I knew elephants could cover as much as twenty miles in a night, I hadn't realized how quickly they can move through the forest. After thirty minutes, we still hadn't caught up with him. Muuk signaled me to be still. We were on the side of a hill and I leaned against a tree, grateful for the rest. This elephant obviously didn't care about following the path of least resistance, and the terrain had proven much rougher than expected. Muuk went over the top of the hill and soon came rushing back.

"He's right below us," he whispered.

I climbed the hill and peered down. The first thing I made out was sparse long strands of reddish-brown hair atop a gray wrinkled head. He was not in a hurry now, and his trunk swayed gently from side to side exploring the vegetation along the bank as he meandered in the stream. As I shifted into a more comfortable position to watch him, a rock came loose, tumbling down the hill. The elephant froze, then thundered up the bank and disappeared.

"Let's follow him a little longer," I said. Muuk glanced at my foot, but said nothing. I was already limping.

It had started to rain when Muuk waved me over and pointed to an open patch of ground dotted with fresh piles of feces. The big male was close, but he was no longer alone. Muuk swung his rifle off his shoulder and carried it in front of him.

We heard them up ahead, snapping bamboo and ambling along, unaware of our presence. We got off their trail and started circling around, eventually kneeling behind the trunk of a large fallen tree. Then we waited. Soon I was able to make out the head of the bull we had followed, his tusks gleaming white against the forest background. A crashing to his left brought my gaze upon another bull, slightly smaller but with longer tusks. Muuk took out his cigarette lighter and checked the wind direction, making sure we were downwind so they wouldn't catch our scent.

All of a sudden there was a squeal behind us, and we both turned in the direction of the sound. Two more elephants were coming through the forest. As my eyes adjusted to the forest configuration, I found the source of the sound—a baby elephant below one of the larger elephant's legs. She squealed again, as her mother's rear leg bumped her. The second elephant ran her trunk gently over the little one's body. She must be the "aunt," I realized, a female attendant that helps a mother elephant with her young.

I watched the baby for a while, thinking how precious she must be to this group. After a gestation period of nearly two years, only a single offspring is born to an adult female elephant. This baby wouldn't reach sexual maturity until at least ten years of age. Hopefully she would survive a good part of her seventy-year life expectancy and help sustain the population here.

The female suddenly bellowed, and Muuk grabbed my shoulder, pulling me low to the ground. We were downwind from the males, but the females and the baby were downwind from us. She must have caught our scent. The forest went silent. The two bulls were staring in our direction. The eyes of the larger bull were looking directly at me.

We started slinking off between the females and the bulls, when Muuk grabbed me again. Another large elephant head was peering through the trees almost directly in front of us. Muuk motioned me to lie down and remain still. He picked his head up and looked around, then signaled me with his hands. There were fifteen of them!

As we tried to get back behind the fallen tree, one of the two bulls snorted and made a short charge in our direction. Then he turned away from us and charged again. He didn't know where we were, but he was waving his trunk in the air to catch our scent. If a breeze came right now we were in trouble. There was a baby to protect.

We flattened ourselves against the ground and picked out nearby trees to climb in case we had to run for it. I was scared but exhilarated. This was why I had come to this forest. After ten frightening minutes of false charges, the elephant herd moved off. I counted twelve and heard several others. This group was small compared with the herds of years ago, which would often number up to two hundred or more, but these few animals comprised 5 to 10 percent of the elephants still thought to exist in the sanctuary, and maybe as much as 1 percent of those still left in the forests of Thailand.

When we could no longer hear them, we moved off quietly in the opposite direction, forced to take a roundabout way back to camp. It took three and a half hours to get back. That night my foot swelled so badly that I was back on a cane for nearly a week afterward. Sue scolded me for my foolishness, but I didn't regret it for a second.

On the night of the first full moon in November, the Thais give thanks to *mae khong kha*, the goddess of water. This seven-hundred-year-old tradition is a time of feasting and rejoicing called the Loy Kratong Festival. *Kratong*, or little banana-leaf boats, each carrying a lighted candle, an incense stick, and a coin, are launched along streams and rivers. The launching of a boat is an act of contrition for having used and polluted the goddess's waters during the past year. Supposedly your sins float away with the small *kratong*.

But the goddess was not so forgiving this year. She had taken too much abuse. Before the month was out, she would play a role in a disaster that shocked the country, made international news, and overshadowed all the other environmental issues.

Although the rainy season had ended in central and northern Thailand, heavy rains continued to batter the southern part of the country. In areas that had been heavily logged and rapidly deforested, the bare, degraded soils could no longer regulate the natural flow of the rain water. Thus, floods were born.

Overnight, thousands of legally and illegally felled logs were swept up in massive numbers by the water and carried like tidal waves into several southern villages. Whole villages were buried under the logs and hundreds of people were killed. The circumstances and the magnitude of the disaster outraged the Thai people. For the first time, the government was forced to face the consequences of their un-controlled exploitation of the forest. Because of the intense public outcry, the Thai government suspended and later banned all logging activities in Thailand.

The permanent logging ban was hailed internationally as a major environmental victory. Prime Minister Chatichai and Agriculture Minister Sanan were honored by Prince Philip of Britain, chairman of the World Wildlife Fund, for their outstanding contributions to forest and wildlife preservation in Thailand. They were lauded as men of foresight and strength who had set an important example for other environmentalists throughout the world.

But the devastation and grief caused by the floods made it a Pyrrhic victory at best. And when the smoke finally cleared and the floods were forgotten, it became obvious that there had been no victory at all. Any environmental "foresight" on the part of the government was really just an act of desperation. Although logging in the country's protected areas, such as Huai Kha Khaeng, ceased temporarily, ex-ploitation and mismanagement of the country's remaining forest re-serve lands accelerated. Resort developments, tree plantations, and "reforestation schemes" quickly took the place of the lumber mills.

Wealthy and influential timber merchants, with government assis-tance, signed logging deals with their neighbors: Laos, Burma, and

∴ **R**elaxing in camp with Supakit and his wife, Amporn. Supakit is holding my dog, Chai Lai. (PHOTO BY SUSAN WALKER.)

∴ **M**y monk friend, Boonchuay, waiting on the coffee-drinking platform before accompanying me on my morning rounds to check the traps.

∴A male common palm civet captured in one of the small wire traps. A chicken placed inside as bait is in the rear compartment.

∴Lung Soowan posing with the newly captured female leopard, Jangair, before placing her back inside the trap to recover from sedation.

∴ **S**usan Walker fitting a radio collar to the adult male leopard that was later named Supanyo. (PHOTO BY LUNG SOOWAN.)

∴ **T**he male leopard Supanyo, only slightly drugged, being released from the trap after he walked back into it a second time. (PHOTO BY THUSSANAD PACHKONG.)

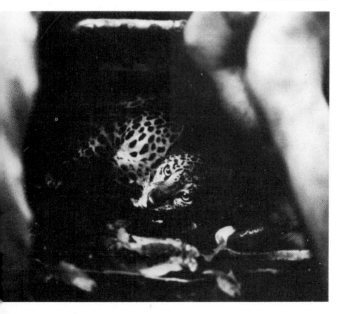

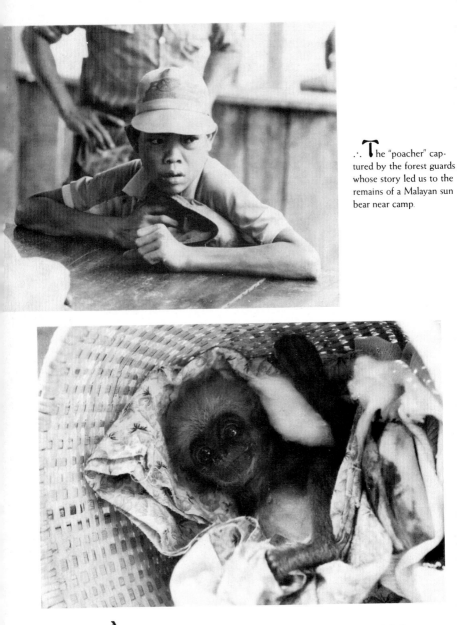

∴ The "poacher" captured by the forest guards whose story led us to the remains of a Malayan sun bear near camp.

∴ A baby gibbon captured by poachers for the pet trade after they'd killed its mother in the forest around Dancing Woman Mountain.

∴ Tiger penises being sold for $200–$300 each at a local Chinese pharmacy. The penises, used primarily as an aphrodisiac, are often placed in bottles of whiskey that are then drunk as a tonic.

∴ Thai graduate student, Saksit, testing the radio collar we attached to the sedated male leopard cat Basho.

∴ The workers from the station constructing a log bridge over a section of muddy road that the rains had made impassable.

∴ A domesticated elephant pulling the station's truck across a stream. The bridge had been washed away by heavy rains.

∴ Telling animal stories to the local children at the "Auk Pansa" ceremony in Uthai Thani. (PHOTO BY SUSAN WALKER.)

∴ Following fresh tracks of the male tiger Payak, accompanied by Muuk, one of the forest guards.
(PHOTO BY BELINDA STEWART-COX.)

∴ The youngest worker at the station, Anant, with his new fifteen-year-old bride. This picture was taken shortly before his death.

∴ The four markers erected in memory of the local forest guards killed by poachers at Dancing Woman Mountain. The marker on the far left is for Anant.

Cambodia. At the same time Thai companies continued to cut Thai forests, claiming they needed to clear passages to bring logs in, or that they couldn't tell where Thailand's border was. Some low-level government workers offered bribes of as much as three million baht ($120,000) to higher-ranking officials in order to be appointed a provincial forestry officer in the province of Mae Hong Son on the Thai-Burmese border. Such a position would enable them to pocket millions of baht in "timber fees."

When the initial figures came out showing how much Thai forest was still being cut in spite of the logging ban, the director general of the Forestry Department claimed these figures represented "raw data" that had yet to be "filtered." Eventually illegal logging became so widespread and blatant that the director general had to admit that the corruption among local officials was so extensive that it had spread beyond his control. The amount of forest cover and the numbers of wild animals in Thailand continued to plummet.

Because of all the press generated by the floods and the Nam Choan Dam project, international conservation organizations began to take more notice of the Huai Kha Khaeng Wildlife Sanctuary. Visitors and consultants from various countries came like carpetbaggers with promises of money and management schemes. They spoke with the government officials, then wrote dozens of reports full of phrases like "sustainable use of forest resources," "buffer zone management," and "socioeconomic changes in hill tribe settlements." I read their recommendations for new buildings, vehicles, state-of-the-art scientific equipment, trips for government officials to visit other countries, and even video cameras.

By December, the forest guards in Thailand's protected areas stopped getting paid. This happened every year at this time while the bureaucrats worked out the next year's budget for each sanctuary in Bangkok. The government staff, whose salaries were separate from the sanctuary's budget, continued receiving their monthly checks. Some station chiefs paid the men out of their own pockets as long as they could. Others had to let their workers go back to their villages until the money came through.

Most of the men at Dancing Woman Mountain had no place else to go, so they stayed on, borrowing money, searching the forest for food, and building up a large bill of credit (with interest) in town. If they were sent out on patrol, they spent their time looking for edible plants instead, and then would sit out the rest of the day until it was time to return. This made it a profitable time of year for the poachers. When we checked the salt licks around the station, we found the poached carcasses of two more gaur, a banteng, and four sambar deer.

I had been in this forest two years now, and I was tired. The radio signals on several of the collared animals were fading, and no new animals had been radio-collared after my accident. Scientifically, I had accomplished what I had set out to do here. Our data, if used properly, would help protect and manage this sanctuary and could serve as a foundation for more detailed work in the future.

My new knowledge of the tigers and leopards in the area would provide Phairote with what he had said the government wanted: a handle on the relative densities of these two species in different habitats and an idea of how much forest some of these big cats needed in order to survive. But the data went beyond that. It also showed that the preservation of certain key components of the forest system—namely, the waterways and lowland evergreen forest—were vital to the survival of good-sized cat populations.

The data on small carnivores was, in some ways, more important, because none of these species had ever been closely studied before. The data on the leopard cats showed that small, solitary flesh-eating carnivores had difficult lives. The leopard cat was thought to be adaptable because it catches small rodents easily and is found in many different kinds of habitats. But forests affected by fires, clear-cutting, or human habitation are not the best living conditions for this species' survival. Local populations of the leopard cat in this area, which are already relatively small, may become genetically impoverished and even disappear in time. The civet community presented an even more complex picture. A large number of civet species live side by side in the sanctuary through habitat and resource partitioning. But as with the leopard cat, small populations may have problems with long-term stability.

Regardless of the large size of the Huai Kha Khaeng Wildlife Sanctuary, it is still an island surrounded by a sea of humanity. Anything affecting key components of this forest will cause repercussions throughout the entire forest system that may well be irreversible. This dry tropical forest is an extremely dynamic system which undergoes both seasonal and long-term changes in habitat composition. Human-related changes brought about by things such as fires, dams, and the expansion of villages must be controlled if the natural forest and wildlife community is to remain intact.

Our work on the small carnivores presents a warning signal for wildlife management and conservation. Over the long term, it is important to study more than just the species that are immediately threatened. We also need to keep an eye on the seemingly omnipresent and adaptable species that may be slowly disappearing. The loss or reduction of some of these species' populations can affect the forest structure in ways we don't even realize.

After talking it over, Sue and I decided to give a big New Year's Eve celebration for the forest workers at my house. It had been a hard year for these families and I wanted to give everyone a feast that they wouldn't soon forget. This would be my parting gift. New Year's Eve was my thirty-fifth birthday, a good year according to the Thai astrologers, and I felt it was a good time to bring the project to a close.

On the morning of the party, the women came early with their pots and pans, and the men started building a fire pit. Pork, beef, and chicken were roasted, fish and rice cooked, and vegetables made into numerous spicy Thai dishes. Fruits were cut up into sweet desserts. A festive spirit infected the camp for the first time in months. The hardships of the monsoon season, the illnesses, the lack of food and money, were all temporarily forgotten. By late afternoon bamboo mats were laid out in the dirt in front of my house and the generator was started up early to run the cassette player. I turned the music up to full volume. It was time to celebrate.

Along with an abundance of food, there was soda, candy, and trinkets for the women and children, and more than enough whiskey for even these hard-drinking men. Sue helped several of the women sneak whiskey into their Cokes without their husbands' knowledge. As the party continued into the early-morning hours, people told stories, sang, and swayed in rhythm to Thai classical music. Long after the women and children had gone to bed, most of the men were still up drinking.

Finally I went off to bed. For a while, I lay near the window and listened to the men's voices, feeling satisfied that I had given them a little happiness for the day. As I drifted off to sleep, I heard Muuk and Riap joking with Anant. He had recently found himself a fifteen-year-old wife from a nearby village, but after he criticized her cooking she had run back to her mother's house. He was leaving in the morning to try to get her back, and the men were making up lines for him to woo her with. I smiled to myself, thinking that Anant wouldn't be exercising with me for a while. I wouldn't have smiled had I known I'd never see Anant alive again.

19

HUAI KHA KHAENG, FEBRUARY 1989

Saksit and Suwat left during the first two weeks of January. We made plans to meet again later in Bangkok. I had promised to help Saksit with his thesis. For Sue, their departure signaled the end of her time in Thailand and she was depressed. She was heading north for a long-overdue holiday, and afterward she planned to return to the sanctuary for one last season of rodent trapping. Then I'd shut down the project and she'd return to the United States.

I decided to take a last trip into the Huai Kha Khaeng Valley. I wanted to hike along a part of the main river that I hadn't yet seen and gather more conclusive data on the relative abundance of tigers there. My old team was gone or incapacitated; Supakit was working in northern Thailand, Intah had fractured his skull falling from the rear of the truck, Sombat had returned to his village, Soowan was still convalescing, and Lung Galong was in the hospital with malaria. I took three other men with me instead: Muuk, Daworn, and Riap.

The water was high for February, so when we couldn't walk along the river we bushwhacked and cut new trails. On the third day, we stopped for lunch on a small island. While the men fished, I explored the sandy beaches around the perimeter, intrigued by the large number of tiger tracks. There were at least three different individuals regularly crossing this island. Since the river here was wide and shallow with gently sloping banks, it was a good crossing place for larger animals. This made it a good place for tigers to stalk prey.

I told the men we'd stay there on the river's banks for the night, so we set up camp several hundred yards downstream. Before sunset, I grabbed a light meal and went back to the island. There was a place I'd seen earlier where I would be hidden by boulders but could peek out for a clear view around me. Muuk and his gun came with me.

By 11 P.M. I was ready to give up. Despite my admonitions, Muuk kept dozing off and snoring, his head sagging and banging against the rock in front of him. Then he'd jerk awake with a grunt, only to do it again. I was about to move out from behind the rocks when I heard a rustling in the grass to my right. It continued for a minute, then stopped. I looked over at Muuk, but he was asleep.

A stone rolled in the darkness on the other side of the boulder directly behind me, and my heart went into my throat. Whatever was out there, it was no more than a few feet away. There were no more sounds. I waited a minute and then I turned on my flashlight to peer around the rock. Nothing. I shook Muuk awake. I wanted to get out of there.

We walked along the river back to the camp. As we reached Daworn and Riap, who were sitting around the fire, a gruff cough came from the forest edge, right where we had just crossed the river. Muuk shined his flashlight toward the noise and caught two spots of emerald green flashing back at us. It was a tiger. I turned my flashlight on him and saw his head peering out from the brush. Then he was gone.

"Goddamn. He was there all the time," I whispered, thinking how tigers like to stalk their prey from the rear so that they can get as close as possible before pouncing.

"He followed us back," Muuk said, looking not at all pleased. "He wants us to know he's here."

"I don't think he wants anything to do with us," I said, the hairs on my neck standing on end.

Some Malaysians say that tigers only attack from behind because on the forehead of every person a verse from the Koran is inscribed which proclaims man's superiority over all other creatures. The tiger doesn't dare face this inscription. The Chinese believe that a tiger that hunts men may be a "were-tiger," possessed by a person who has been devoured and has become a spirit known as Chang Kwei. I was glad the men kept their guns loaded by their side that night.

The tigers were in trouble in Thailand, even in Huai Kha Khaeng, one of their last strongholds. I was now convinced that there were probably less than two hundred tigers left in the entire country. The basic requirements of this species—a good water supply, adequate ground cover, and relatively large prey species—were becoming increasingly scarce because of hunting pressures and loss or encroachment of good lowland forest areas. Still, in this valley there were at least three times as many tigers as there were around Dancing Woman Mountain.

The riverine forest here abounded with life. We often crossed the tracks of the rare green peafowl, sometimes flushing the bird itself. At a salt lick, I hid in the undergrowth and watched two of these birds go through their courtship ritual, the long train of the male repeatedly lifting and fanning out in a mesmerizing display of kaleidoscopic colors. When his emerald plumage caught the sunlight, it was like watching a mythological creature come to life.

After dark, civets scavenged nearby and elephants trumpeted in the distance. Over dinner one evening, we listened to the heart-wrenching shrieks of a sambar deer being taken down by a tiger. Once, I woke to the sound of otters digging in the sand. By the light of the stars they looked like small children playing on the beach.

The Huai Kha Khaeng Valley was definitely the heart of this forest. This area was the stronghold for the tigers, elephants, and tapirs, and a rich area for wild boar, packs of dholes, and sambar deer. This area was also one of the last refuges for three otter species, wild water buffalo, green peafowl, and the white-winged wood duck. Dancing Woman Mountain was like a little sister to the Huai Kha Khaeng Valley. If the biological wealth of this valley was lost or damaged, the repercussions in surrounding forest areas would be magnified a hundredfold. It was already happening. This valley was the victim of the heaviest poaching in the sanctuary.

Between 1986 and 1988, the poached wildlife recorded by sanctuary workers included twenty-one gaur, ten banteng, one serow, one wild water buffalo, seven sambar deer, six barking deer, one Malaysian sun bear, sixty-six monkeys, forty-six small mammals, seven birds, twenty-five lizards, one civet, one tiger, and two elephants. And these numbers grossly underrepresented the true extent of the damage wrought by illegal hunters who were causing changes to the forest community that were difficult to quantify. The workers spoke of smaller and fewer fish in the rivers, less frequent sightings of sambar deer, gaur in herds of five or six instead of fifty.

Once I came upon a female gibbon with a baby clinging tightly to her belly, I was surprised to see that when she saw me, she pushed her baby away from her and swung off in the opposite direction. Gibbons usually keep their young close to them when they feel threatened. Muuk explained that so many female gibbons had been killed for their babies that the mothers had learned to react the only way they could to stay alive. I hoped the mother spirit here would be strong enough to protect them.

That night the men fished for our dinner. But instead of spearing the fish as they usually did, they staked a long net across a narrow part of the river. Within half an hour we had more fish than we could eat.

The fish were thrown in the dirt, while Riap prepared the fire. A short time later Muuk staked the fish out over the hot coals, spearing them through their gills and mouth with a stick. I watched the fish slowly stew in their own body juices, mouths gaping trying to arch their bodies away from the heat until the life finally passed out of them. Every now and then an eyeball popped.

"I want you to kill the fish first," I said to Muuk after watching five fish die this way. "There's no reason for this." I pointed to a fish struggling against the stake. Muuk and Riap laughed. I picked up the remaining fish and severed their spines.

The next afternoon I returned from several hours of following small-cat tracks and was met by a sight that made me think I had stumbled into the wrong camp. Stretched out between two trees was a fifteen-foot reticulated python, half skinned, and still alive. It was held to one tree with a vine around its neck and its head was bleeding from a shotgun wound. I could still hear its ragged gasping. Muuk and Daworn pulled at the live snake's skin as if engaged in a tug-of-war. I watched the snake's muscles quiver and undulate as the skin was ripped from its body.

"What the hell is going on here?" I asked.

"It was too close to camp," Muuk grunted. "I had to shoot it. Help us. This is hard." He ripped a few more inches of skin off.

"This is not our camp," I said. "This is the forest and that's a protected species. And it's still alive," I hollered. "Kill it!"

"They're easier to skin alive," Riap grunted, nonplussed by my anger. Now the three of them were tugging at the skin.

I pulled out my knife and cut through the top of the spinal cord where it joined with the skull.

"If you killed it for the skin, then say so. Don't bullshit me with this crap about it hurting us, and don't pretend to care about the wildlife just because it pays your salary," I ranted in English, not even thinking about what I was saying. Then I stomped out of camp.

That night, I sat off by myself, away from the fire. The men talked among themselves loud enough so that I could hear them. They were afraid I'd report them to Ong-art. They knew that what they had done could get them fired or at the very least severely reprimanded.

In fact, I never planned to report them. I knew that they hadn't been paid in two months and that the snake's skin meant a few extra dollars to them. The government officials in Bangkok didn't care whether the men and their families were hungry or not. Still, I couldn't excuse their behavior. They had chosen to be forest guards. If they could bend the rules whenever they wanted, then nothing separated them from the poachers. They became a part of the problem instead of part of the solution. But the root of this problem went way beyond the boundaries of this sanctuary. These impoverished, undereducated men had to fight just to stay alive, and if they were fired or punished, I had no doubt that the wildlife would suffer even more in their absence.

What enraged me the most, however, was their complete insensitivity to an animal's pain and suffering. I had seen this kind of behavior too often in Thailand: frogs skinned alive in the market, monkeys chained in the temples. The list went on and on. Let them wonder if I'm going to turn them in, I thought.

I had made this last trip to the river for several reasons. More than anything, I'd hoped to recapture some of the magic I had felt during my first visit here. But much of that magic had been born of an innocence and naïveté that was now long gone. I'd seen too much. Everything in this area was changing too rapidly. Even if the borders of the Huai Kha Khaeng Wildlife Sanctuary remained intact, it might never recover from the damage being inflicted on it by humans on a daily basis.

During our last night along the river, two monks appeared in our camp. They had been walking among some of the tribal villages in Thung Yai and were now on their way out of the forest. The men and I showed them the best route to follow and cleared a place for them to rest for the night. We also invited them to join us for breakfast the next morning.

The following day, as I took my turn putting food in the monks' bowls, one of them kept glancing at the amulet around my neck. I wondered if he thought it strange to see a foreigner wear such a thing.

"Do you know a monk named Boonchuay by any chance?" I asked, about to explain how I had gotten the charm that had become my talisman.

Both monks smiled.

"We know of him," one of them said. "We know of you too."

20

THE
PLACE
OF
KNOWING

Shortly after we returned to the field station, a patrol of forest guards from the sanctuary's headquarters followed the same route we had taken along the river and stumbled upon a group of Hmong poachers in the area of our last camp. The patrol charged the camp and the Hmong fought back. In the ensuing gun battle, two forest guards went down. One was killed instantly; the second took a bullet in his stomach. The second guard was Anant, my young friend who had so badly wanted to grow up quickly. After the night of the New Year's Eve party, Anant had transferred to headquarters so that his new wife could be closer to her family. He died while being carried out of the forest. His wife was two months pregnant with their first son.

Afterward, soldiers were sent into the first Hmong village across the border in Thung Yai, where the poachers had come from. I remembered that village. It was there that I'd lost a crossbow shooting contest and had sat among a group of children playing their bamboo mouth pipes and singing. The village was evacuated and resettled outside the sanctuary, as were many others in the ensuing months.

The wildlife was safer, but the circumstances that finally brought about these actions were tragic.

Following the shootings, the Hmong tribesmen involved hid out in the forest and swore revenge on any forest guards they encountered. In response to their actions, the river valley was declared off-limits and the gates at each substation were manned for the first time since I'd been in the sanctuary. Nobody left camp without a gun. Sue finished up her last season of rodent trapping, but neither of us wandered far into the forest by ourselves.

Soon the sounds of crackling fires and bursting bamboo could be heard around camp again. Another fire season had begun. Large areas of forest took on the ashen, dead look that had shocked me so much on my first survey trip. But now I looked upon the whole scene a little differently. I knew so much more about how these fires shaped the forest mosaic and affected the different wildlife species here.

I now knew that, despite the predictability of these seasonal fires, the carnivore species and the forest as a whole were being adversely affected. The bigger animals—bears, tigers, and leopards—moved away or became scarce in response to the burning. Smaller mammals didn't have that luxury. They had to survive as best they could, sometimes sustaining higher mortality rates than usual. The end result for both big and small carnivore species was low population densities compared with what might otherwise exist in the absence of fires. Only if the burning was controlled and managed would the situation improve.

After the shooting, monks were no longer accorded special privileges in the sanctuary. Several monks were discovered fishing illegally at a waterfall near headquarters. It was decided that even the monks should not be trusted all the time. There were no longer any monks living in the huts at Dancing Woman Mountain, and with no one to maintain them, the huts themselves would soon be gone as well. When the fires reached that area of our station, I went to take a last look.

I sat alone on the coffee-drinking platform, watching and listening to the approaching fire. I knew the platform would be the last thing to go because it was surrounded by a cleared area. One hut had already burned to the ground and I watched as another hut caught fire. The dried palm leaf walls and the pole frameworks went up like kindling. Within minutes the hut was gone.

I was saddened to see a place that had been so much a part of this forest and of my life here over the last two years lost forever. I pictured Boonchuay waiting for me by the side of the road each morning. I remembered the many mysteries this place held for me.

Then I remembered Supanyo sitting next to me on this platform, telling me to feel instead of think. He had taught me to reach down inside myself and create a life for myself that was a little fuller than before, and a little less tumultuous. Certain things in life will go as they are meant to go. I believed that now. And if actions are carried out with good intentions and with no anticipation of the outcome, then there can be no failures. Any path is the right one. I smiled as my sadness disappeared. I realized that the huts themselves were not important to me anymore.

In the days that followed, Sue and I gave away most of our clothes, our food, and our household utensils. The house belonged to the station now. On the last morning, only Beng and Lung Galong were there to see us off. Ong-art was in Bangkok, and most of the men were out clearing trees that had fallen across the road. Tears welled up in Sue's eyes as she held hands and talked quietly with Beng.

I embraced Lung Galong in a bear hug, then grabbed him by the shoulders and held him at arm's length, looking into that weather-beaten, gnomelike face. It was a face that represented so much of what I had been through here over the last two years. In the deep crevices and bloodshot eyes, I could see elephants and tribal people, countless pipes of opium and bottles of whiskey; I could feel the ancient forest before me in Galong's gaze.

I took Beng inside the house and gave her an envelope containing ten thousand baht ($500). With this money, Beng would have finally saved up enough to buy a little patch of land in her village where she hoped to build a home and settle with her family. Now she could start her house. She bowed her head as tears dropped from her eyes. I kissed her lightly on the cheek.

"I will miss you, Beng," I said. "I will miss you more than I can tell you."

"It is the same for me," she whispered.

As Sue waited in the truck, I pulled out my portable antenna and plugged it into the radio receiver to listen one last time to Nit's signal. She was nearby as usual. There were still radios on Supanyo, Nit, and several civets, but they would all eventually fall off when the connecting link on the collars weakened. Then Sue and I drove away.

We passed the wives and children in front of their houses and the men working along the road. They waved to us casually and smiled as if we were just going out into town and would be back by evening. It was a good way to leave. As I passed the spirit house, I honked the horn three times and nodded in its direction.

Just before we reached headquarters, I stopped the truck and looked out into the same little clearing I had looked into nearly three years earlier. Where there had been two black memorial markers, now there were four. I now knew why no one had wanted to tell me about these memorials during my first visit here, why they had seemed so ominous to me.

I got out of the truck and went over to the last marker. This black stump with Anant's name carved on it was the best testimonial I had seen to the progress being made toward protecting Thailand's forests. I took off my gold amulet and laid it at the base of the marker. Boonchuay had said that this piece of metal symbolized respect for compassion and wisdom. I could only hope that it would start here.

EPILOGUE

I stayed in Thailand after leaving Huai Kha Khaeng, in order to compile our data and put it into a form that could be used to manage and protect the sanctuary. But when this task was finished and I looked at the 164-page scientific report for the Royal Thai Forestry Department, I knew it wasn't enough. The sense of urgency I had felt when I first came here was now stronger than ever. The forest was dying. Drastic measures were needed if Thailand's last protected areas were to be saved.

The government of Thailand declared 1989 the Year of Nature and Environmental Protection. Yet more than one million households illegally occupied over twelve million acres of land in Thailand's forest reserves, and this country still had no comprehensive land-reform program. Bangkok was a vast labyrinth of mushrooming high rises, choking traffic, and dangerous pollution levels, and still the city lacked a zoning plan and pollution controls. Logging and forest encroachment were continuing at an alarming rate nationwide, and there was no comprehensive forest policy to deal with these crucial environmental conflicts. Illegal wildlife shipments bound for Japan, Hong

Kong, and Taiwan were intercepted containing binturongs, slow loris, spotted cats, gibbons, pangolins, pythons, and many other members of Thailand's rapidly disappearing species. Street vendors openly sold fierce-looking gibbon heads, obtained by injecting embalming fluid into the brains of live animals. And Thailand's antiquated wildlife law hadn't been revised since 1960.

In October 1989, Phairote was appointed director general of the Forestry Department. He had finally gotten what he had most wanted, but he was powerless to reverse the flow of events that stemmed, not from a lack of understanding among Thais, but from the greed and corruption that had become all-pervasive. During Phairote's first six months in office, his officials arrested nearly five thousand people for destroying wildlife or encroaching on protected forest areas. More than twenty million dollars of illegal logs were seized. Among those arrested or implicated were prominent businessmen, senior police and government officials, and politicians. Three forestry officials were killed and twelve injured bringing these criminals in. One newspaper called 1989 the Year of Greed.

The Thai smiles, the seemingly gentle nature of the Thai people, their Buddhist philosophy and animistic beliefs, all add up to very little effective protection of the forest and its wildlife. Instead the country's resources are viewed simply as a commodity, a bank account to be drawn upon indefinitely. I had come to realize that if real conservation is to be carried out into the twenty-first century, then the few special areas that are still left, areas like Huai Kha Khaeng, must be kept inviolate at all costs. These are the "core areas" that will help seed the future. There can be no chipping away at the edges, no human settlements, no sustainable or multi-use schemes, no commercial exploitation—*inviolate*. Research will be crucial to understand, protect, and manage these intact natural systems. Education will be needed to firmly implant the inviolability of these areas into the national consciousness. But first, these few special areas must be protected by physical and legal forces that will meet the day-to-day threats. The forest guards must be better paid, better taken care of, better trained and better armed than the poachers. Otherwise the battle is lost from the beginning.

On New Year's Day of 1990, I went back to Dancing Woman Mountain. I paid my respects at the spirit house, walked the old trails, and slept in the now empty field station. The families greeted me as if I'd only been gone a few days. But nothing was the same.

It was the end of the fiscal year and, once again, the workers hadn't been paid in months. Just before my arrival, some of the men went on one of their food-gathering forays into the forest. It was Muuk who first saw the little spotted coat peaking out through the underbrush. Only after he shot it did he see the radio around its neck. He had killed Nit.

BIBLIOGRAPHY

BOOKS

ARBHABHIRAMA, ANAT, D. PHANTUMVANIT, J. ELKINGTON, and P. INGKASUWAN (Editors). *Thailand: Natural Resources Profile.* Bangkok: Thailand Development Research Institute, 1987.

CORBETT, JIM. *Man-Eaters of Kumaon.* Delhi: Oxford University Press, 1944.

————. *The Man-Eating Leopard of Rudrapranag.* Bombay: Oxford University Press, 1948.

EVANS, MAJOR G. P. *Big-Game Shooting in Upper Burma.* London: Longmans, Green, 1911.

GERVAISE, NICHOLAS. *The Natural and Political History of the Kingdom of Siam.* Bangkok: White Lotus Co., 1989. (Original from 1688, British Library, London.)

GITTLEMAN, J. L. (Editor). *Carnivore Behavior, Ecology, and Evolution.* Ithaca: Cornell University Press, 1989.

HALFPENNY, JAMES. *A Field Guide to Mammal Tracking in North America.* Boulder: Johnson Books, 1986.

JONES, R. L., and HAROLD C. HANSON. *Mineral Licks, Geophagy, and Biogeochemistry of North American Ungulates.* Ames: Iowa State University Press, 1985.

KENWARD, ROBERT. *Wildlife Radio Tagging.* New York: Academic Press, 1987.

KHANTIPALO, PHRA. *Buddhism Explained.* Bangkok: Mahamkut Rajavidyalaya Press, 1986.

KLAUSNER, WILLIAM. *Reflections on Thai Culture*. Bangkok: The Siam Society, 1987.

KOCH-ISENBURG, LUDWIG. *Through the Jungle Very Softly*. London: Hodder & Stoughton, 1963.

LEKAGUL, BOONSONG, and JEFFREY MCNEELY. *Mammals of Thailand*. Bangkok: Association for the Conservation of Wildlife, 1977.

LEWIS, PAUL, and ELAINE LEWIS. *Peoples of the Golden Triangle*. London: Thames & Hudson, 1984.

MEYERS, NORMAN. *The Sinking Ark*. New York: Pergamon Press, 1979.

MILLER, S. DOUGLAS, and DANIEL EVERETT (Editors). *Cats of the World: Biology, Conservation, and Management*. Washington, D.C.: National Wildlife Federation, 1986.

MOUHOT, H. *Travels in Indo-China*. Bangkok: White Lotus Co., 1986. (Original from 1864, London: John Murray.)

NATIONAL IDENTITY OFFICE. *Thailand in the 80's*. Bangkok: Muang Boran Publishing House, 1984.

OSBORNE, MILTON. *Southeast Asia: An Introductory History*. Sydney: Allen & Unwin, 1985.

PEACOCK, E. H. *A Game-Book for Burma and Adjoining Territories*. London: H. F. & G. Witherby, 1933.

PERRY, RICHARD. *Life in Forest and Jungle*. New York: Taplinger, 1976.

RAJADHON, PHYA ANUMAN. *Popular Buddhism in Siam and Other Essays on Thai Studies*. Bangkok: Thai Inter-Religious Commission for Development, 1986.

————. *Some Traditions of the Thai*. Bangkok: Thai Inter-Religious Commission for Development, 1987.

SCHALLER, GEORGE. *The Deer and the Tiger: A Study of Wildlife in India*. Chicago: University of Chicago Press, 1967.

————. *The Serengeti Lion: A Study of Predator-Prey Relations*. Chicago: University of Chicago Press, 1972.

SHEARER, ALISTAIR. *Thailand: The Lotus Kingdom*. London: John Murray, 1989.

SIAM SOCIETY. *Culture and Environment in Thailand*. Bangkok: Siam Society Publications, 1989.

STODDART, D. M. (Editor). *Ecology of Small Mammals*. London: Chapman & Hall, 1979.

SUKAWANIT, NONGPA-NGA. *Before Shooting the Last Bullet*. Bangkok: Today Printing Press, 1989. (In Thai.)

TILSON, RONALD, and ULYSSES SEAL (Editors). *Tigers of the World*. Park Ridge, N.J.: Noyes Publications, 1987.

TOTH, MARIAN DAVIES. *Tales from Thailand*. Tokyo: Charles E. Tuttle, 1971.

WAUGH, ALEX. *Bangkok: The Story of a City*. Bangkok: Orientations Ltd., 1987.

WELLS, KENNETH. *Thai Buddhism: Its Rites and Activities*. Bangkok: Suriyabun Publishers, 1975.

WHITNEY, CASPAR. *Jungle Trails and Jungle People.* New York: Charles Scribner's Sons, 1905.

WILDLIFE FUND THAILAND. *A Cry from the Forest: Buddhist Perception of Nature.* Bangkok: Wildlife Fund Thailand, 1987.

WILSON, E. O. (Editor). *Biodiversity.* Washington, D.C.: National Academy Press, 1988.

YIN, U TUN. *Wild Animals of Burma.* Rangoon: Rangoon Gazette, 1967.

YOUNG, GORDON. *Tracks of an Intruder.* London: Souvenir Press, 1967.

YOUNGHUSBAND. LT. G. J. *Eighteen Hundred Miles on a Burmese Tat.* London: W. H. Allen & Co., 1888.

ARTICLES

BLYTH, ED. "On the Flat-Horned Taurine Cattle of South-East Asia." Pp. 278–97 in *Essays Relating to Indo-China,* vol. 2. London: Trubner & Co., 1886.

BURNS, D. M. "A Survey of the Valley Huai Kha Khaeng." *Natural History Bulletin of the Siam Society,* vol. 26, nos. 1–2, 1975, pp. 21–26.

CAVALLO, J. A. "Cat in the Human Cradle." *Natural History,* vol. 2, 1990, pp. 53–60.

CHAMPION, F. W. "Tiger Tracks." *Journal of the Bombay Natural History Society,* vol. 33, no. 2, 1929, pp. 282–87.

CONRY, P. J. "Gaur *Bos gaurus* and Development in Malaysia." *Biological Conservation,* vol. 49, 1989, pp. 47–65.

COX, B. S. "Thailand's Nam Choan Dam: A Disaster in the Making." *The Ecologist,* vol. 17, no. 6, 1987, pp. 212–19.

GITTLEMAN, J. L., and P. H. HARVEY. "Carnivore Home-Range Size, Metabolic Needs and Ecology." *Behavioral Ecology and Sociobiology,* vol. 10, 1982, pp. 57–63.

KLEIMAN, D. G., and J. F. EISENBERG. "Comparisons of Canid and Felid Social Systems from an Evolutionary Perspective." *Animal Behavior,* vol. 21, 1973, pp. 637–59.

LAIR, R. C. "The Number and Distribution of Domesticated Elephants in Thailand." *Natural History Bulletin of the Siam Society,* vol. 36, 1988, pp. 143–60.

MITHTHAPALA, S., J. SEIDENSTICKER, L. G. PHILLIPS, S. B. U. FERNANDO, and J. A. SMALLWOOD. "Identification of Individual Leopards (*Panthera pardus kotiya*) Using Spot Pattern Variation." *Journal of Zoology, London,* vol. 218, 1989, pp. 527–36.

MURRAY, J. D. "How the Leopard Gets Its Spots." *Scientific American,* 1988, pp. 80–87.

RABINOWITZ, A. "The Density and Behavior of Large Cats in a Dry Tropical Forest Mosaic in Huai Kha Khaeng Wildlife Sanctuary, Thailand." *Natural History Bulletin of the Siam Society,* vol. 37, no. 2, 1989, pp. 235–51.

——. "Behaviour and Movements of Sympatric Civet Species in Huai Kha Khaeng Wildlife Sanctuary, Thailand." *Journal of Zoology, London*, vol. 223, no. 2, 1991.

——. "Notes on the Behaviour and Movements of Leopard Cats, *Felis bengalensis*, in a Dry Tropical Forest Mosaic in Thailand." *Biotropica*, vol. 22, no. 4, 1990, pp. 397–403.

——. "Fire, Dry Dipterocarp Forest, and the Carnivore Community in a Dry Tropical Forest Mosaic in Huai Kha Khaeng Wildlife Sanctuary." *Natural History Bulletin of the Siam Society*, vol. 38, no. 2, 1990.

—— and SUSAN WALKER. "The Carnivore Community in a Dry Tropical Forest Mosaic in Huai Kha Khaeng Wildlife Sanctuary, Thailand." *Journal of Tropical Ecology*, vol. 7, 1991.

ROSENZWEIG, M. L. "Community Structure in Sympatric Carnivora." *Journal of Mammalogy*, vol. 47, no. 4, 1966, pp. 602–12.

SEIDENSTICKER, J. "On the Ecological Separation between Tigers and Leopards." *Biotropica*, vol. 8, no. 4, 1976, pp. 225–34.

——. "Predation by *Panthera* Cats and Measures of Human Influence in Habitats of South Asian Monkeys." *Journal of Primatology*, vol. 4, no. 3, 1983, pp. 323–26.

SMITH, J. L. D., C. MCDOUGAL, and D. MIQUELLE. "Scent Marking in Free-Ranging Tigers, *Panthera tigris*." *Animal Behavior*, vol. 37, 1989, pp. 1–10.

STOTT, P. "The Spatial Pattern of Dry Season Fires in the Savanna Forests of Thailand." *Journal of Biogeography*, vol. 13, 1986, pp. 345–58.

——. "Savanna Forest and Seasonal Fire in South East Asia." *Plants Today*, November–December 1988, pp. 196–200.

——. "The Forest As Phoenix: Towards a Biogeography of Fire in Mainland South East Asia." *The Geographical Journal*, vol. 154, no. 3, 1988, pp. 337–50.

SUNQUIST, M. "The Social Organization of Tigers in Royal Chitawan National Park, Nepal." *Smithsonian Contributions to Zoology*, no. 336, 1981, 98 pp.

VAN VALKENBURG, B., and C. B. RUFF. "Canine Tooth Strength and Killing Behaviour in Large Carnivores." *Journal of Zoology, London*, vol. 212, 1987, pp. 379–97.

—— and ——. "Incidence of Tooth Breakage among Large, Predatory Mammals." *American Naturalist*, vol. 131, no. 2, 1988, pp. 291–302.

WHARTON. C. H. 1966. Man, Fire and Wild Cattle in North Cambodia. Proceedings of the Annual Tall Timbers Fire Ecology Conference 5:23–65.

——. 1968. Man, Fire and Wild Cattle in Southeast Asia. Proceedings of the Annual Tall Timbers Fire Ecology Conference 8.

ACKNOWLEDGMENTS

The research described in this book was funded by Wildlife Conservation International (WCI) of the New York Zoological Society (NYZS). Assistance for the project was also provided by the Center for Conservation Biology and the Biology Department at Mahidol University, the National Research Council of Thailand, the Royal Thai Forestry Department, and Wildlife Fund Thailand. Heartfelt thanks go to the numerous people who helped me in the field. Foremost among these are the field assistants who were with me the longest: Susan Walker, Saksit Simchareon, and Suwat Kaeosrisuk. Additional field assistance was provided by Ramesh Boonratana and Justina Ray. Field observations, data, and insights that helped in compiling the information in this book were provided by Warren Brockelman, Philip Round, Salisa Satapanawath, Sompoad Srikosamatara and Belinda Stewart-Cox. Cliff Hallam provided an excellent critical review of the initial manuscript. Leslie Lannon was instrumental in getting me together with my editor.

I would also like to thank the two chiefs of the Dancing Woman Mountain Station, Noparat Naksatit and Ong-art Laohawat, as well as all of the workers who were there during my stay. They put up with me during my worst moments and helped me to understand the forest in a way I might not have otherwise.

A very special thanks to my editor, Heidi von Schreiner, for the many hours spent working with me in putting together this book, and for the special warmth and caring that I received from her as an extra bonus. And to my agent, Owen Laster, whose friendship and confidence in me continues to inspire my work.

To my parents, who are never far from my thoughts. Thank you for always being there, and for having convinced a shy, lonely boy that he could do whatever he set his mind to.

Finally, an acknowledgment of two incredible monks, Supanyo and Boonchuay, whose real names I never knew. Thank you for your friendship when I needed it the most, and for helping to make my journey through life a little less burdensome. Thank you for "the place of knowing."

INDEX

ABOUT THE AUTHOR

ALAN RABINOWITZ, a Research Zoologist at Wildlife Conservation International, is one of the world's foremost experts on large cats. His work has been instrumental in the establishment of several nature preserves around the world including the Cockscomb Basin Jaguar Preserve, created especially to protect jaguars in Belize. This project formed the basis of Alan Rabinowitz's first book, *Jaguar: One Man's Battle to Establish the World's First Jaguar Preserve* (Anchor Books). Born and raised in New York City, the author currently resides in Bangkok, Thailand where he is assessing the status of the tigers in this region. For his next project he will research wild cats in Borneo and help to establish a wildlife conservation and management training program to help protect this area's wild species.

Wildlife Conservation International, a division of the New York Zoological Society, supports various projects around the world to understand and protect endangered species and habitats, including endangered great cats—clouded leopards in Malaysia, tigers in India, jaguars in Central America, snow leopards on the Tibetan Plateau, and the wild cat species of Thailand mentioned in this book. You can help. For more information, or to send a contribution, contact:

"Great Cats Fund"
Wildlife Conservation International
New York Zoological Society
Bronx, New York 10460
(212) 220-6891

WILDLIFE
CONSERVATION
INTERNATIONAL
NYZS·1895